KURT SUTTER'S
SISTERS OF SORROW ™

COURTNEY ALAMEDA · HYEONJIN KIM · JEAN-PAUL CSUKA

BOOM!
S T U D I O S

BOOM!
S T U D I O S

SISTERS OF SORROW, June 2018.
Published by BOOM! Studios, a
division of Boom Entertainment,
Inc. Sisters of Sorrow is ™ & © 2018
Sutterink. Originally published in
single magazine form as SISTERS OF SORROW No. 1-4. ™ & ©
2017 Sutterink. All Rights Reserved. BOOM! Studios™ and the
BOOM! Studios logo are trademarks of Boom Entertainment,
Inc., registered in various countries and categories. All
characters, events, and institutions depicted herein are
fictional. Any similarity between any of the names, characters,
persons, events, and/or institutions in this publication to actual
names, characters, and persons, whether living or dead, events,
and/or institutions is unintended and purely coincidental.
BOOM! Studios does not read or accept unsolicited submissions
of ideas, stories, or artwork.

BOOM! Studios, 5670 Wilshire Boulevard, Suite 400, Los
Angeles, CA 90036-5679. Printed in China. First Printing.

ISBN: 978-1-68415-201-8, eISBN: 978-1-64144-016-5

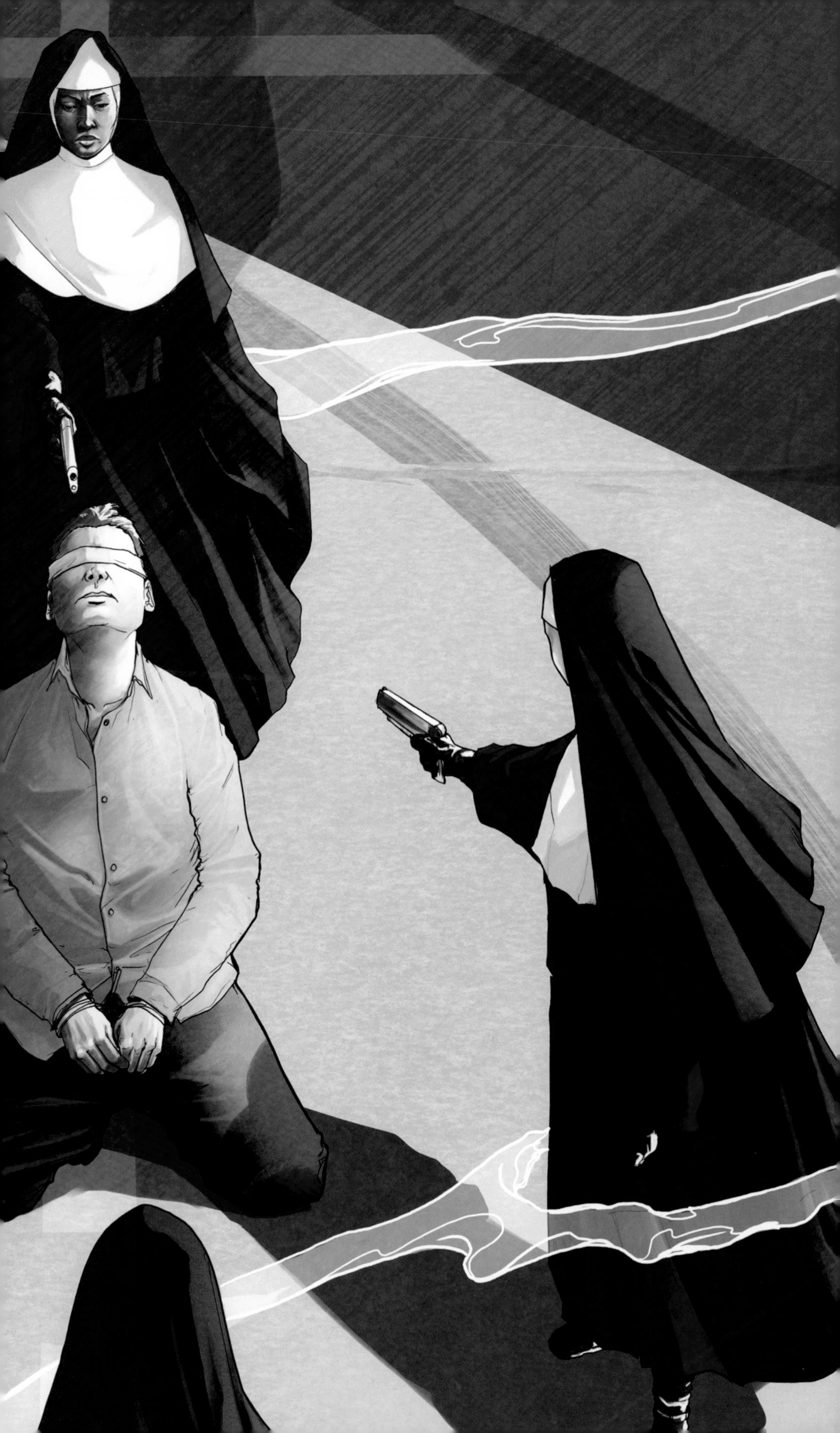

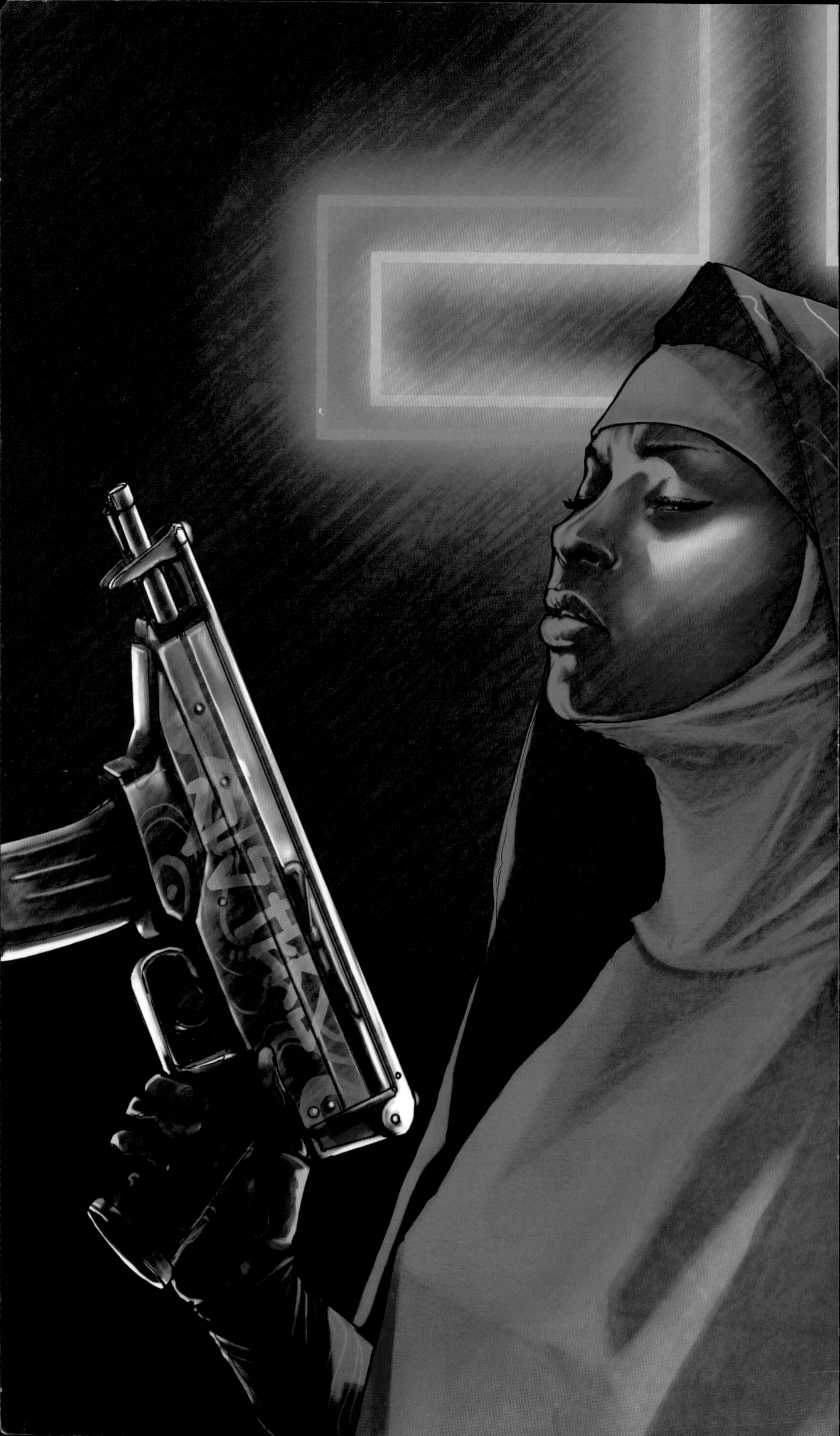

SISTERS OF SORROW

CREATED BY *KURT SUTTER*

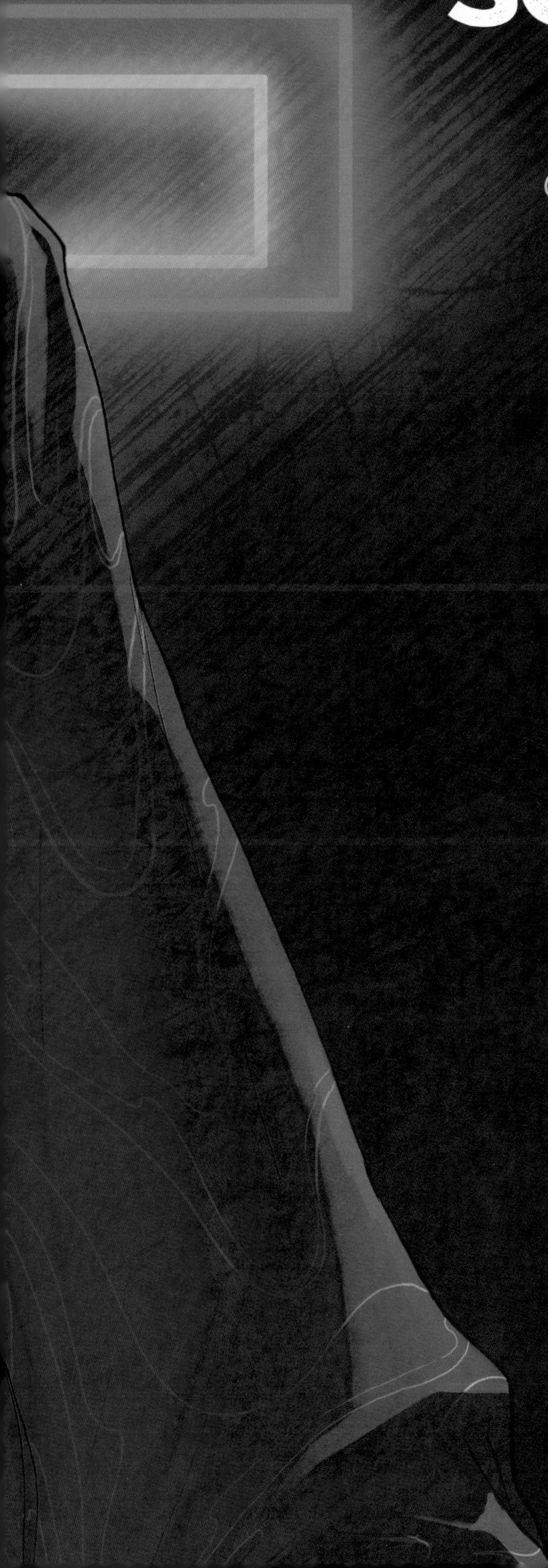

WRITTEN BY
KURT SUTTER &
COURTNEY ALAMEDA

ILLUSTRATED BY
HYEONJIN KIM

COLORED BY
JEAN-PAUL CSUKA

LETTERED BY
JIM CAMPBELL

COVER BY
JAE LEE & JUNE CHUNG

DESIGNER
JILLIAN CRAB **WITH**
MICHELLE ANKLEY

ASSOCIATE EDITOR
CHRIS ROSA

EDITORS
DAFNA PLEBAN &
MATT GAGNON

CHAPTER ONE

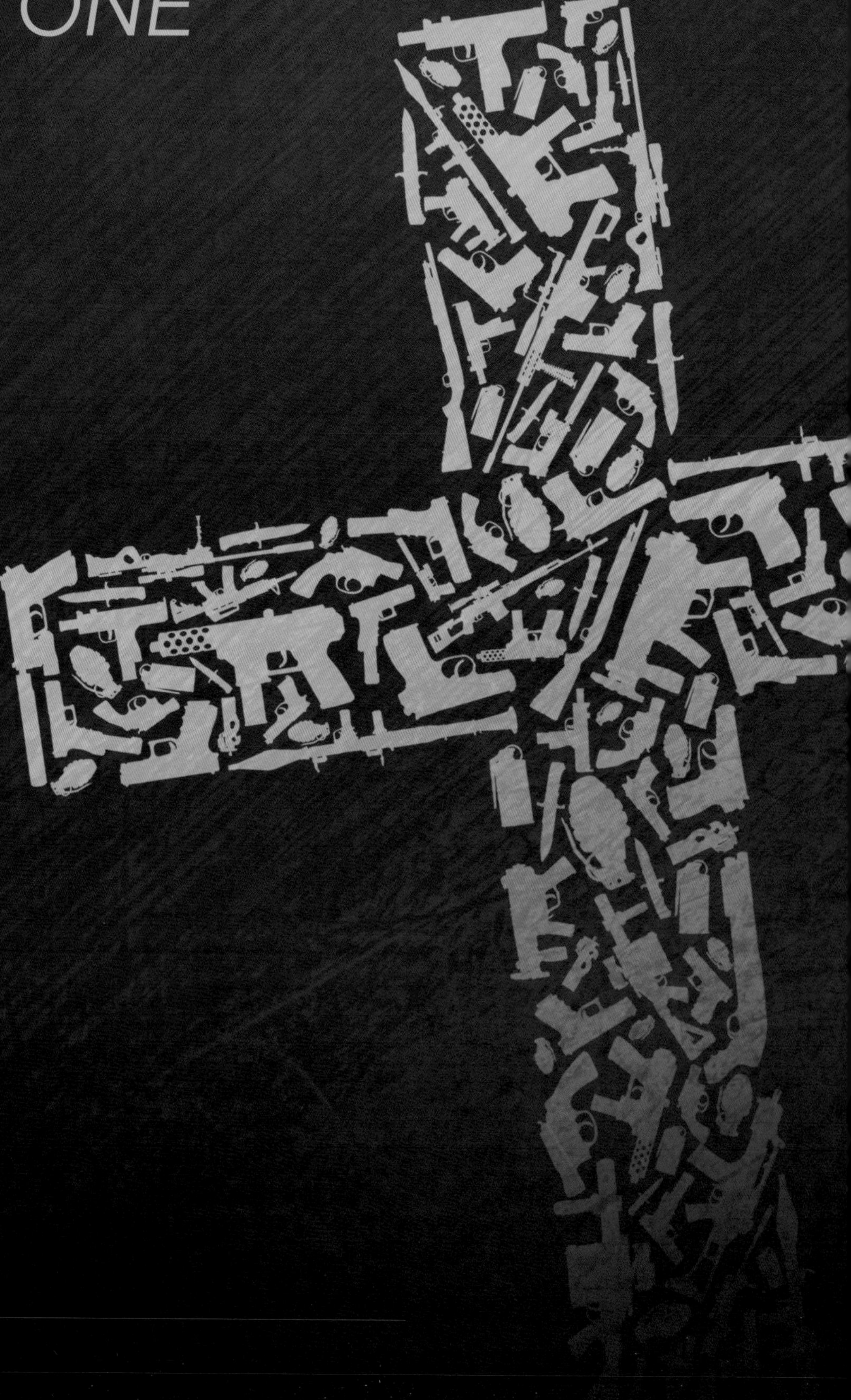

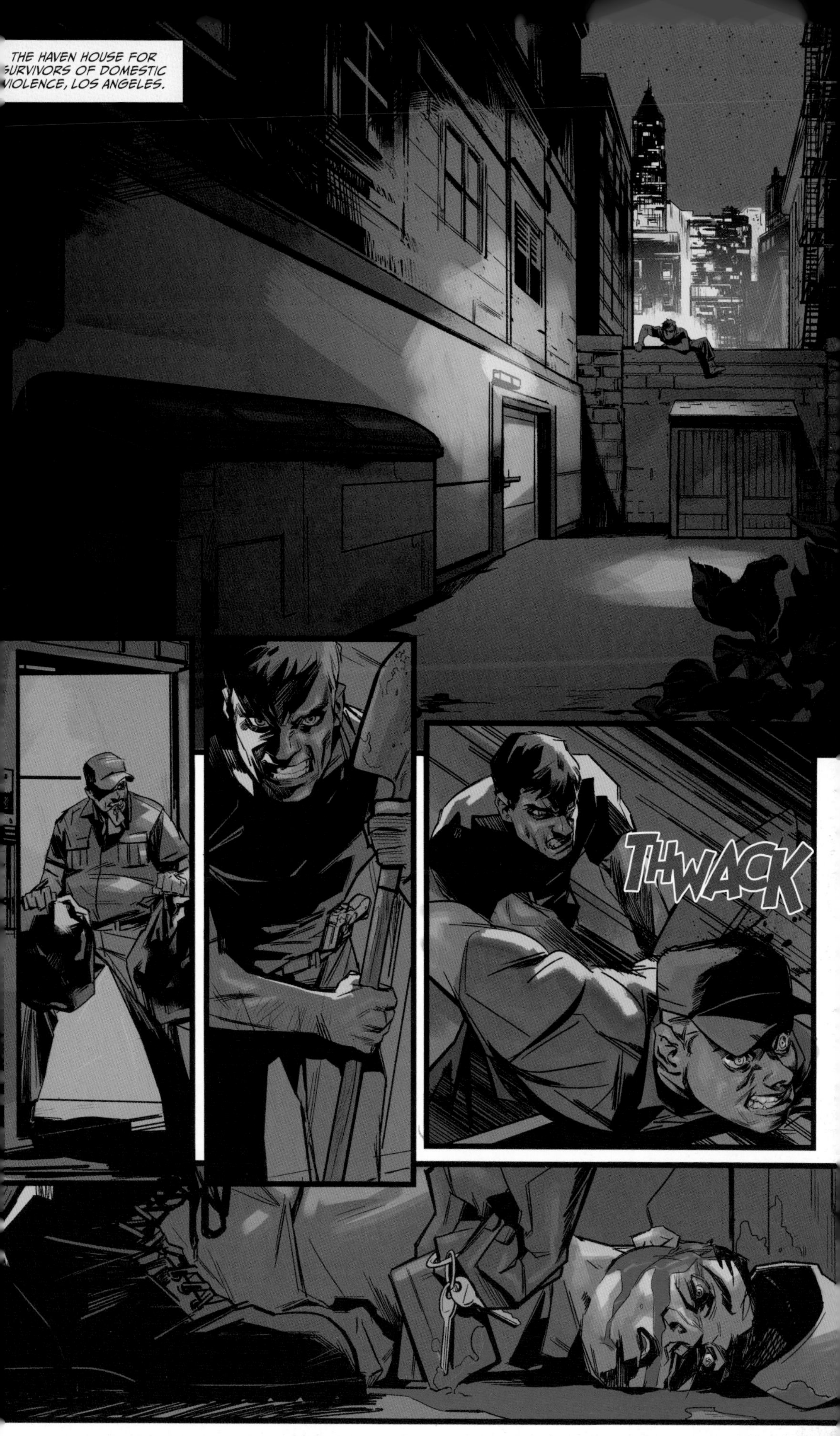
THE HAVEN HOUSE FOR SURVIVORS OF DOMESTIC VIOLENCE, LOS ANGELES.
THWACK

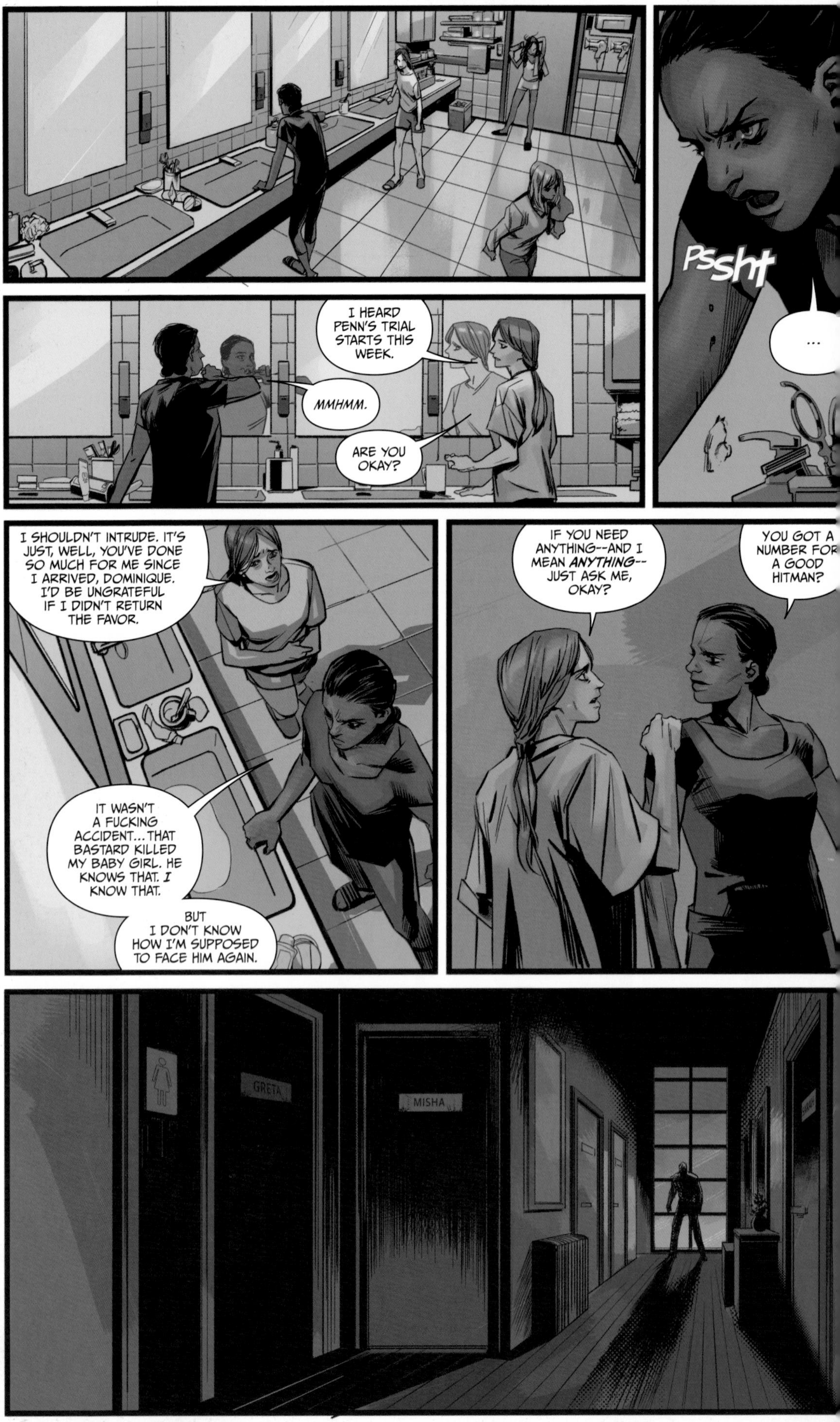
PSSHT
...
I HEARD PENN'S TRIAL STARTS THIS WEEK.
MMHMM.
ARE YOU OKAY?
I SHOULDN'T INTRUDE. IT'S JUST, WELL, YOU'VE DONE SO MUCH FOR ME SINCE I ARRIVED, DOMINIQUE. I'D BE UNGRATEFUL IF I DIDN'T RETURN THE FAVOR.
IT WASN'T A FUCKING ACCIDENT...THAT BASTARD KILLED MY BABY GIRL. HE KNOWS THAT. I KNOW THAT.
BUT I DON'T KNOW HOW I'M SUPPOSED TO FACE HIM AGAIN.
IF YOU NEED ANYTHING--AND I MEAN ANYTHING--JUST ASK ME, OKAY?
YOU GOT A NUMBER FOR A GOOD HITMAN?
GRETA
MISHA

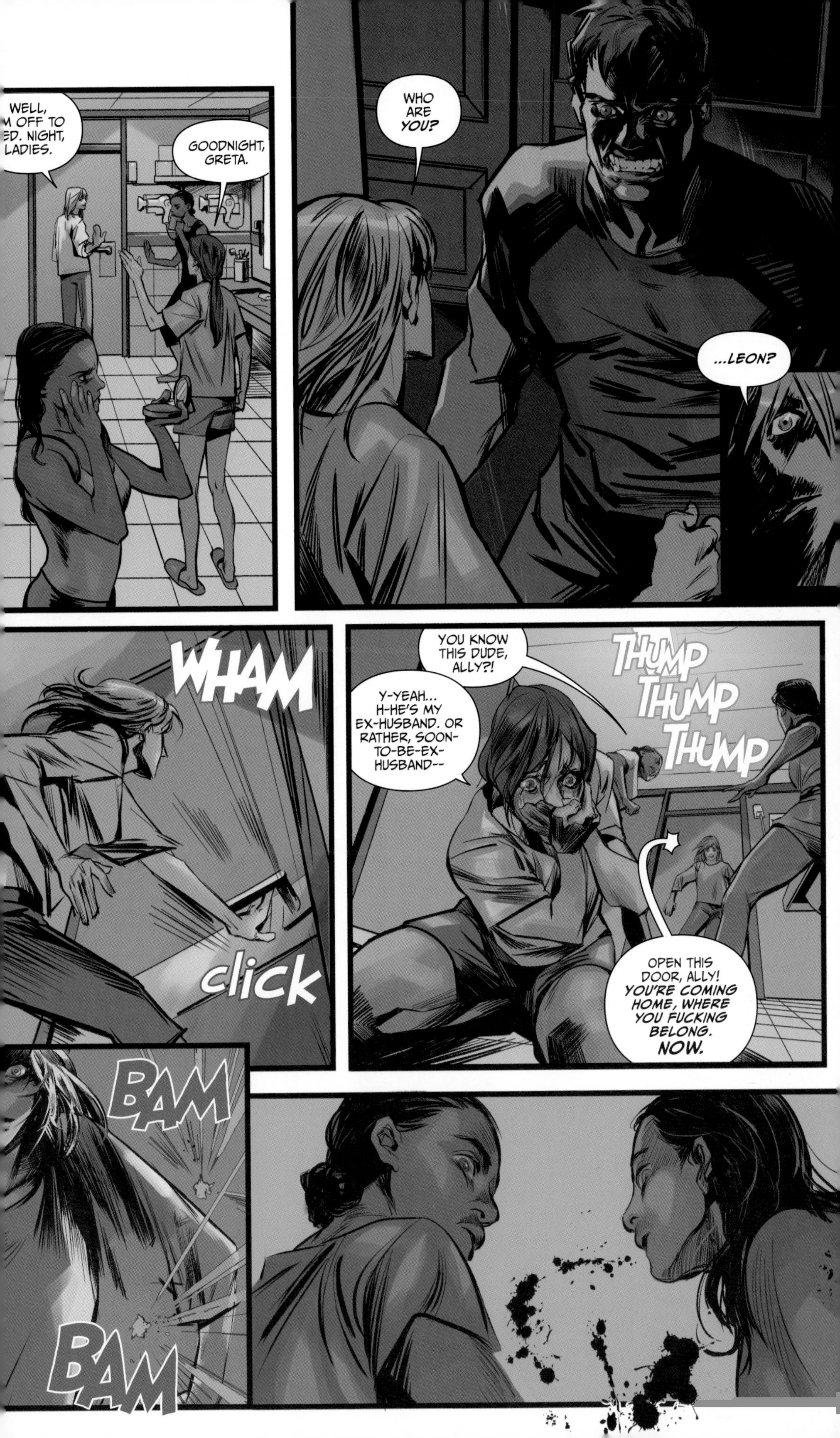
WELL, M OFF TO ED. NIGHT, LADIES.
GOODNIGHT, GRETA.
WHO ARE YOU?
...LEON?
WHAM
click
YOU KNOW THIS DUDE, ALLY?!
Y-YEAH... H-HE'S MY EX-HUSBAND. OR RATHER, SOON-TO-BE-EX-HUSBAND--
THUMP THUMP THUMP
OPEN THIS DOOR, ALLY! YOU'RE COMING HOME, WHERE YOU FUCKING BELONG. NOW.
BAM
BAM

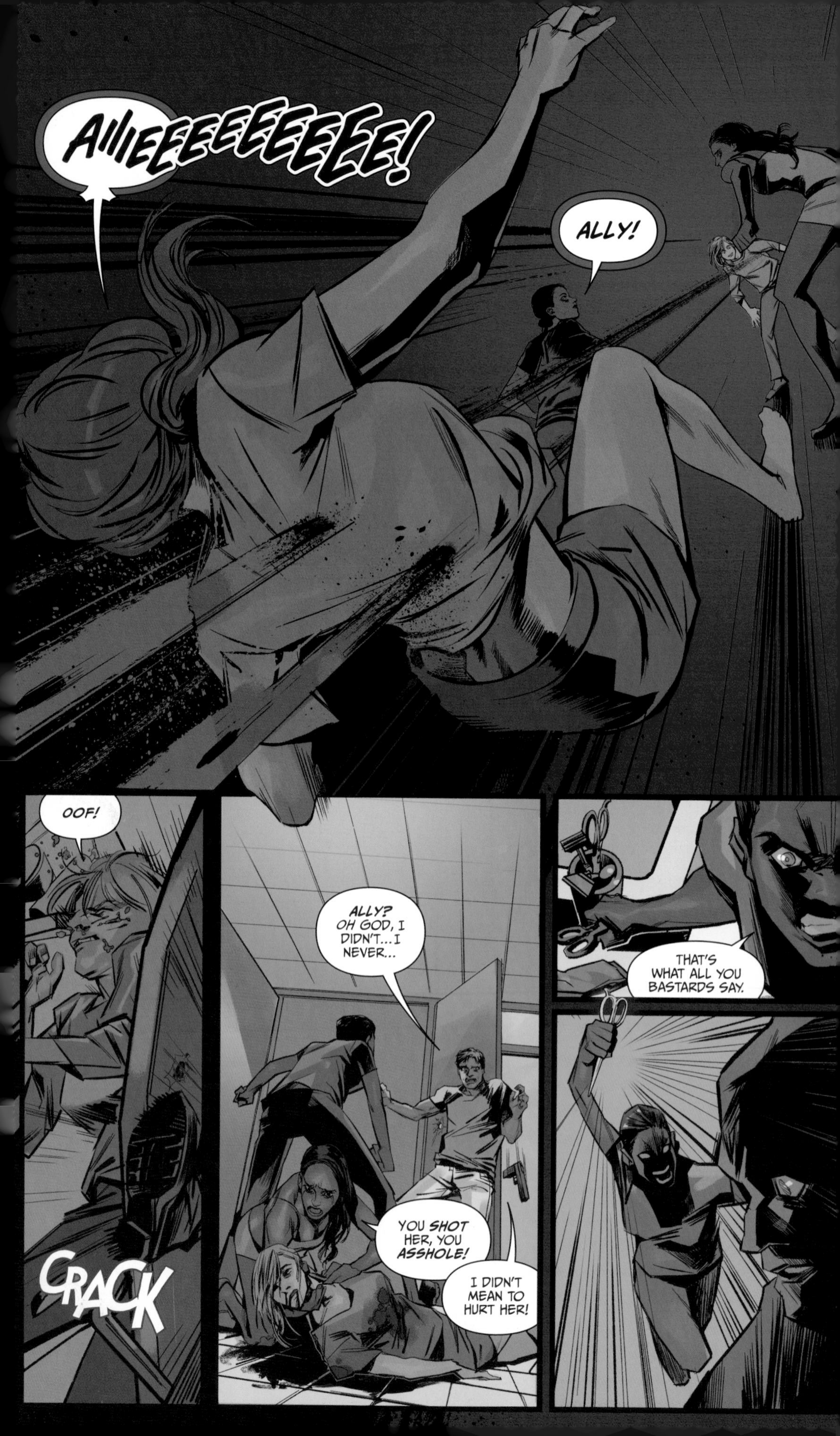
AIIIEEEEEEEEEE!
ALLY!
OOF!
CRACK
ALLY? OH GOD, I DIDN'T... I NEVER...
YOU SHOT HER, YOU ASSHOLE!
I DIDN'T MEAN TO HURT HER!
THAT'S WHAT ALL YOU BASTARDS SAY.

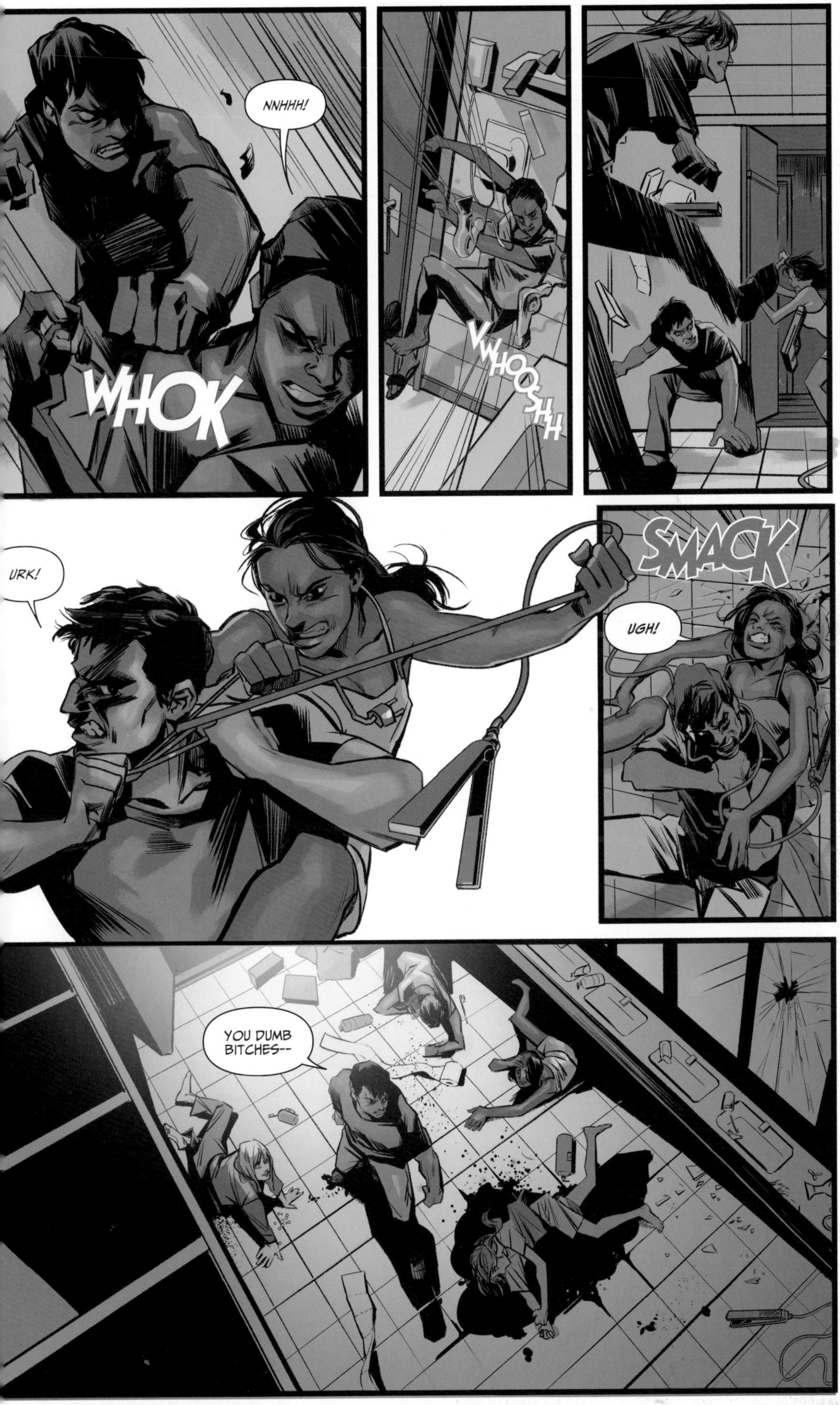
NNHHH!
WHOK
VWHOOSHH
URK!
SMACK
UGH!
YOU DUMB BITCHES--

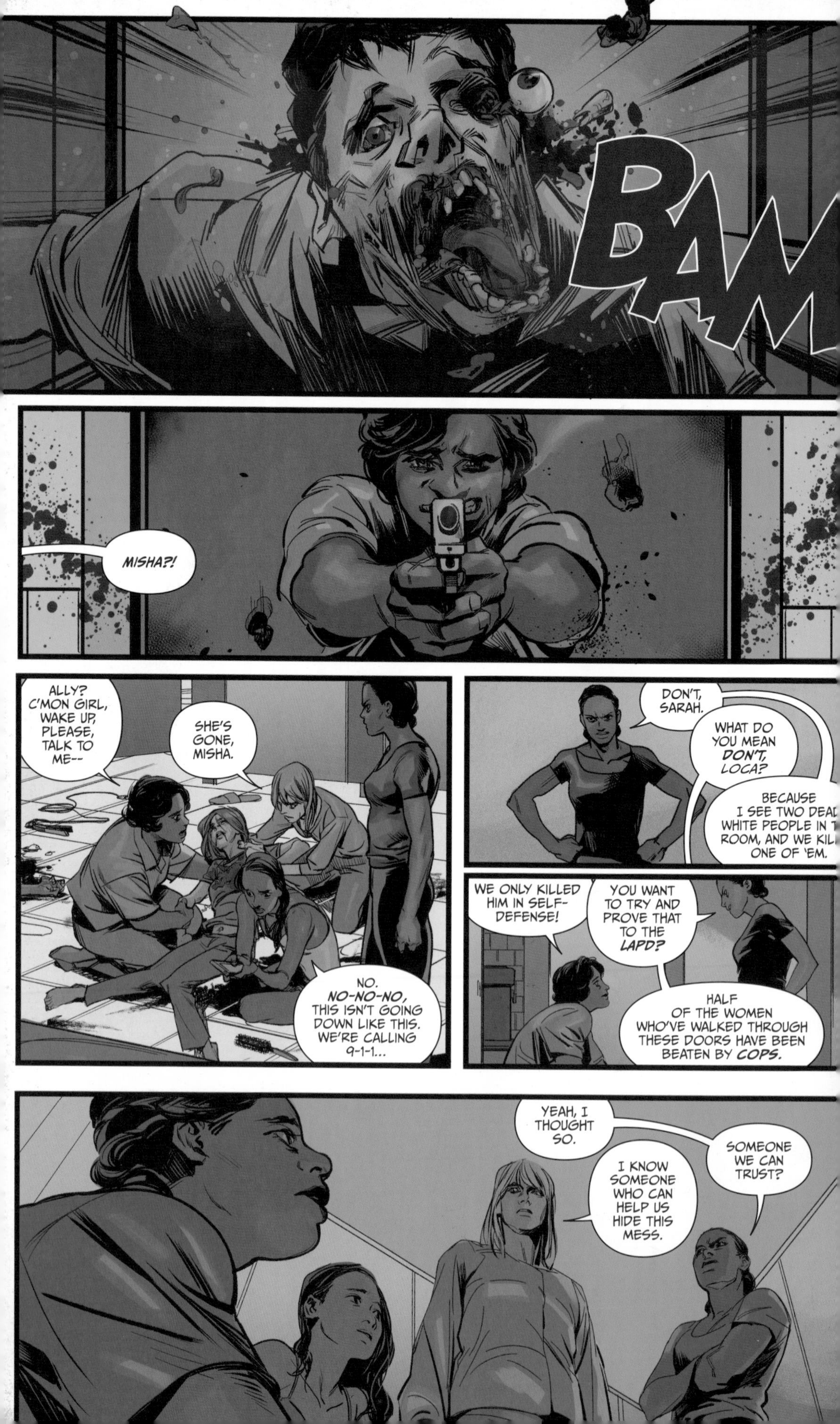
BAM
MISHA?!
ALLY? C'MON GIRL, WAKE UP, PLEASE, TALK TO ME--
SHE'S GONE, MISHA.
NO. *NO-NO-NO,* THIS ISN'T GOING DOWN LIKE THIS. WE'RE CALLING 9-1-1...
DON'T, SARAH.
WHAT DO YOU MEAN *DON'T,* LOCA?
BECAUSE I SEE TWO DEAD WHITE PEOPLE IN T ROOM, AND WE KIL ONE OF 'EM.
WE ONLY KILLED HIM IN SELF-DEFENSE!
YOU WANT TO TRY AND PROVE THAT TO THE *LAPD?*
HALF OF THE WOMEN WHO'VE WALKED THROUGH THESE DOORS HAVE BEEN BEATEN BY *COPS.*
YEAH, I THOUGHT SO.
I KNOW SOMEONE WHO CAN HELP US HIDE THIS MESS.
SOMEONE WE CAN TRUST?

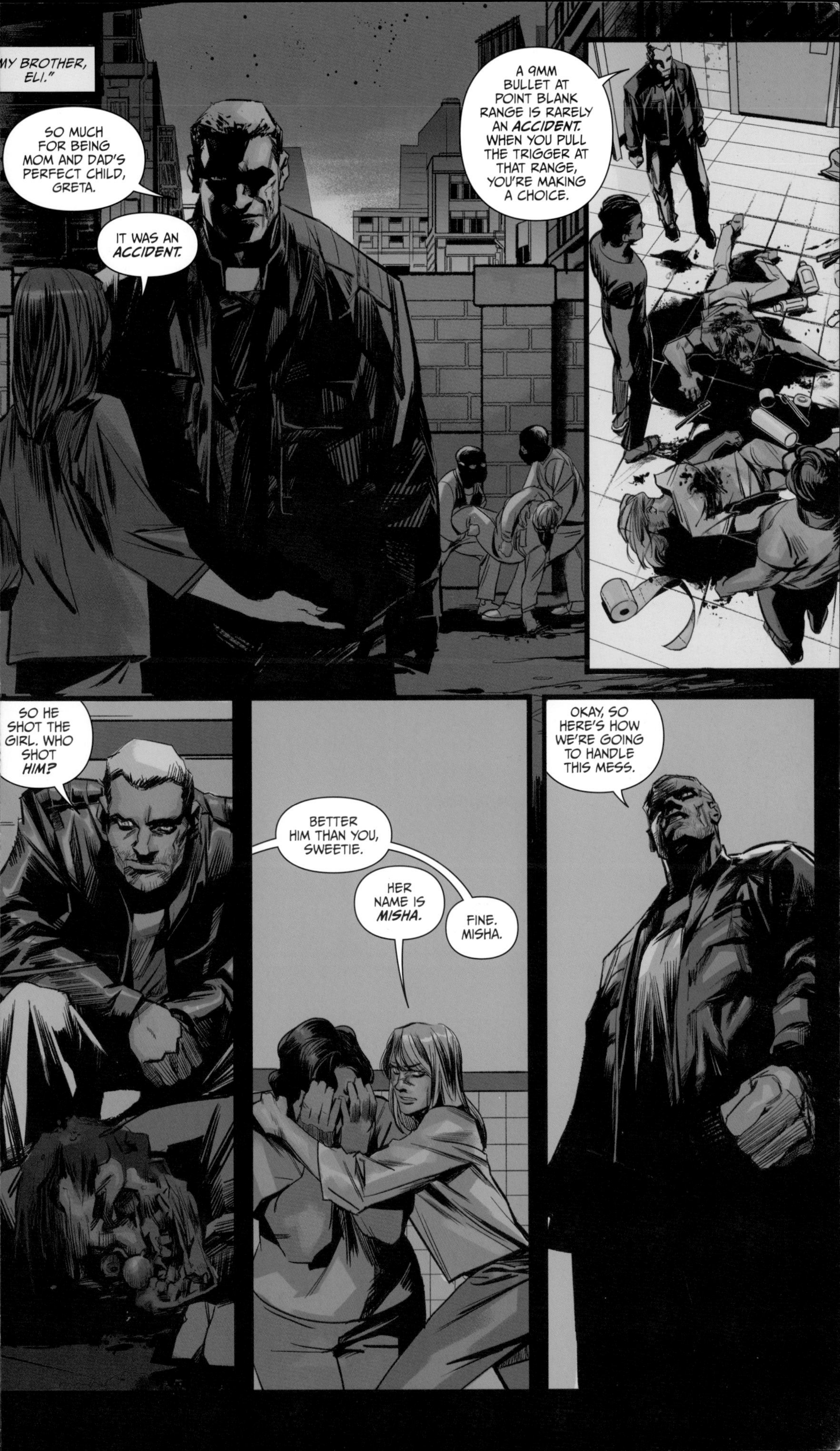
MY BROTHER, ELI."
SO MUCH FOR BEING MOM AND DAD'S PERFECT CHILD, GRETA.
IT WAS AN *ACCIDENT.*
A 9MM BULLET AT POINT BLANK RANGE IS RARELY AN *ACCIDENT.* WHEN YOU PULL THE TRIGGER AT THAT RANGE, YOU'RE MAKING A CHOICE.
SO HE SHOT THE GIRL. WHO SHOT *HIM?*
BETTER HIM THAN YOU, SWEETIE.
HER NAME IS *MISHA.*
FINE. MISHA.
OKAY, SO HERE'S HOW WE'RE GOING TO HANDLE THIS MESS.

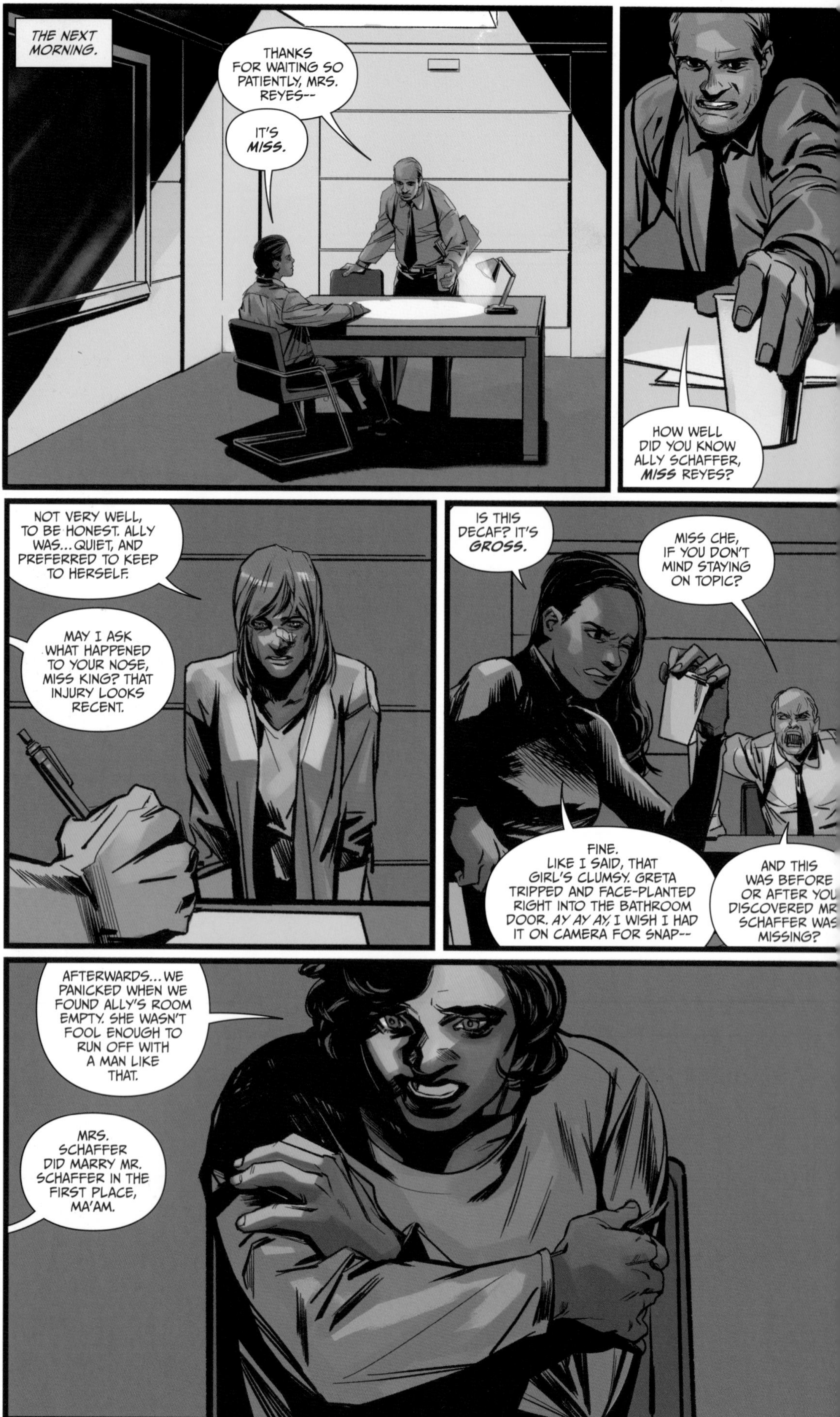
THE NEXT MORNING.
THANKS FOR WAITING SO PATIENTLY, MRS. REYES--
IT'S MISS.
HOW WELL DID YOU KNOW ALLY SCHAFFER, MISS REYES?
NOT VERY WELL, TO BE HONEST. ALLY WAS...QUIET, AND PREFERRED TO KEEP TO HERSELF.
MAY I ASK WHAT HAPPENED TO YOUR NOSE, MISS KING? THAT INJURY LOOKS RECENT.
IS THIS DECAF? IT'S GROSS.
MISS CHE, IF YOU DON'T MIND STAYING ON TOPIC?
FINE. LIKE I SAID, THAT GIRL'S CLUMSY. GRETA TRIPPED AND FACE-PLANTED RIGHT INTO THE BATHROOM DOOR. AY AY AY, I WISH I HAD IT ON CAMERA FOR SNAP--
AND THIS WAS BEFORE OR AFTER YOU DISCOVERED MR SCHAFFER WAS MISSING?
AFTERWARDS...WE PANICKED WHEN WE FOUND ALLY'S ROOM EMPTY. SHE WASN'T FOOL ENOUGH TO RUN OFF WITH A MAN LIKE THAT.
MRS. SCHAFFER DID MARRY MR. SCHAFFER IN THE FIRST PLACE, MA'AM.

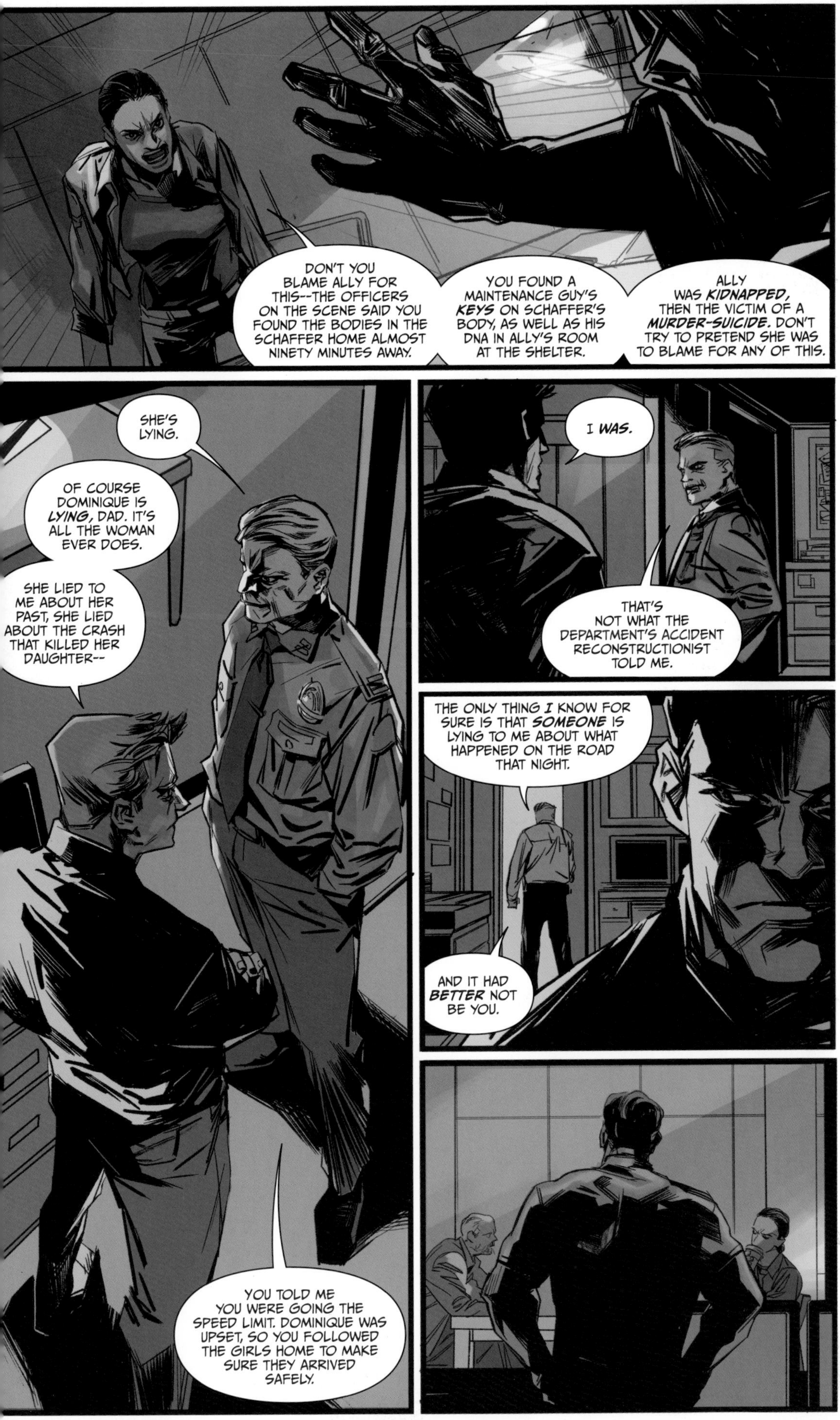
DON'T YOU BLAME ALLY FOR THIS--THE OFFICERS ON THE SCENE SAID YOU FOUND THE BODIES IN THE SCHAFFER HOME ALMOST NINETY MINUTES AWAY.
YOU FOUND A MAINTENANCE GUY'S **KEYS** ON SCHAFFER'S BODY, AS WELL AS HIS DNA IN ALLY'S ROOM AT THE SHELTER.
ALLY WAS **KIDNAPPED,** THEN THE VICTIM OF A **MURDER-SUICIDE.** DON'T TRY TO PRETEND SHE WAS TO BLAME FOR ANY OF THIS.
SHE'S LYING.
OF COURSE DOMINIQUE IS **LYING,** DAD. IT'S ALL THE WOMAN EVER DOES.
SHE LIED TO ME ABOUT HER PAST, SHE LIED ABOUT THE CRASH THAT KILLED HER DAUGHTER--
YOU TOLD ME YOU WERE GOING THE SPEED LIMIT. DOMINIQUE WAS UPSET, SO YOU FOLLOWED THE GIRLS HOME TO MAKE SURE THEY ARRIVED SAFELY.
I **WAS.**
THAT'S NOT WHAT THE DEPARTMENT'S ACCIDENT RECONSTRUCTIONIST TOLD ME.
THE ONLY THING **I** KNOW FOR SURE IS THAT **SOMEONE** IS LYING TO ME ABOUT WHAT HAPPENED ON THE ROAD THAT NIGHT.
AND IT HAD **BETTER** NOT BE YOU.

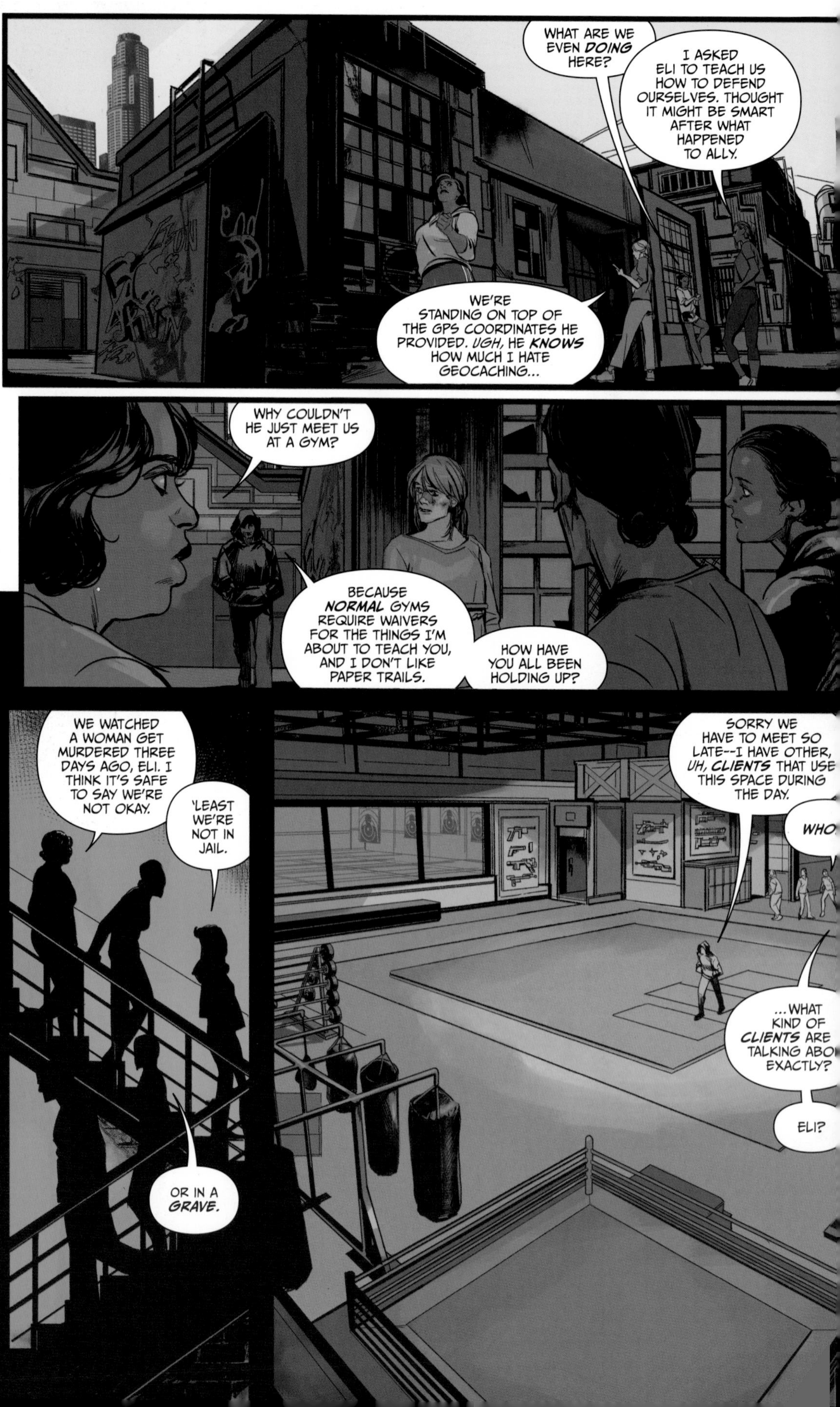

WHAT ARE WE EVEN *DOING* HERE?
I ASKED ELI TO TEACH US HOW TO DEFEND OURSELVES. THOUGHT IT MIGHT BE SMART AFTER WHAT HAPPENED TO ALLY.
WE'RE STANDING ON TOP OF THE GPS COORDINATES HE PROVIDED. *UGH*, HE ***KNOWS*** HOW MUCH I HATE GEOCACHING...
WHY COULDN'T HE JUST MEET US AT A GYM?
BECAUSE ***NORMAL*** GYMS REQUIRE WAIVERS FOR THE THINGS I'M ABOUT TO TEACH YOU, AND I DON'T LIKE PAPER TRAILS.
HOW HAVE YOU ALL BEEN HOLDING UP?
WE WATCHED A WOMAN GET MURDERED THREE DAYS AGO, ELI. I THINK IT'S SAFE TO SAY WE'RE NOT OKAY.
'LEAST WE'RE NOT IN JAIL.
OR IN A ***GRAVE***.
SORRY WE HAVE TO MEET SO LATE--I HAVE OTHER, *UH*, ***CLIENTS*** THAT USE THIS SPACE DURING THE DAY.
WHO
...WHAT KIND OF ***CLIENTS*** ARE TALKING ABO
EXACTLY?
ELI?

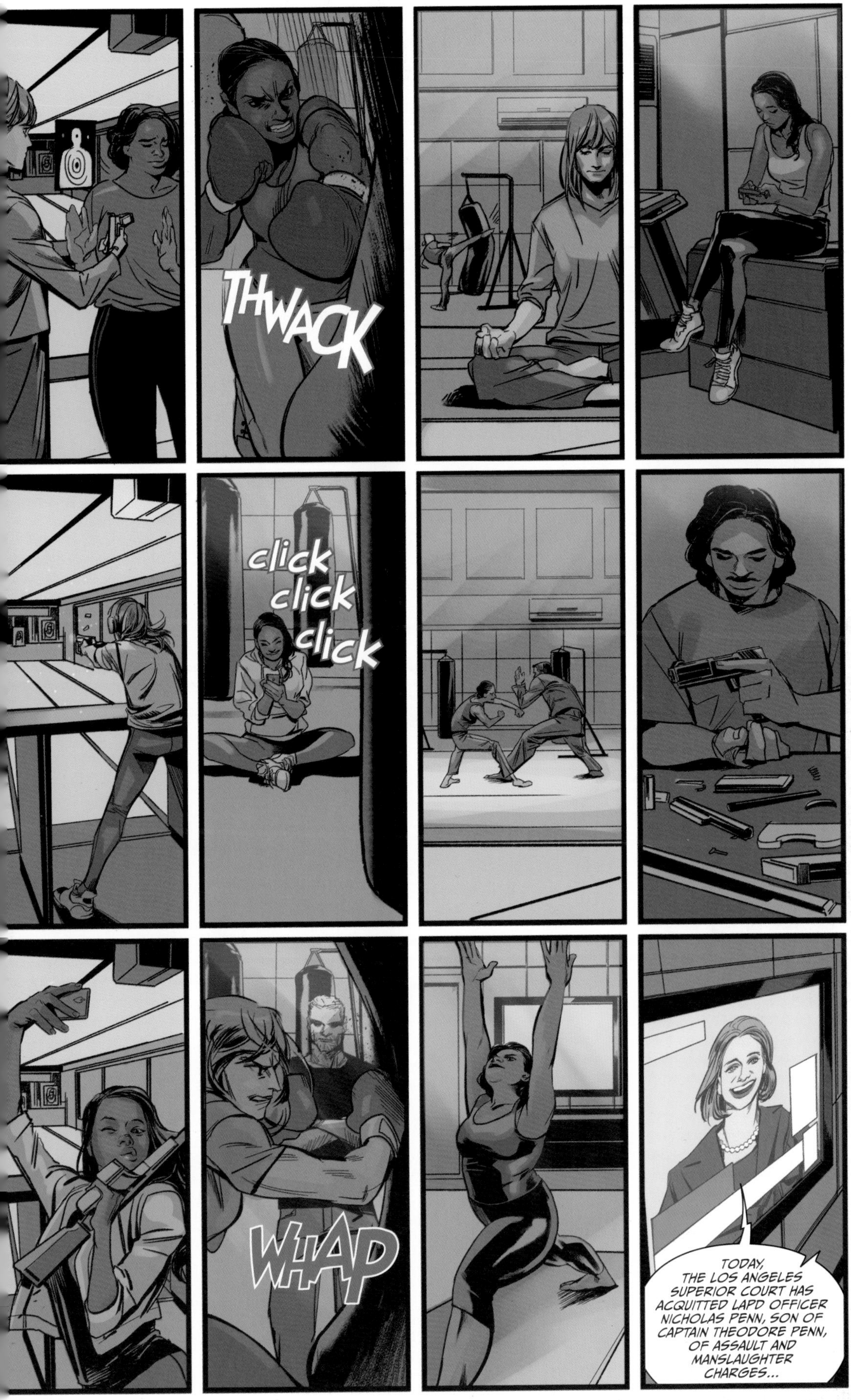
THWACK
click
click
click
WHAP
TODAY, THE LOS ANGELES SUPERIOR COURT HAS ACQUITTED LAPD OFFICER NICHOLAS PENN, SON OF CAPTAIN THEODORE PENN, OF ASSAULT AND MANSLAUGHTER CHARGES...

DOMINIQUE? WE SAW THE NEWS... YOU OKAY, HON?

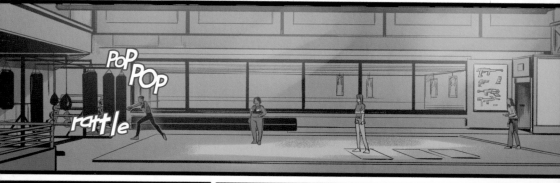

POP POP

rattle

POW

DOMINIQUE...?

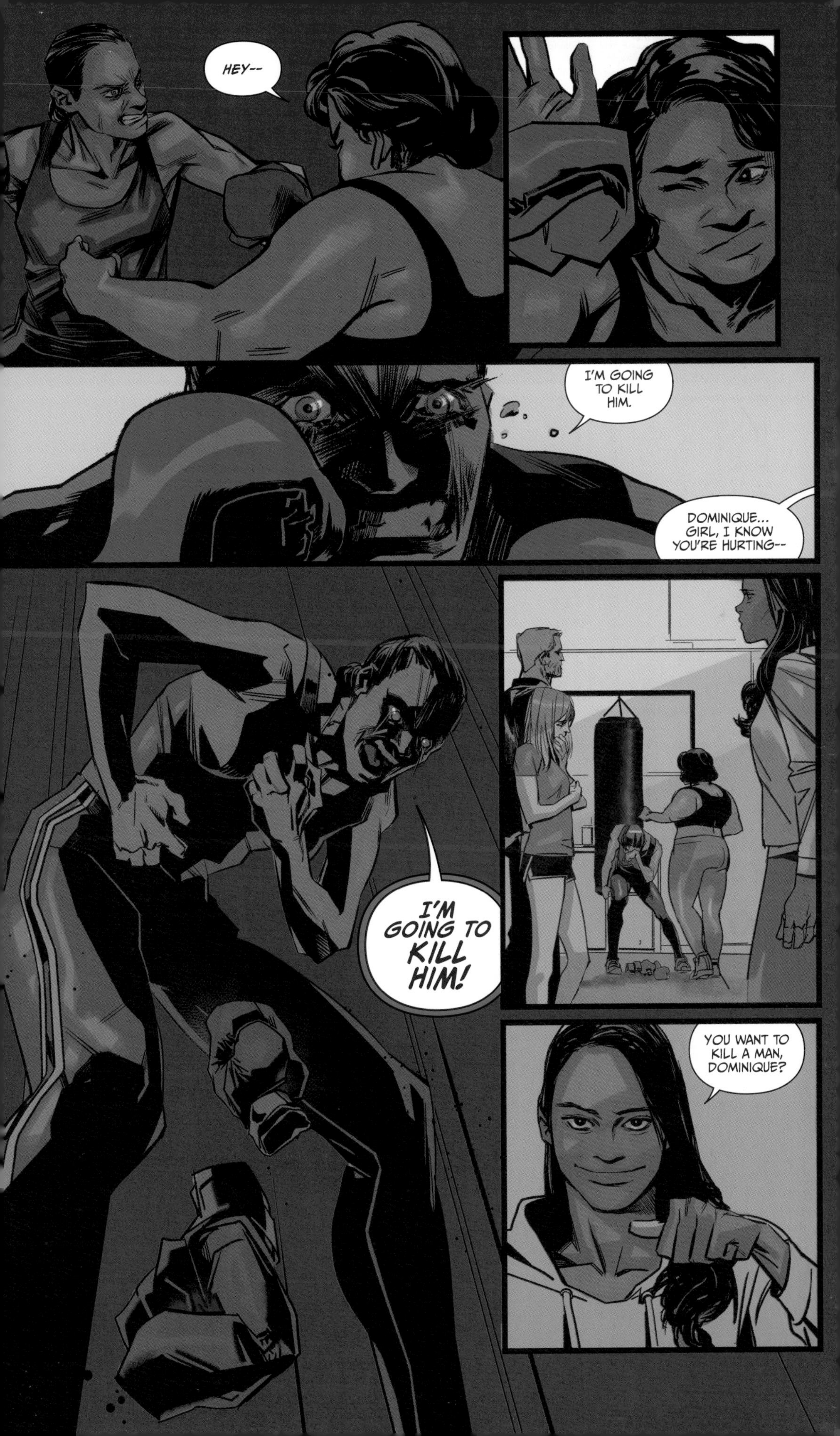

HEY--
I'M GOING TO KILL HIM.
DOMINIQUE... GIRL, I KNOW YOU'RE HURTING--
I'M GOING TO KILL HIM!
YOU WANT TO KILL A MAN, DOMINIQUE?

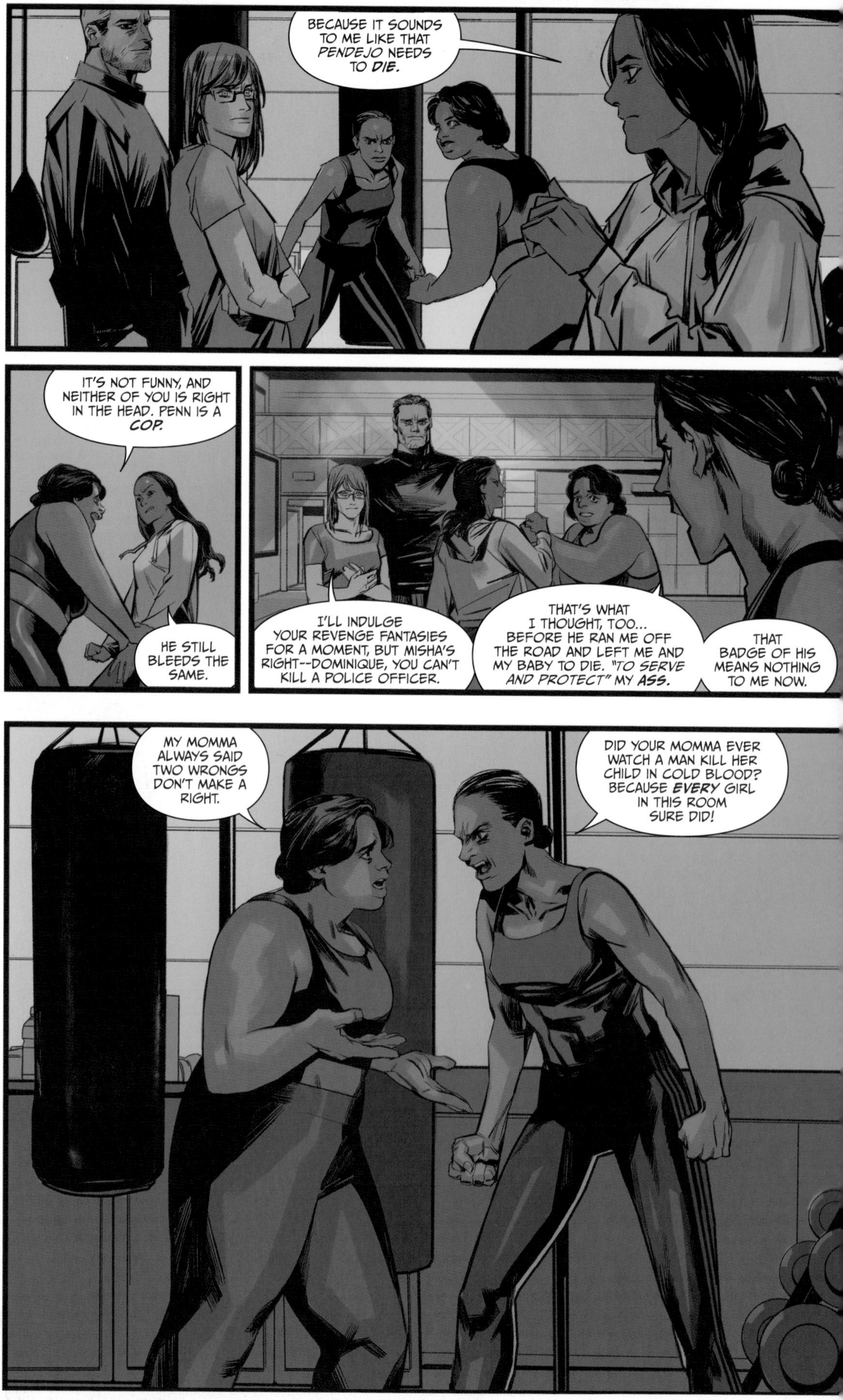
BECAUSE IT SOUNDS TO ME LIKE THAT *PENDEJO* NEEDS TO ***DIE.***
IT'S NOT FUNNY, AND NEITHER OF YOU IS RIGHT IN THE HEAD. PENN IS A ***COP.***
HE STILL BLEEDS THE SAME.
I'LL INDULGE YOUR REVENGE FANTASIES FOR A MOMENT, BUT MISHA'S RIGHT--DOMINIQUE, YOU CAN'T KILL A POLICE OFFICER.
THAT'S WHAT I THOUGHT, TOO... BEFORE HE RAN ME OFF THE ROAD AND LEFT ME AND MY BABY TO DIE. *"TO SERVE AND PROTECT"* MY ***ASS.***
THAT BADGE OF HIS MEANS NOTHING TO ME NOW.
MY MOMMA ALWAYS SAID TWO WRONGS DON'T MAKE A RIGHT.
DID YOUR MOMMA EVER WATCH A MAN KILL HER CHILD IN COLD BLOOD? BECAUSE ***EVERY*** GIRL IN THIS ROOM SURE DID!

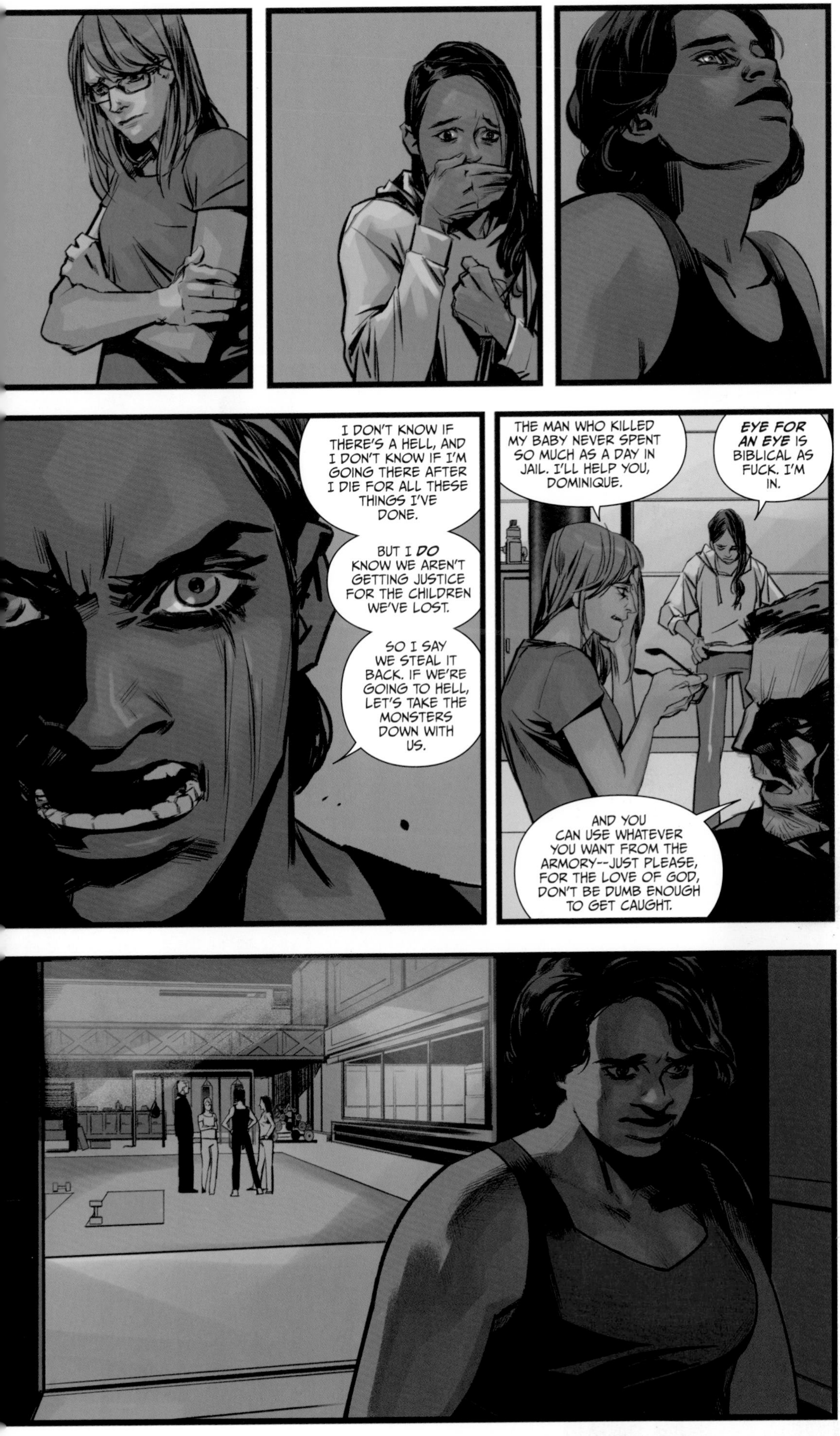
I DON'T KNOW IF THERE'S A HELL, AND I DON'T KNOW IF I'M GOING THERE AFTER I DIE FOR ALL THESE THINGS I'VE DONE.
BUT I *DO* KNOW WE AREN'T GETTING JUSTICE FOR THE CHILDREN WE'VE LOST.
SO I SAY WE STEAL IT BACK. IF WE'RE GOING TO HELL, LET'S TAKE THE MONSTERS DOWN WITH US.
THE MAN WHO KILLED MY BABY NEVER SPENT SO MUCH AS A DAY IN JAIL. I'LL HELP YOU, DOMINIQUE.
EYE FOR AN EYE IS BIBLICAL AS FUCK. I'M IN.
AND YOU CAN USE WHATEVER YOU WANT FROM THE ARMORY--JUST PLEASE, FOR THE LOVE OF GOD, DON'T BE DUMB ENOUGH TO GET CAUGHT.

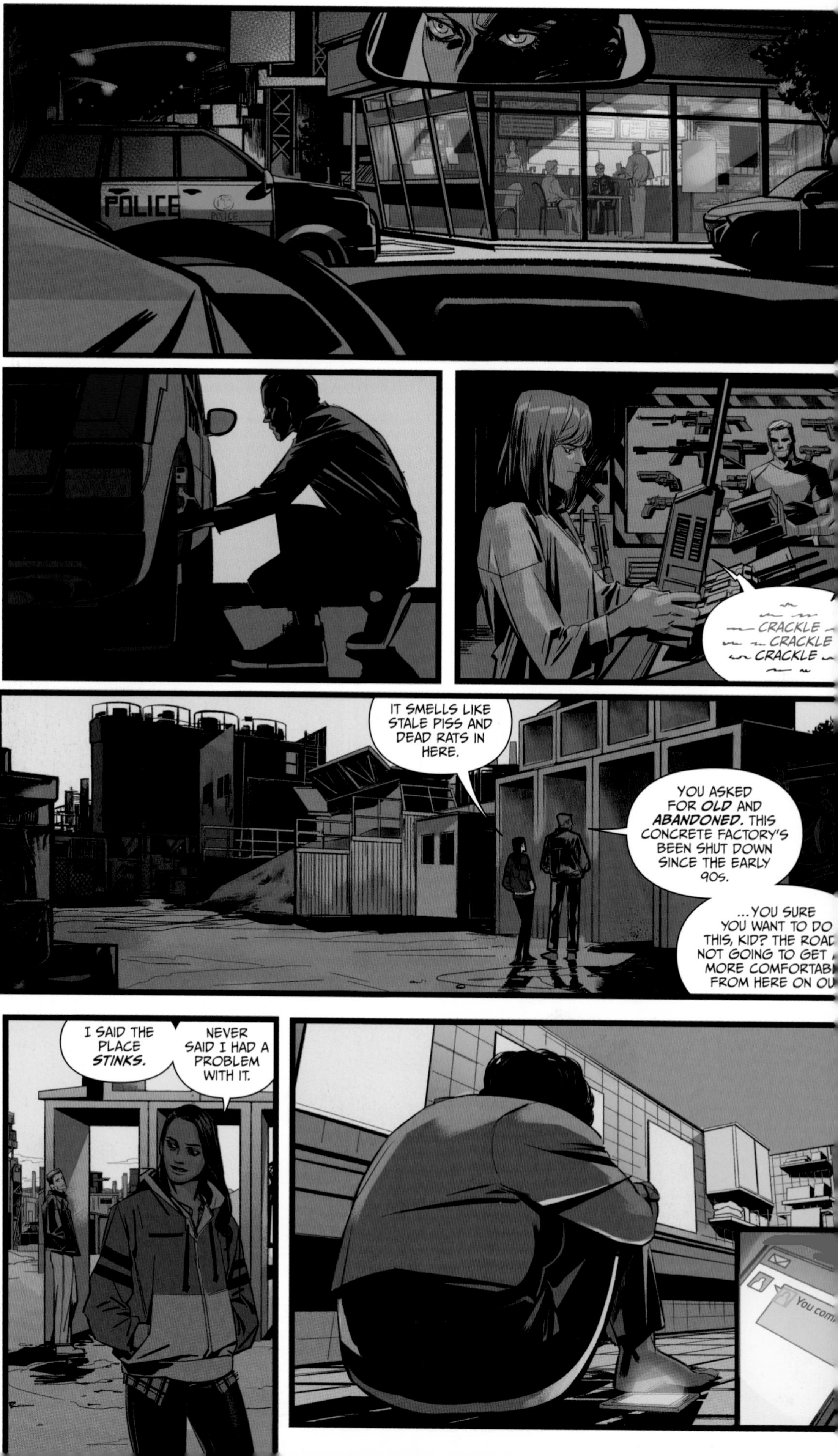
POLICE
POLICE
CRACKLE CRACKLE CRACKLE
IT SMELLS LIKE STALE PISS AND DEAD RATS IN HERE.
YOU ASKED FOR OLD AND ABANDONED. THIS CONCRETE FACTORY'S BEEN SHUT DOWN SINCE THE EARLY 90S.
...YOU SURE YOU WANT TO DO THIS, KID? THE ROAD NOT GOING TO GET MORE COMFORTAB FROM HERE ON OU
I SAID THE PLACE STINKS.
NEVER SAID I HAD A PROBLEM WITH IT.
You com

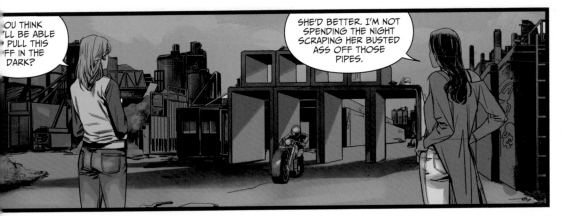

OU THINK 'LL BE ABLE PULL THIS FF IN THE DARK?

SHE'D BETTER. I'M NOT SPENDING THE NIGHT SCRAPING HER BUSTED ASS OFF THOSE PIPES.

THIS RADIO JAMMER WILL ONLY WORK IN A THIRTY METER RADIUS AROUND YOUR BIKE, DOMINIQUE. YOU'LL NEED TO KEEP PENN WITHIN RANGE.

I HEARD YOU THE FIRST TIME, GRETA. PUTTING A HELMET ON DIDN'T MAKE ME DEAF.

I'VE WIRED THE WAREHOUSE'S FLOODLIGHTS TO COME ON FIVE SECONDS AFTER YOU PASS THE FRONT GATES.

'TIL THEN, I'VE PLACED REFLECTIVE STRIPS ON THE BOX CULVERTS TO HELP GUIDE YOU. IT'S NOT MUCH, BUT IT'LL HAVE TO DO.

WE'LL BACK YOU UP, DOM, BUT THIS ONE'S YOURS.

THIS ONE? YOU EXPECT THERE TO BE OTHERS?

CALL IT A HUNCH.

NO, NO, THIS IS A ONE-TIME OPERATION, LADIES.

MMHMM.

I'VE GOT PENN'S LOCATION--HE'S DOWNTOWN, NEAR ELI'S CHURCH.

YOU'RE SURE ABOUT THIS, DOMINIQUE?

NO DOUBTS, NO REGRETS. LET'S GO.

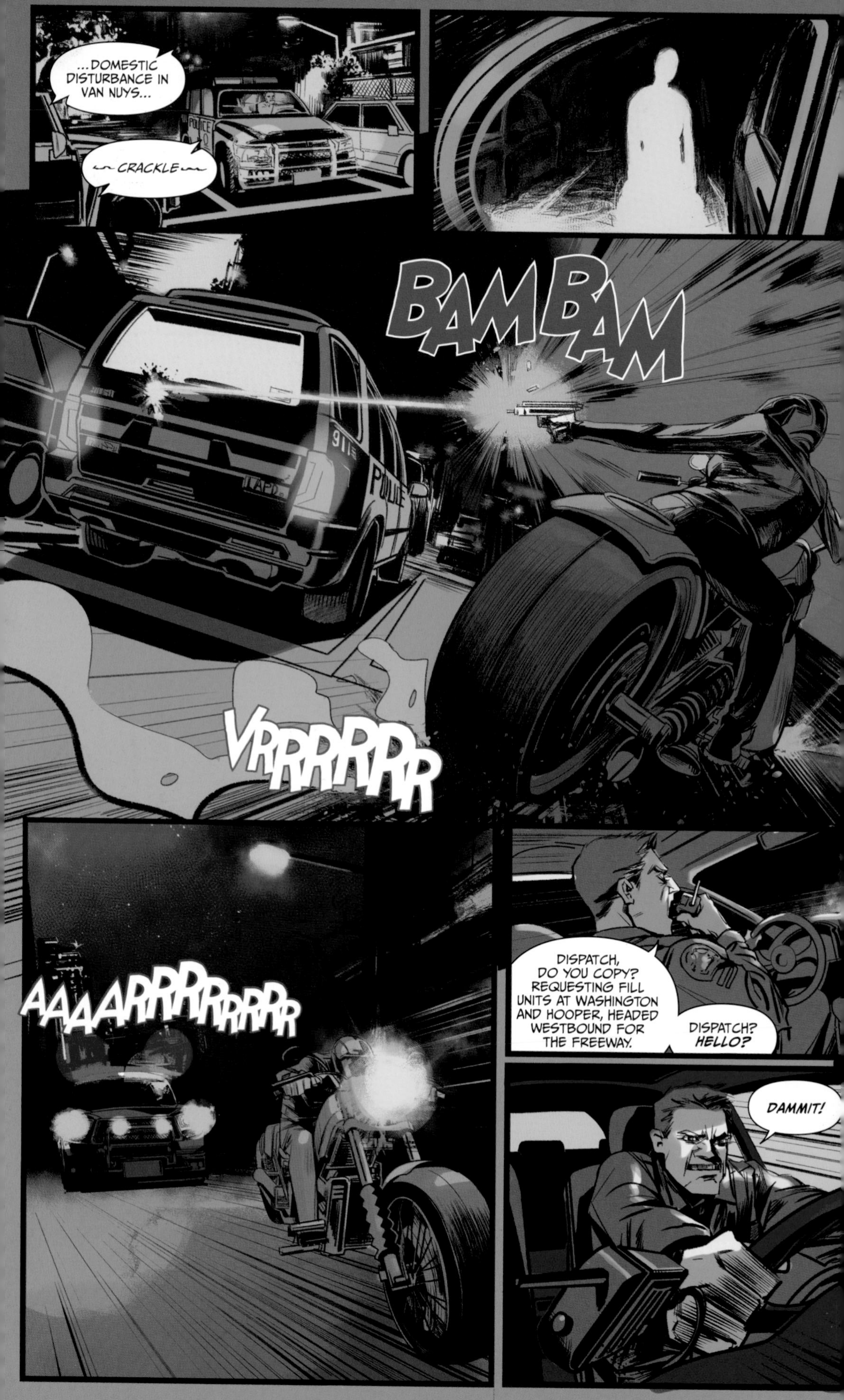

...DOMESTIC DISTURBANCE IN VAN NUYS...
CRACKLE
BAM BAM
VRRRRRRR
AAAARRRRRRRRR
DISPATCH, DO YOU COPY? REQUESTING FILL UNITS AT WASHINGTON AND HOOPER, HEADED WESTBOUND FOR THE FREEWAY.
DISPATCH? *HELLO?*
DAMMIT!

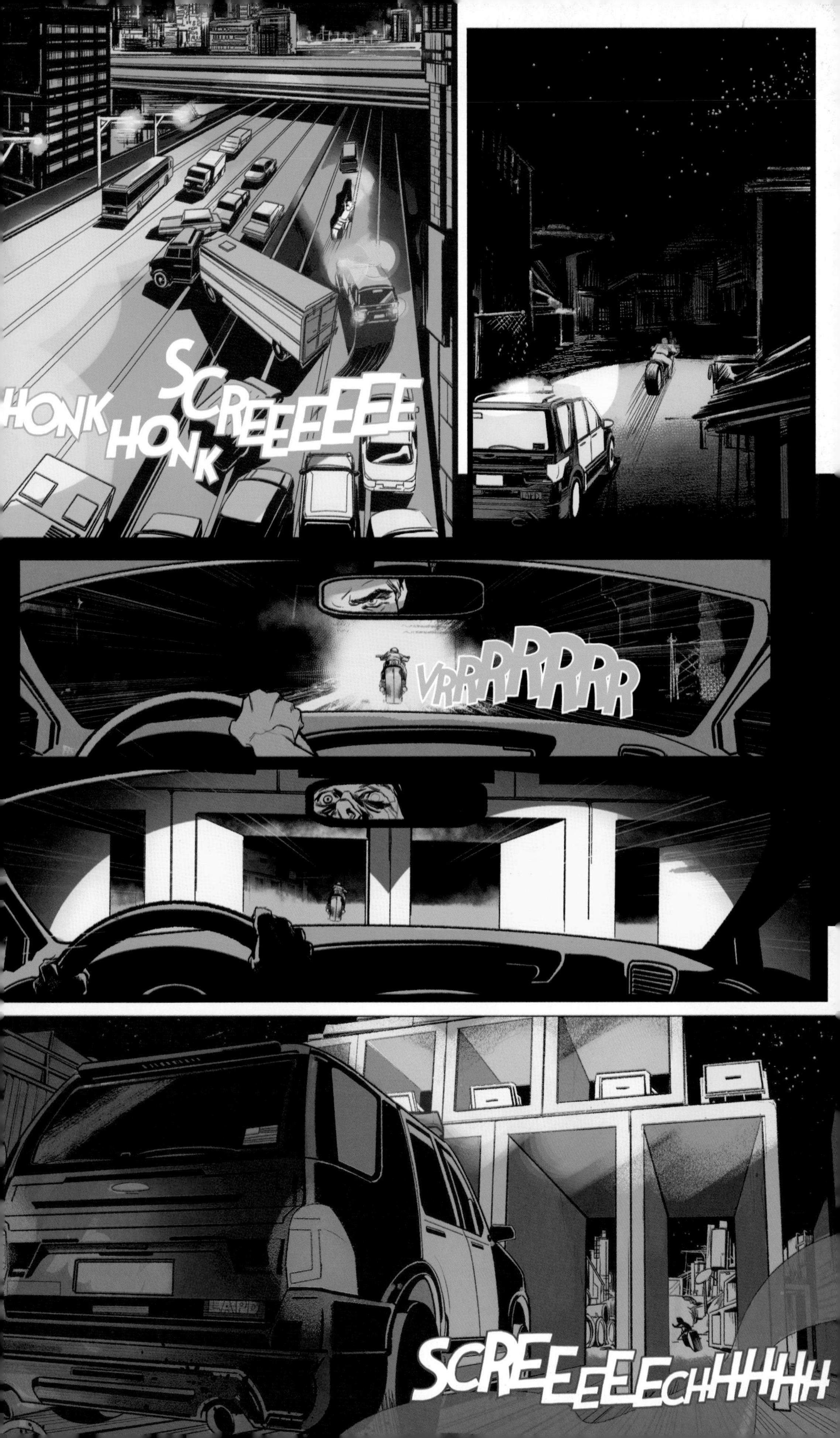
SCREEEEEEEE
HONK
HONK
VRRRRRRRR
SCREEEEECHHHHHH

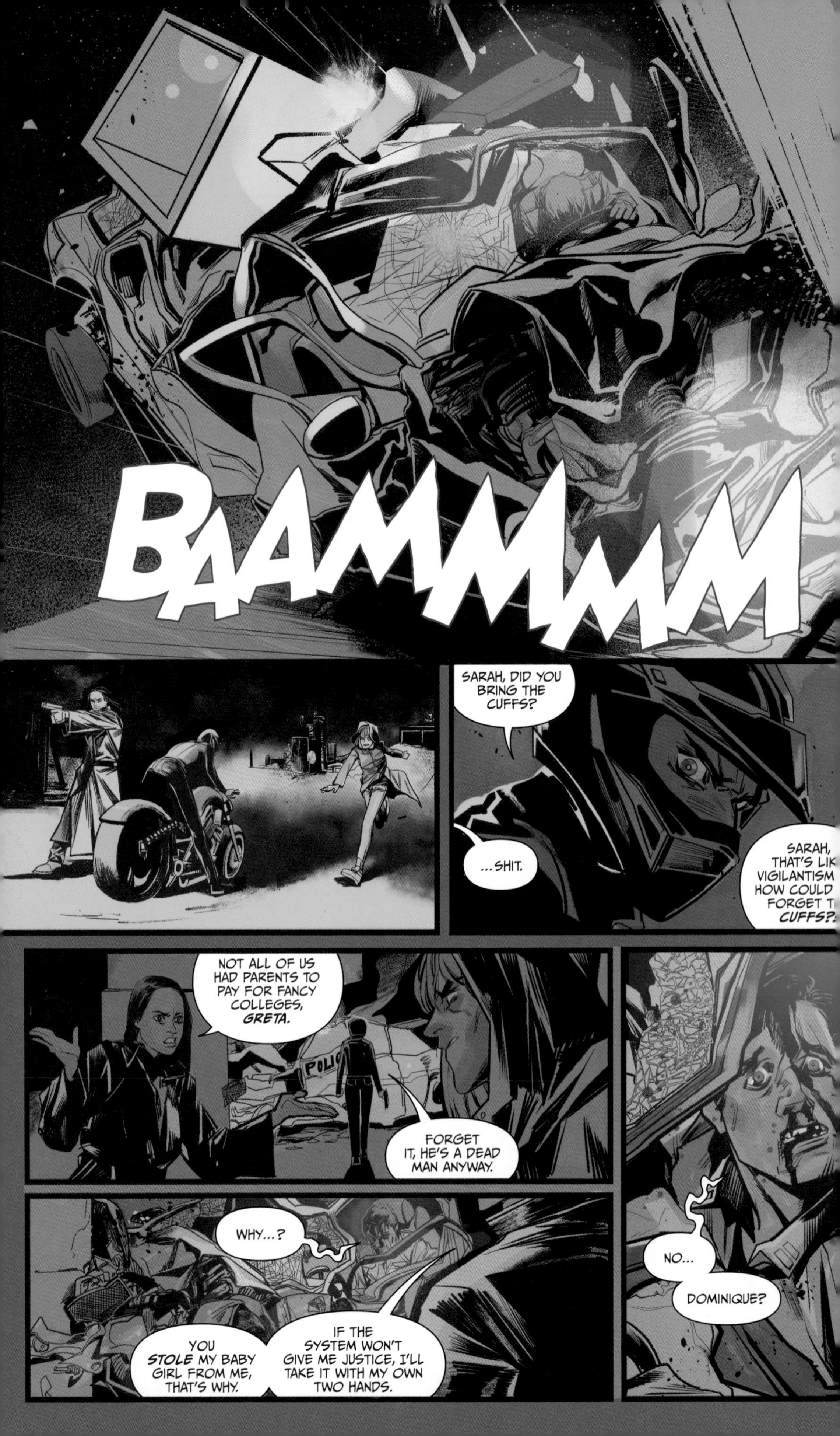
BAAMMMM
SARAH, DID YOU BRING THE CUFFS?
...SHIT.
SARAH, THAT'S LIK
VIGILANTISM
HOW COULD
FORGET T
CUFFS?
NOT ALL OF US HAD PARENTS TO PAY FOR FANCY COLLEGES, GRETA.
FORGET IT, HE'S A DEAD MAN ANYWAY.
NO...
DOMINIQUE?
WHY...?
YOU STOLE MY BABY GIRL FROM ME, THAT'S WHY.
IF THE SYSTEM WON'T GIVE ME JUSTICE, I'LL TAKE IT WITH MY OWN TWO HANDS.

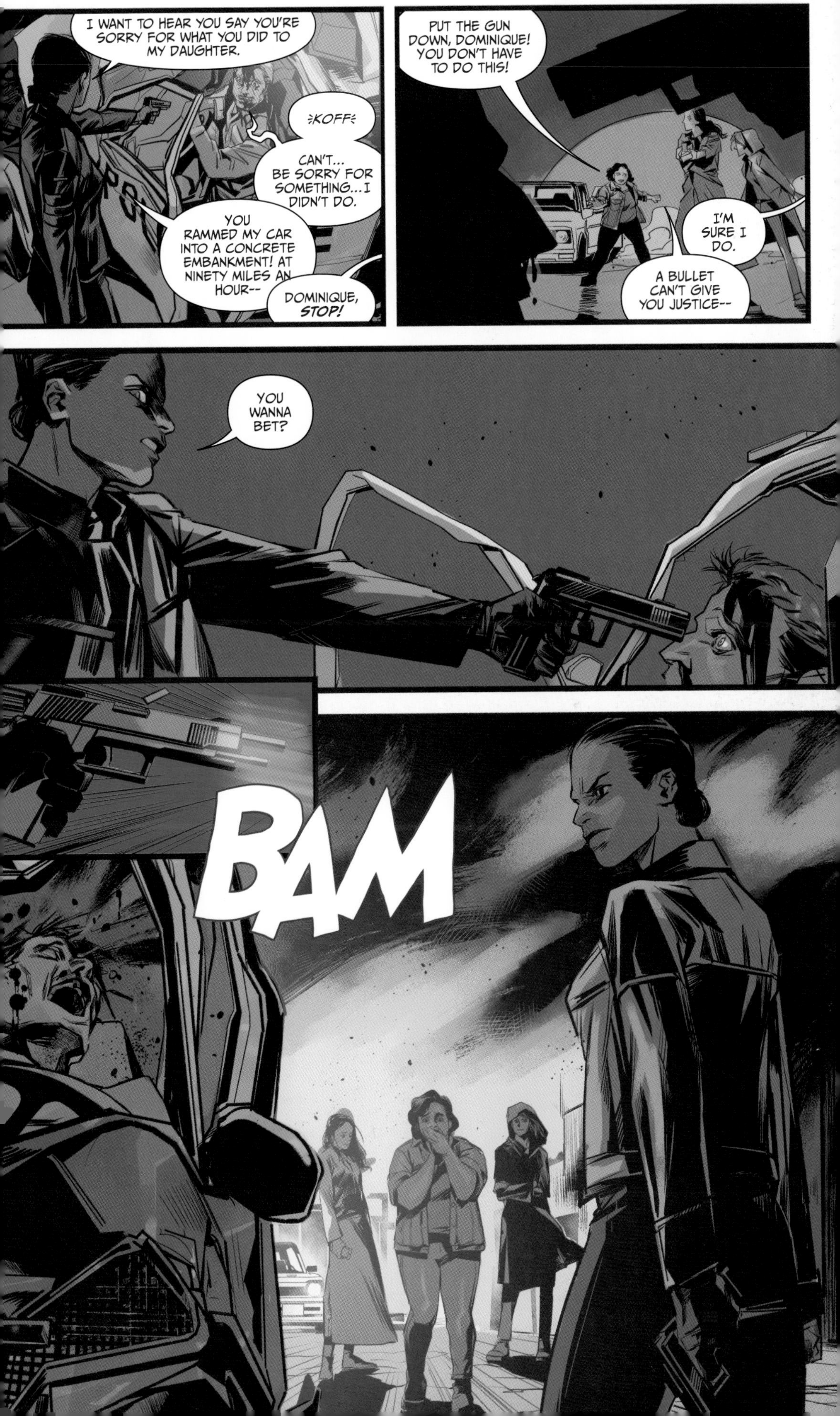
I WANT TO HEAR YOU SAY YOU'RE SORRY FOR WHAT YOU DID TO MY DAUGHTER.
≷KOFF≶
CAN'T... BE SORRY FOR SOMETHING...I DIDN'T DO.
YOU RAMMED MY CAR INTO A CONCRETE EMBANKMENT! AT NINETY MILES AN HOUR--
DOMINIQUE, STOP!
PUT THE GUN DOWN, DOMINIQUE! YOU DON'T HAVE TO DO THIS!
I'M SURE I DO.
A BULLET CAN'T GIVE YOU JUSTICE--
YOU WANNA BET?
BAM

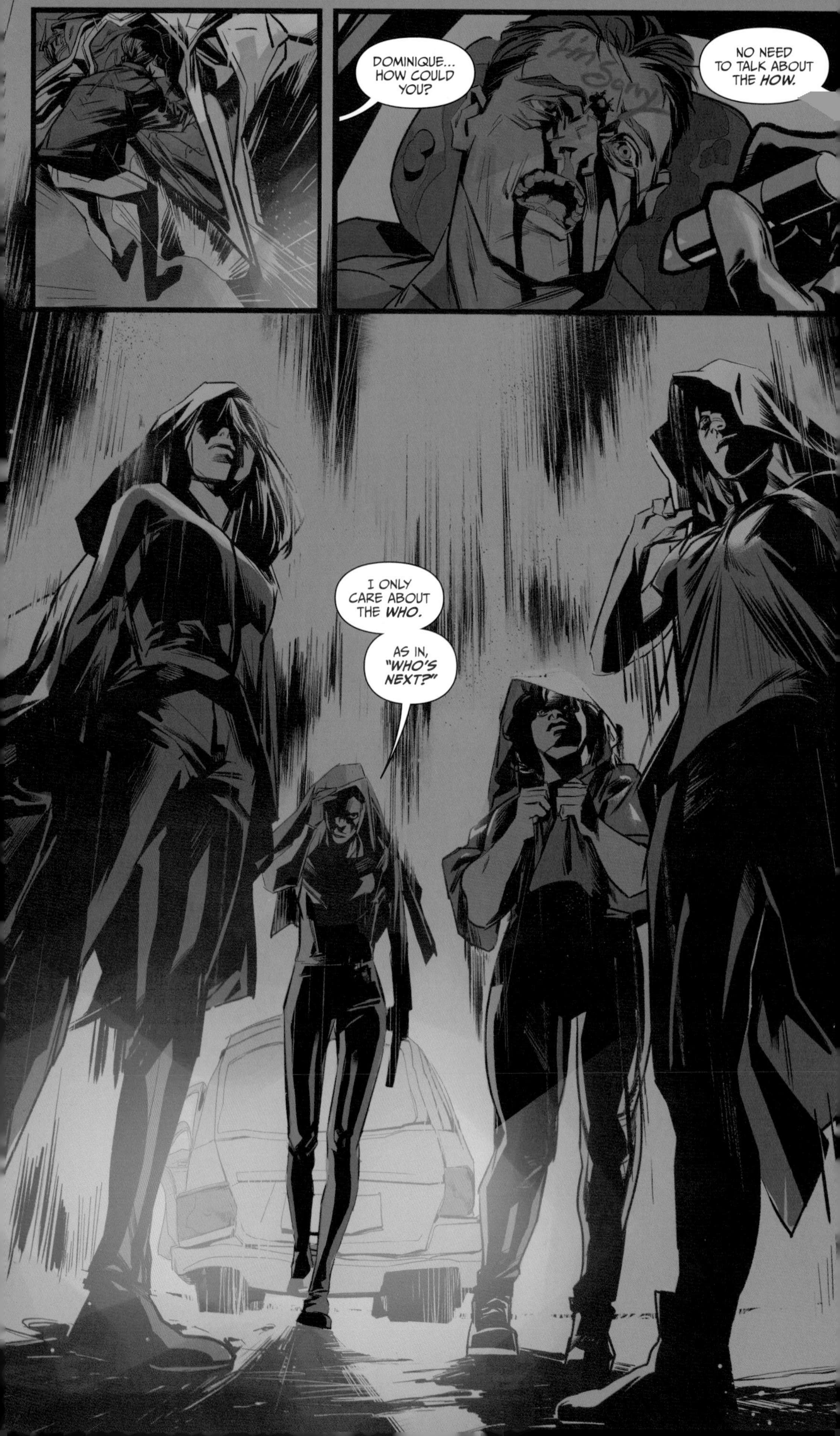
DOMINIQUE... HOW COULD YOU?
NO NEED TO TALK ABOUT THE HOW.
I ONLY CARE ABOUT THE WHO.
AS IN, "WHO'S NEXT?"

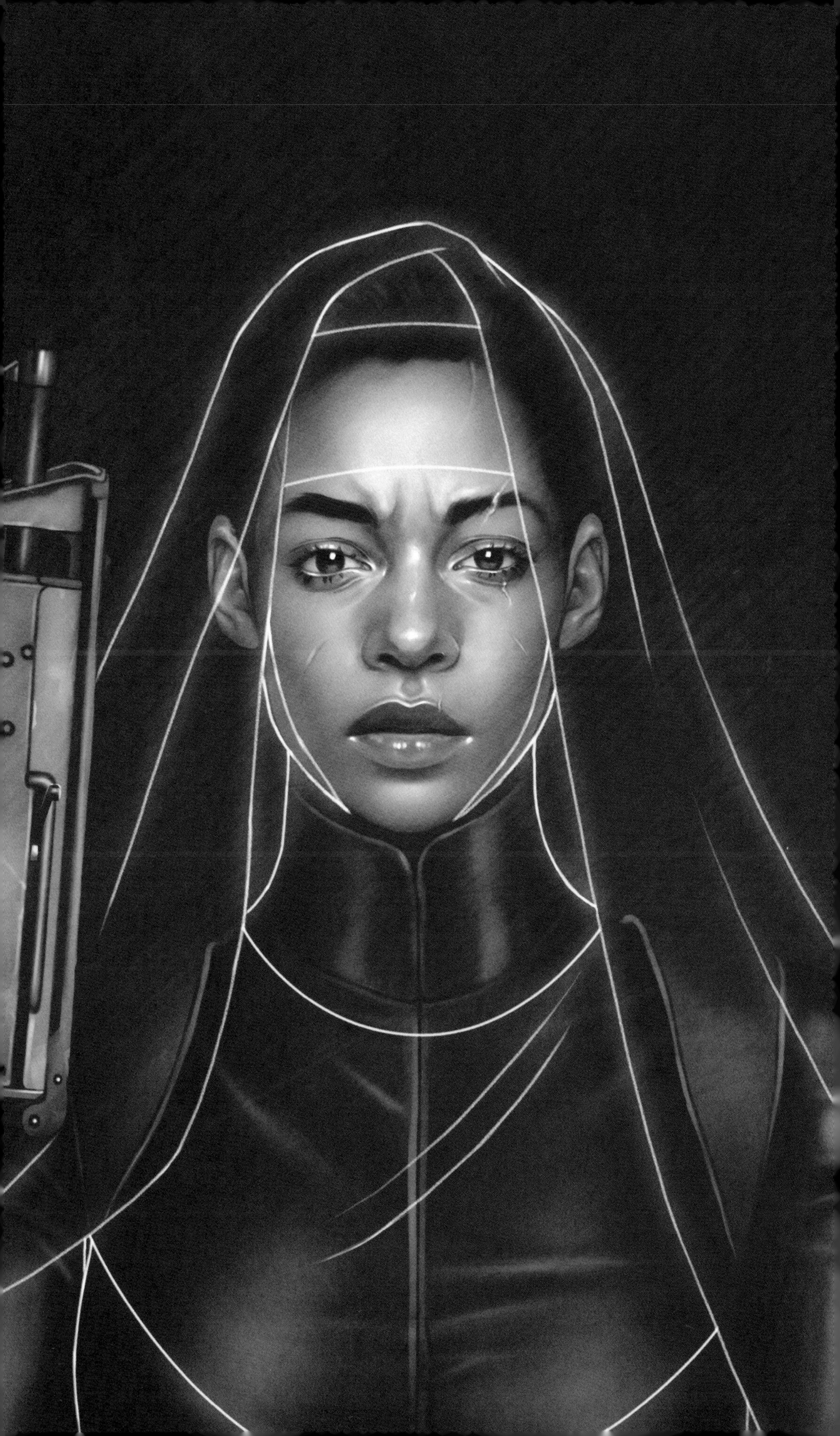

CHAPTER TWO

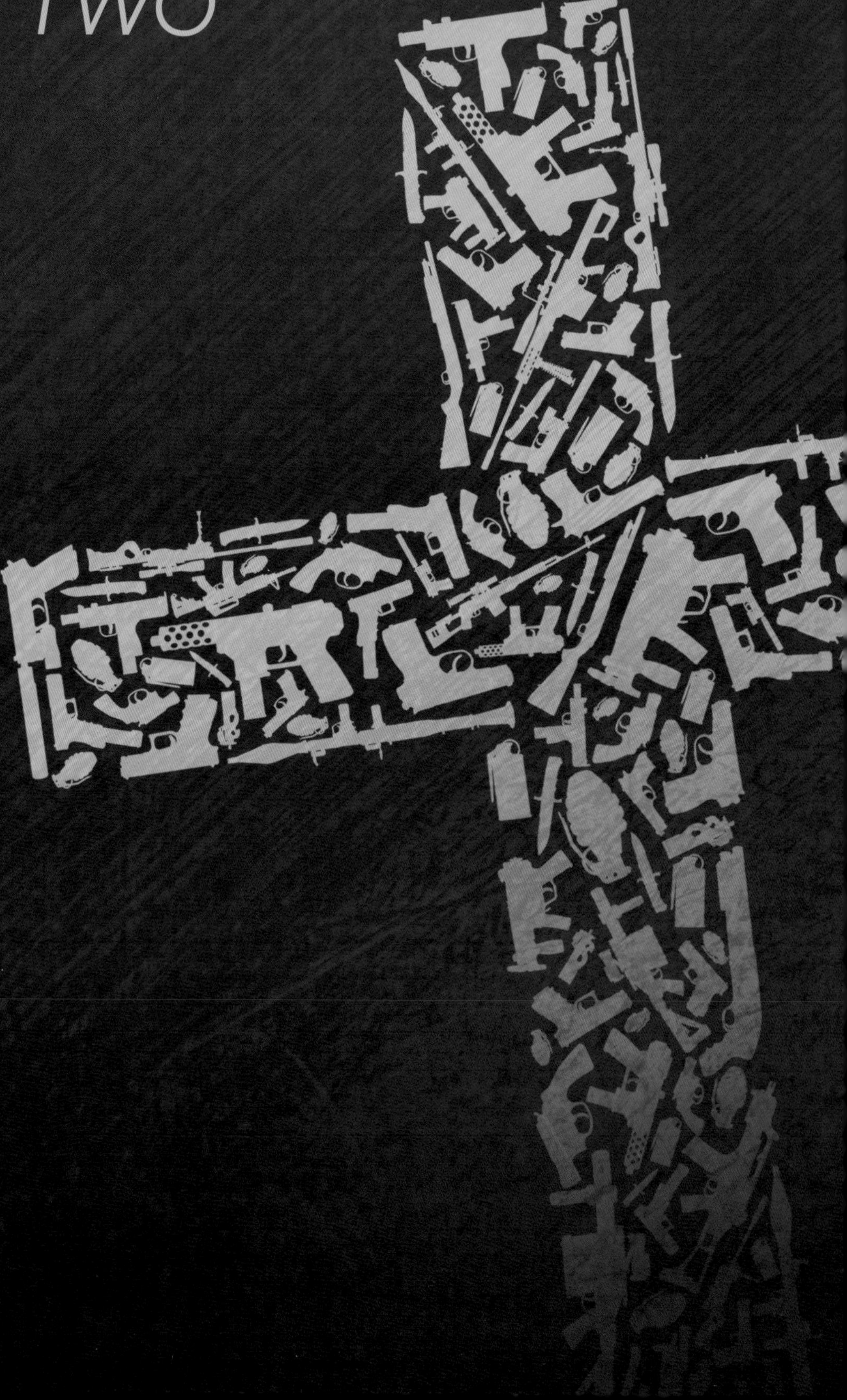

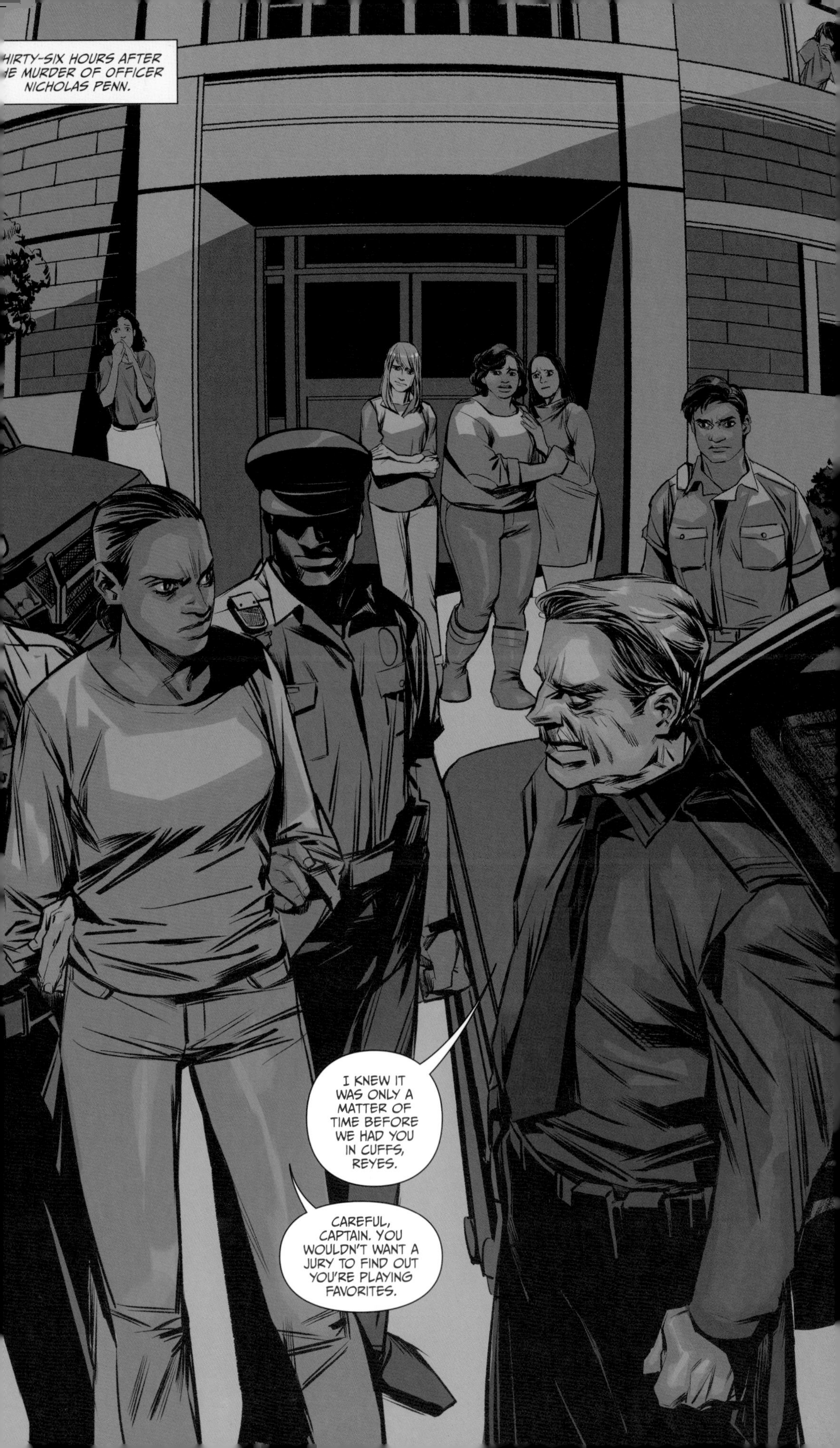
HIRTY-SIX HOURS AFTER
HE MURDER OF OFFICER
NICHOLAS PENN.
I KNEW IT WAS ONLY A MATTER OF TIME BEFORE WE HAD YOU IN CUFFS, REYES.
CAREFUL, CAPTAIN. YOU WOULDN'T WANT A JURY TO FIND OUT YOU'RE PLAYING FAVORITES.

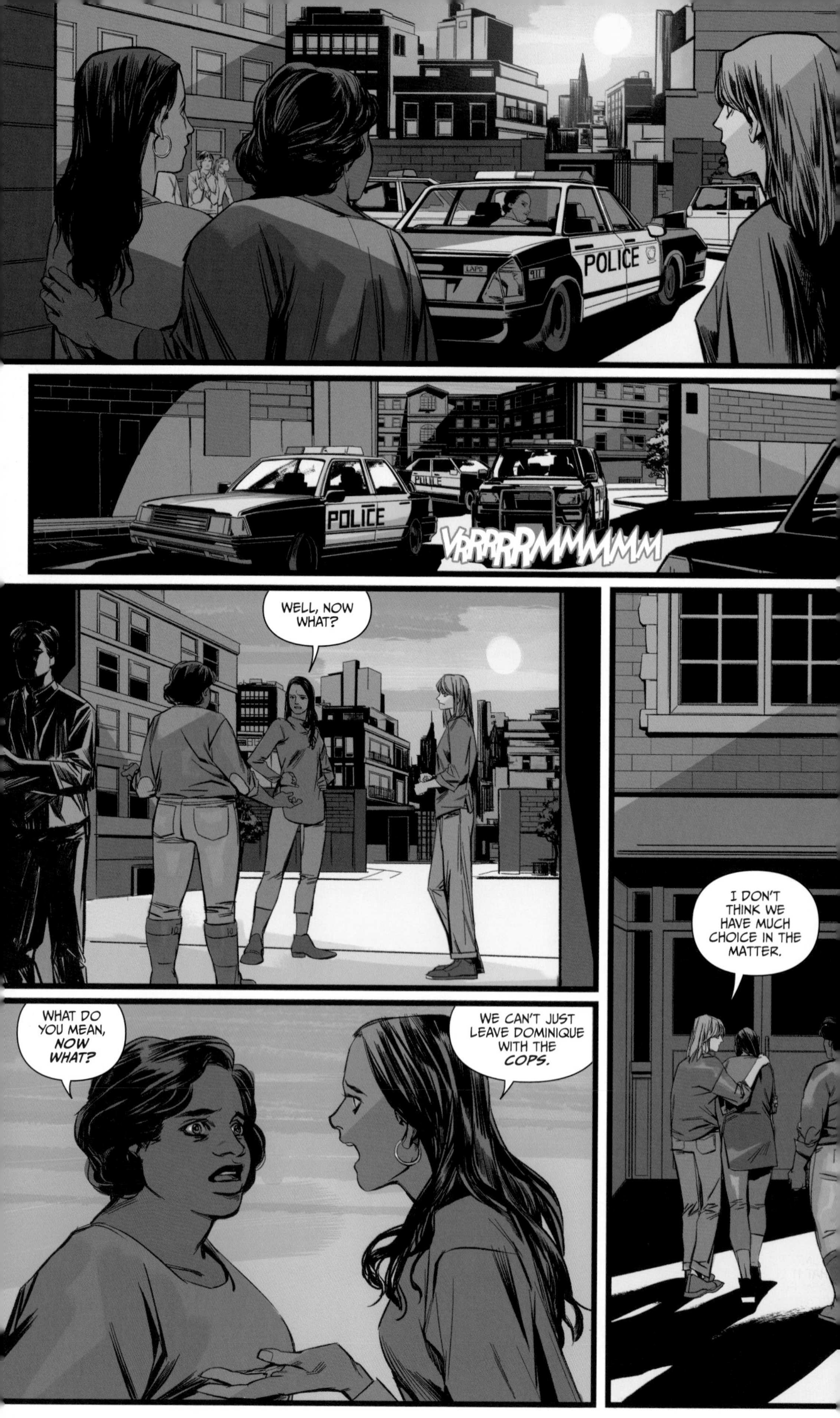
POLICE
LAPD
POLICE
POLICE
VRRRRRMMMMMM
WELL, NOW WHAT?
I DON'T THINK WE HAVE MUCH CHOICE IN THE MATTER.
WHAT DO YOU MEAN, *NOW WHAT?*
WE CAN'T JUST LEAVE DOMINIQUE WITH THE *COPS.*

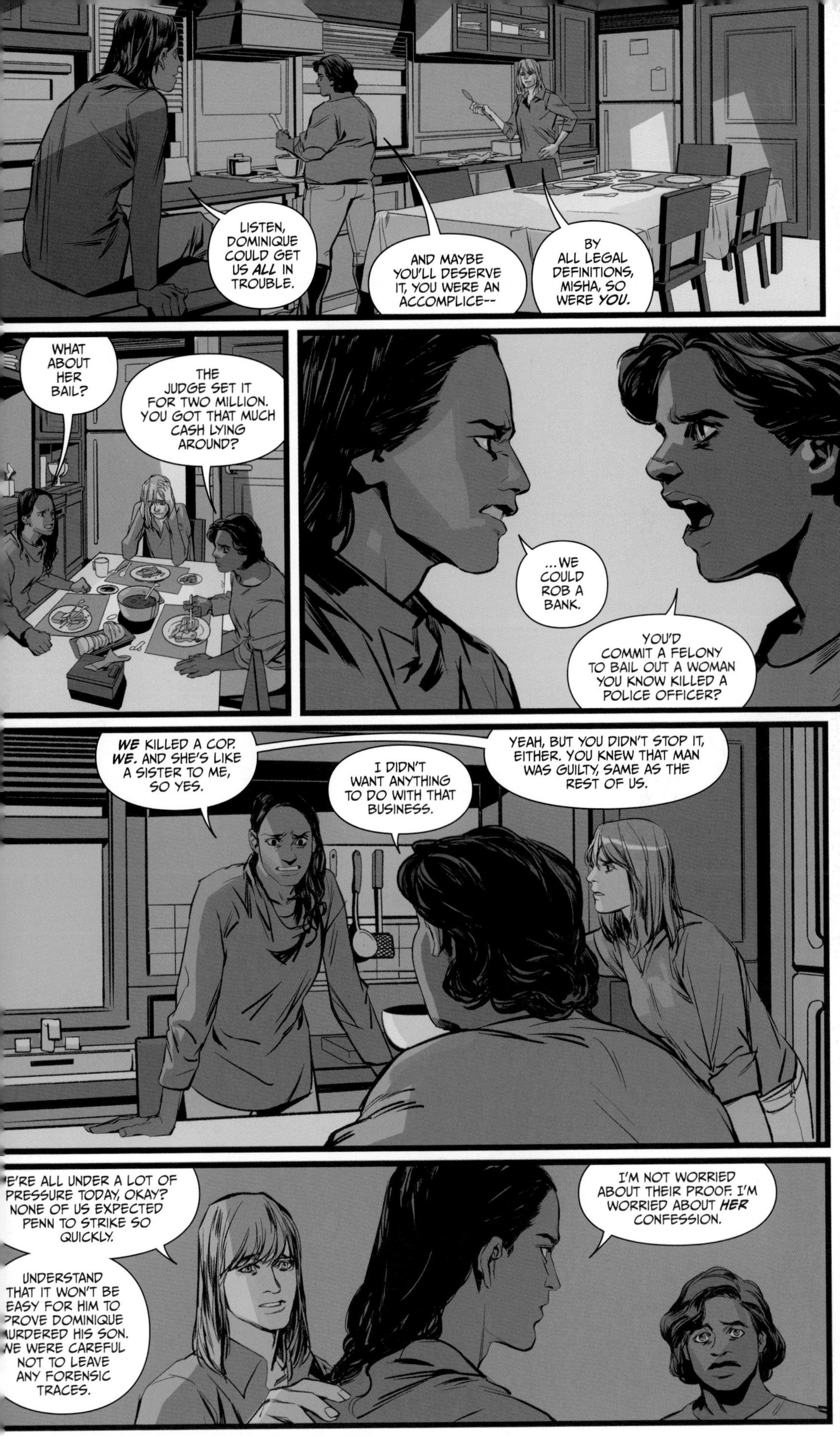
LISTEN, DOMINIQUE COULD GET US *ALL* IN TROUBLE.
AND MAYBE YOU'LL DESERVE IT, YOU WERE AN ACCOMPLICE--
BY ALL LEGAL DEFINITIONS, MISHA, SO WERE *YOU.*
WHAT ABOUT HER BAIL?
THE JUDGE SET IT FOR TWO MILLION. YOU GOT THAT MUCH CASH LYING AROUND?
...WE COULD ROB A BANK.
YOU'D COMMIT A FELONY TO BAIL OUT A WOMAN YOU KNOW KILLED A POLICE OFFICER?
WE KILLED A COP. *WE.* AND SHE'S LIKE A SISTER TO ME, SO YES.
I DIDN'T WANT ANYTHING TO DO WITH THAT BUSINESS.
YEAH, BUT YOU DIDN'T STOP IT, EITHER. YOU KNEW THAT MAN WAS GUILTY, SAME AS THE REST OF US.
'E'RE ALL UNDER A LOT OF PRESSURE TODAY, OKAY? NONE OF US EXPECTED PENN TO STRIKE SO QUICKLY.
UNDERSTAND THAT IT WON'T BE EASY FOR HIM TO PROVE DOMINIQUE URDERED HIS SON. VE WERE CAREFUL NOT TO LEAVE ANY FORENSIC TRACES.
I'M NOT WORRIED ABOUT THEIR PROOF. I'M WORRIED ABOUT *HER* CONFESSION.

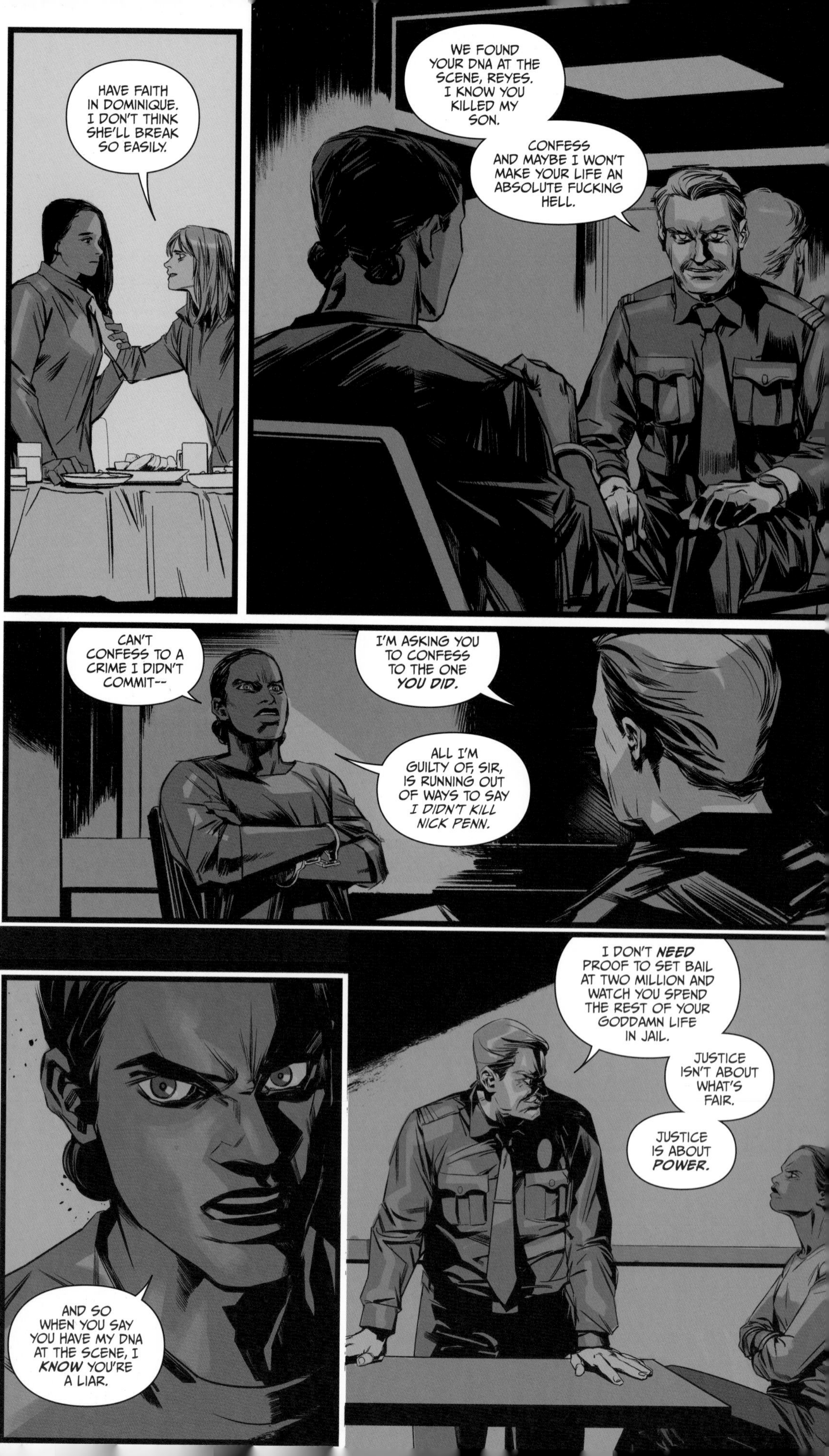

HAVE FAITH IN DOMINIQUE. I DON'T THINK SHE'LL BREAK SO EASILY.
WE FOUND YOUR DNA AT THE SCENE, REYES. I KNOW YOU KILLED MY SON.
CONFESS AND MAYBE I WON'T MAKE YOUR LIFE AN ABSOLUTE FUCKING HELL.
CAN'T CONFESS TO A CRIME I DIDN'T COMMIT--
I'M ASKING YOU TO CONFESS TO THE ONE *YOU DID.*
ALL I'M GUILTY OF, SIR, IS RUNNING OUT OF WAYS TO SAY *I DIDN'T KILL NICK PENN.*
I DON'T ***NEED*** PROOF TO SET BAIL AT TWO MILLION AND WATCH YOU SPEND THE REST OF YOUR GODDAMN LIFE IN JAIL.
JUSTICE ISN'T ABOUT WHAT'S FAIR.
JUSTICE IS ABOUT ***POWER.***
AND SO WHEN YOU SAY YOU HAVE MY DNA AT THE SCENE, I ***KNOW*** YOU'RE A LIAR.

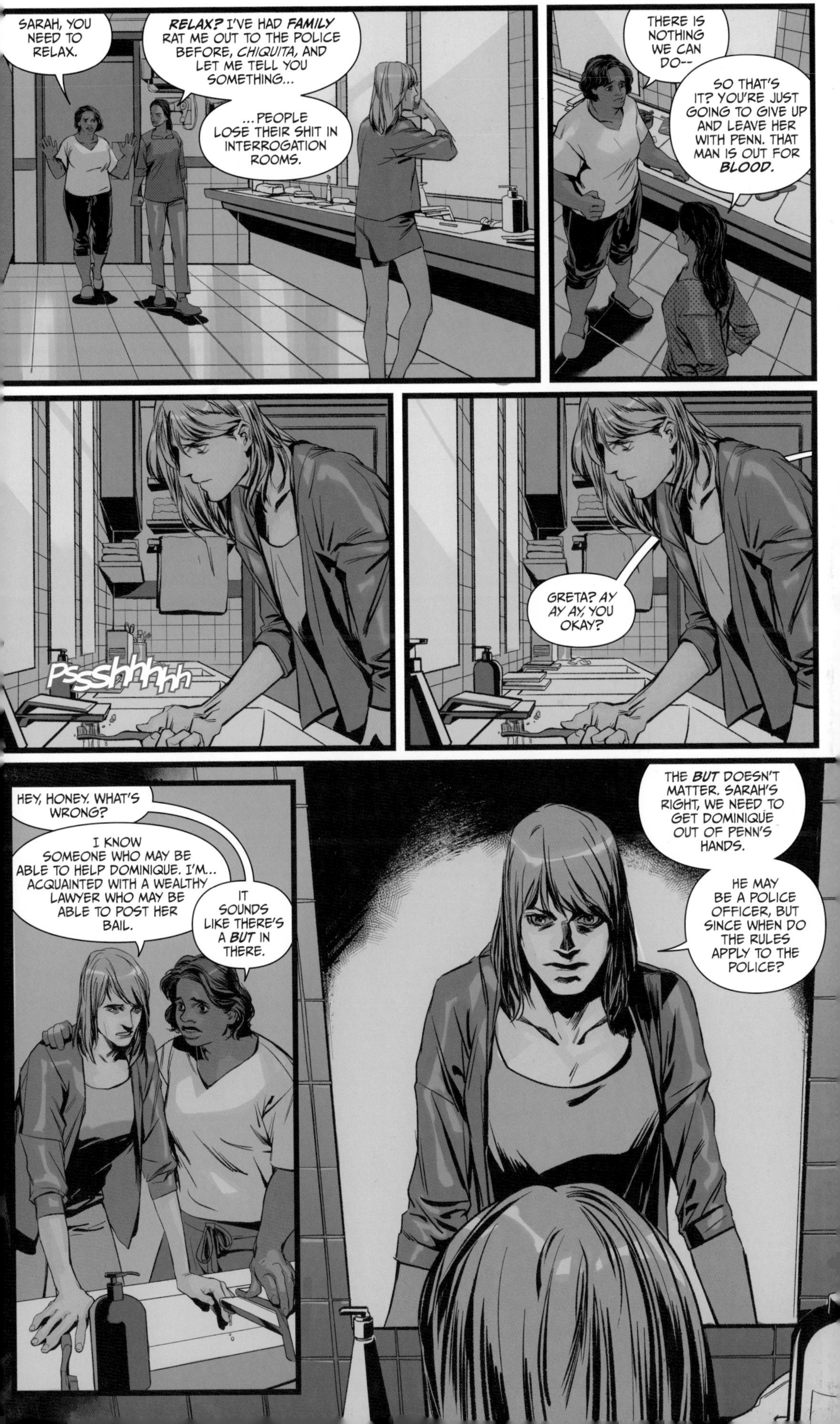
SARAH, YOU NEED TO RELAX.
RELAX? I'VE HAD FAMILY RAT ME OUT TO THE POLICE BEFORE, CHIQUITA, AND LET ME TELL YOU SOMETHING...
...PEOPLE LOSE THEIR SHIT IN INTERROGATION ROOMS.
THERE IS NOTHING WE CAN DO--
SO THAT'S IT? YOU'RE JUST GOING TO GIVE UP AND LEAVE HER WITH PENN. THAT MAN IS OUT FOR BLOOD.
PSSSHHHHH
GRETA? AY AY AY, YOU OKAY?
HEY, HONEY. WHAT'S WRONG?
I KNOW SOMEONE WHO MAY BE ABLE TO HELP DOMINIQUE. I'M... ACQUAINTED WITH A WEALTHY LAWYER WHO MAY BE ABLE TO POST HER BAIL.
IT SOUNDS LIKE THERE'S A BUT IN THERE.
THE BUT DOESN'T MATTER. SARAH'S RIGHT, WE NEED TO GET DOMINIQUE OUT OF PENN'S HANDS.
HE MAY BE A POLICE OFFICER, BUT SINCE WHEN DO THE RULES APPLY TO THE POLICE?

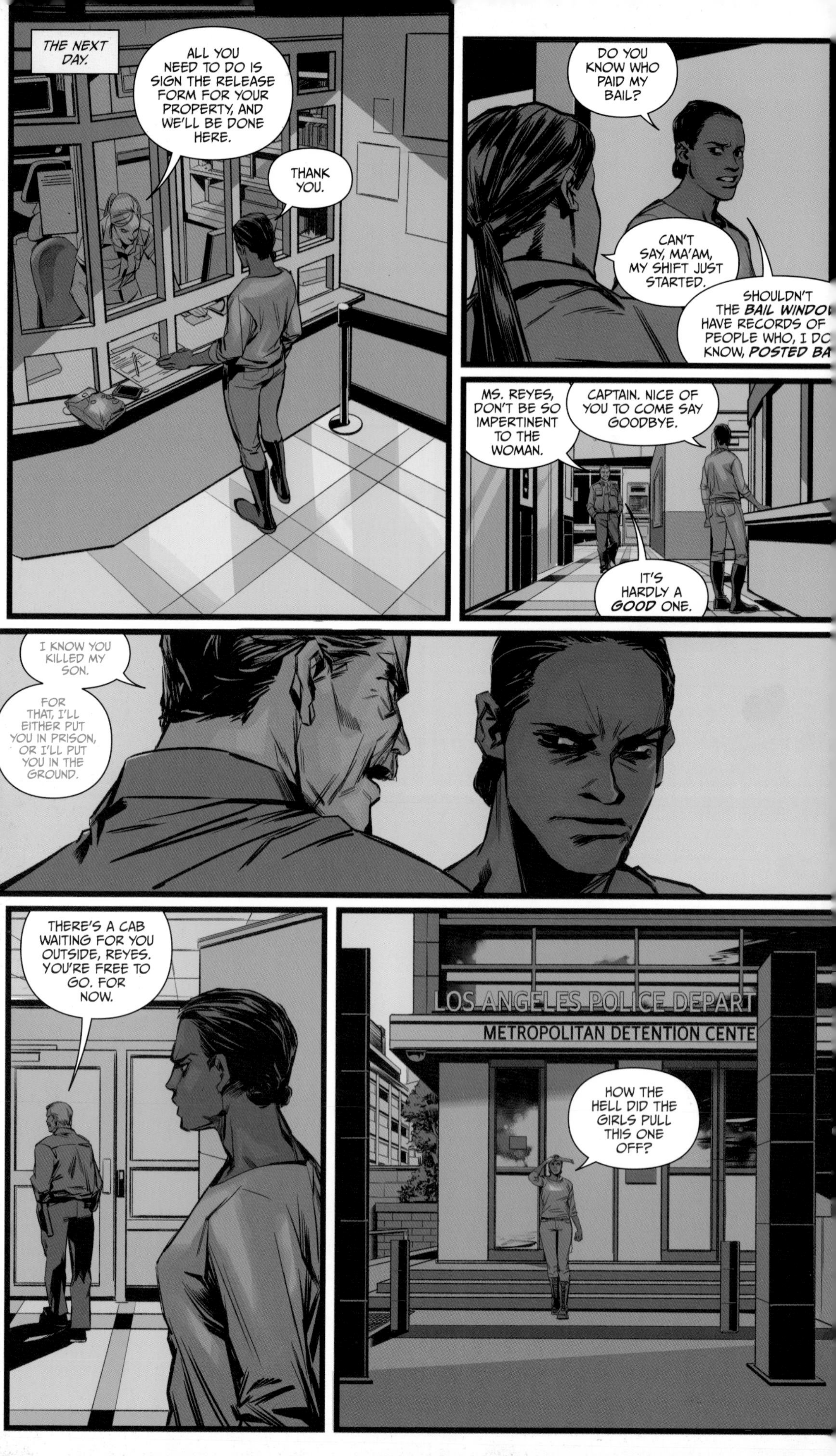
THE NEXT DAY.
ALL YOU NEED TO DO IS SIGN THE RELEASE FORM FOR YOUR PROPERTY, AND WE'LL BE DONE HERE.
THANK YOU.
DO YOU KNOW WHO PAID MY BAIL?
CAN'T SAY, MA'AM, MY SHIFT JUST STARTED.
SHOULDN'T THE BAIL WINDOW HAVE RECORDS OF PEOPLE WHO, I DO KNOW, POSTED BA
MS. REYES, DON'T BE SO IMPERTINENT TO THE WOMAN.
CAPTAIN. NICE OF YOU TO COME SAY GOODBYE.
IT'S HARDLY A GOOD ONE.
I KNOW YOU KILLED MY SON.
FOR THAT, I'LL EITHER PUT YOU IN PRISON, OR I'LL PUT YOU IN THE GROUND.
THERE'S A CAB WAITING FOR YOU OUTSIDE, REYES. YOU'RE FREE TO GO. FOR NOW.
LOS ANGELES POLICE DEPART
METROPOLITAN DETENTION CENTE
HOW THE HELL DID THE GIRLS PULL THIS ONE OFF?

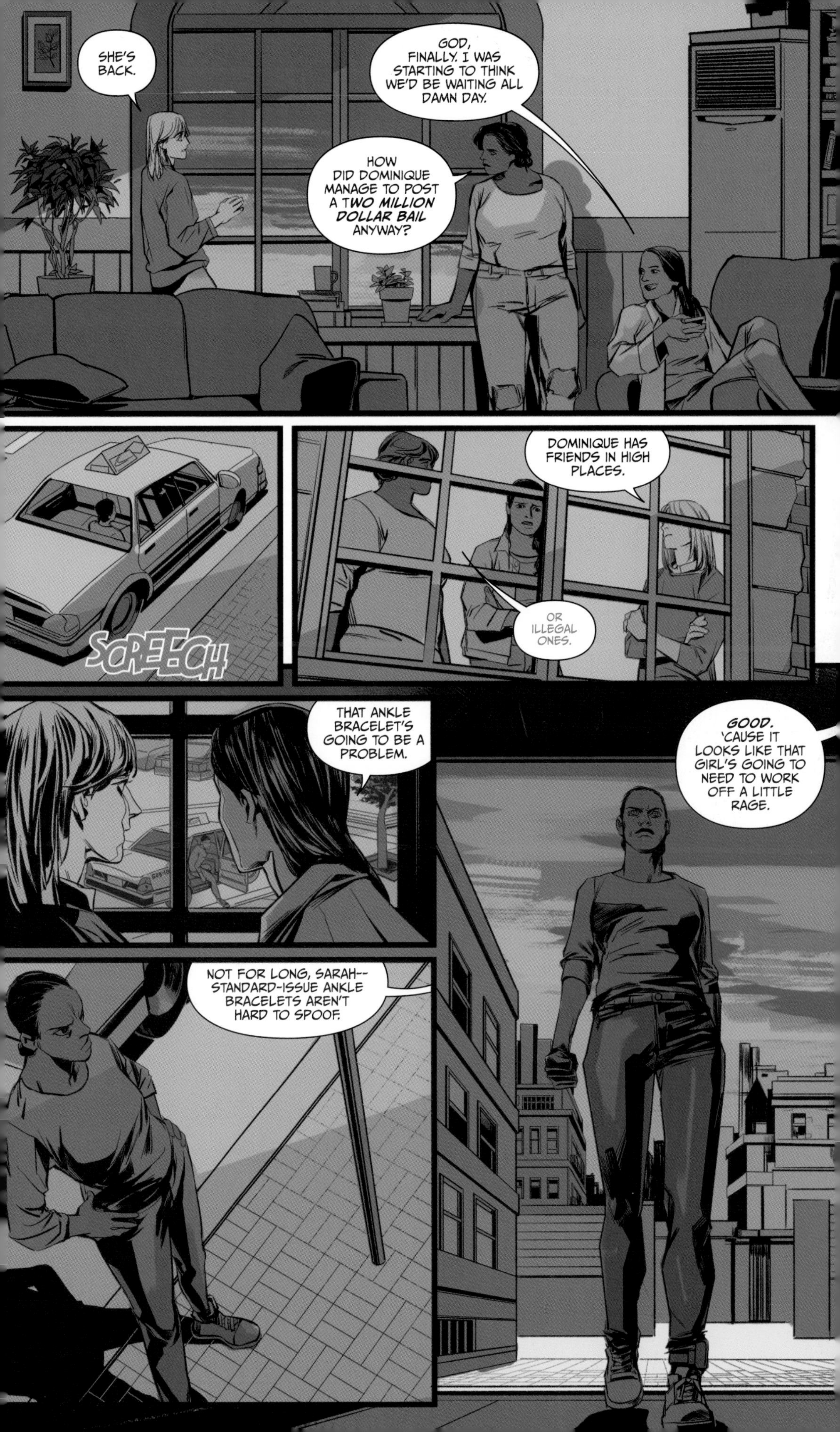
SHE'S BACK.
GOD, FINALLY. I WAS STARTING TO THINK WE'D BE WAITING ALL DAMN DAY.
HOW DID DOMINIQUE MANAGE TO POST A TWO MILLION DOLLAR BAIL ANYWAY?
SCREECH
DOMINIQUE HAS FRIENDS IN HIGH PLACES.
OR ILLEGAL ONES.
THAT ANKLE BRACELET'S GOING TO BE A PROBLEM.
NOT FOR LONG, SARAH-- STANDARD-ISSUE ANKLE BRACELETS AREN'T HARD TO SPOOF.
GOOD. 'CAUSE IT LOOKS LIKE THAT GIRL'S GOING TO NEED TO WORK OFF A LITTLE RAGE.

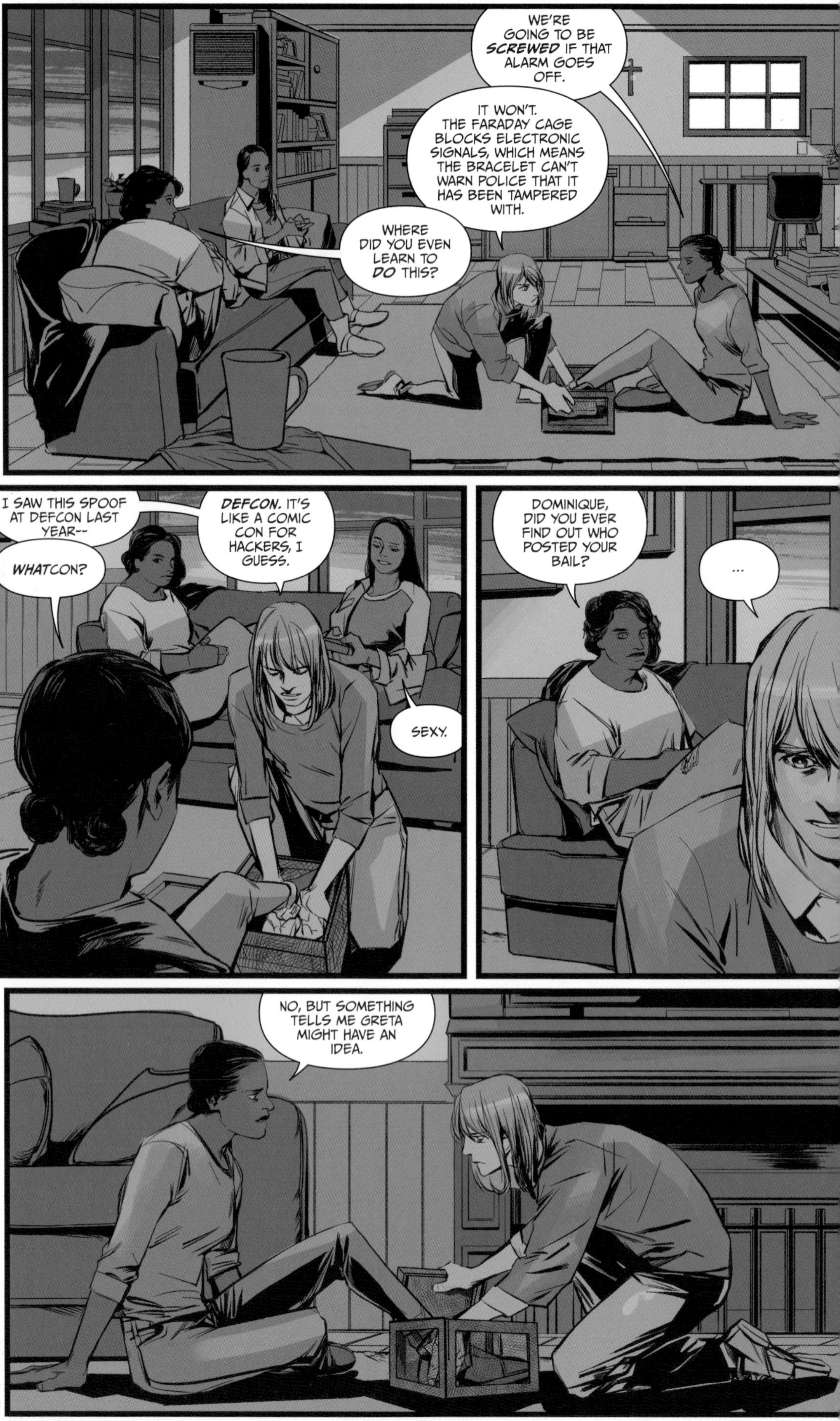
WE'RE GOING TO BE SCREWED IF THAT ALARM GOES OFF.
IT WON'T. THE FARADAY CAGE BLOCKS ELECTRONIC SIGNALS, WHICH MEANS THE BRACELET CAN'T WARN POLICE THAT IT HAS BEEN TAMPERED WITH.
WHERE DID YOU EVEN LEARN TO DO THIS?
I SAW THIS SPOOF AT DEFCON LAST YEAR--
WHATCON?
DEFCON. IT'S LIKE A COMIC CON FOR HACKERS, I GUESS.
SEXY.
DOMINIQUE, DID YOU EVER FIND OUT WHO POSTED YOUR BAIL?
...
NO, BUT SOMETHING TELLS ME GRETA MIGHT HAVE AN IDEA.

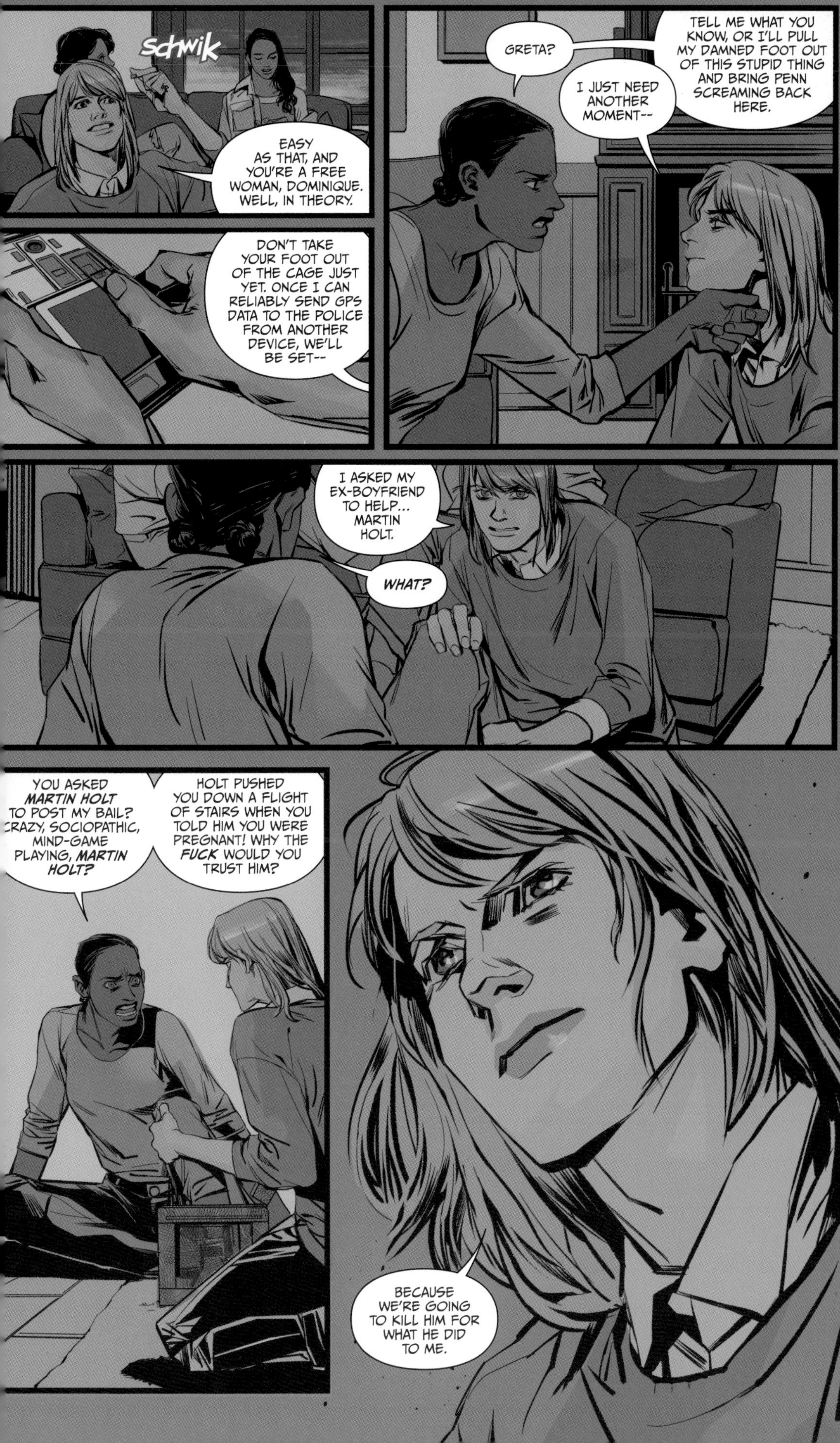
SCHWIK
EASY AS THAT, AND YOU'RE A FREE WOMAN, DOMINIQUE. WELL, IN THEORY.
DON'T TAKE YOUR FOOT OUT OF THE CAGE JUST YET. ONCE I CAN RELIABLY SEND GPS DATA TO THE POLICE FROM ANOTHER DEVICE, WE'LL BE SET--
GRETA?
TELL ME WHAT YOU KNOW, OR I'LL PULL MY DAMNED FOOT OUT OF THIS STUPID THING AND BRING PENN SCREAMING BACK HERE.
I JUST NEED ANOTHER MOMENT--
I ASKED MY EX-BOYFRIEND TO HELP... MARTIN HOLT.
WHAT?
YOU ASKED MARTIN HOLT TO POST MY BAIL? CRAZY, SOCIOPATHIC, MIND-GAME PLAYING, MARTIN HOLT?
HOLT PUSHED YOU DOWN A FLIGHT OF STAIRS WHEN YOU TOLD HIM YOU WERE PREGNANT! WHY THE FUCK WOULD YOU TRUST HIM?
BECAUSE WE'RE GOING TO KILL HIM FOR WHAT HE DID TO ME.

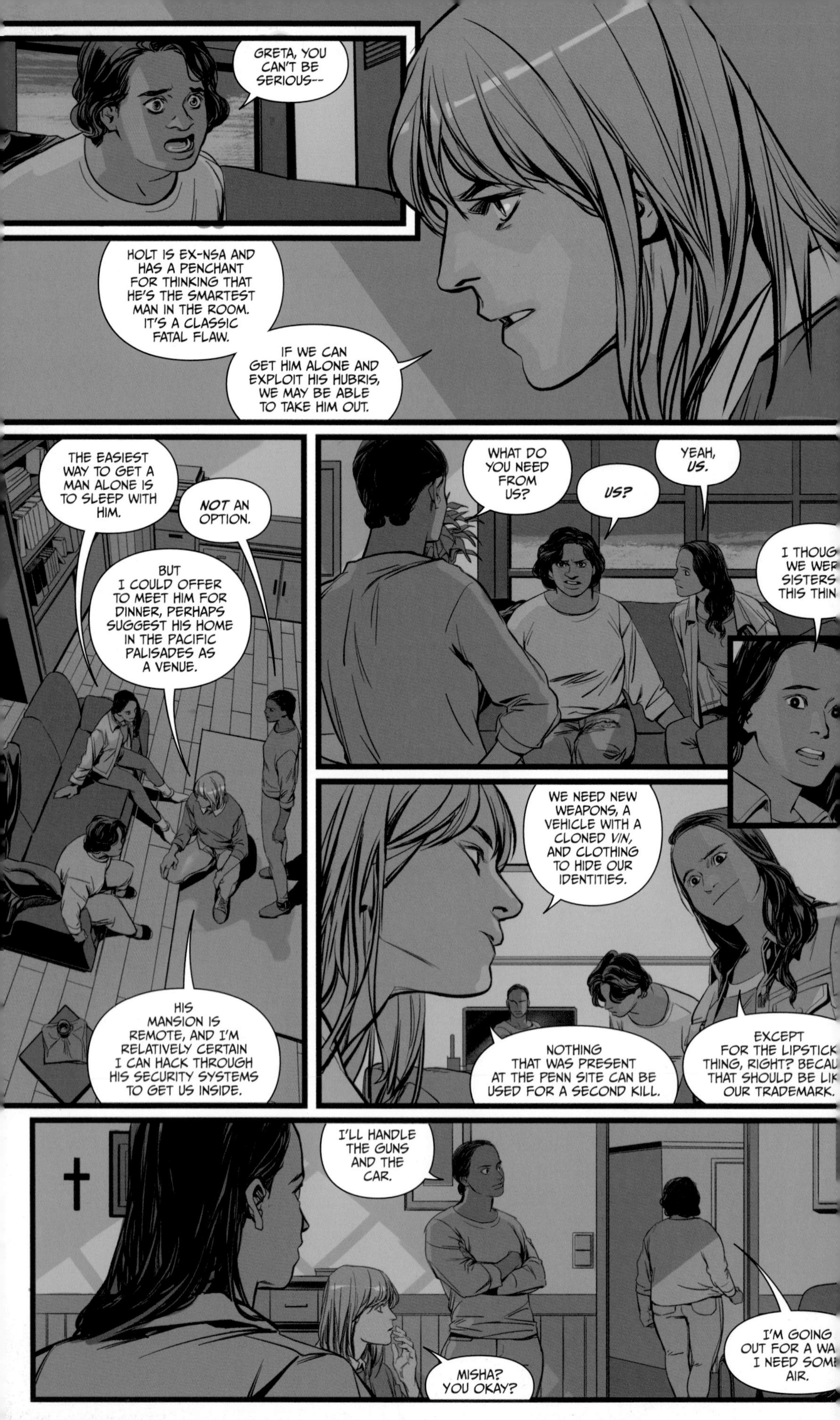
GRETA, YOU CAN'T BE SERIOUS--
HOLT IS EX-NSA AND HAS A PENCHANT FOR THINKING THAT HE'S THE SMARTEST MAN IN THE ROOM. IT'S A CLASSIC FATAL FLAW.
IF WE CAN GET HIM ALONE AND EXPLOIT HIS HUBRIS, WE MAY BE ABLE TO TAKE HIM OUT.
THE EASIEST WAY TO GET A MAN ALONE IS TO SLEEP WITH HIM.
NOT AN OPTION.
BUT I COULD OFFER TO MEET HIM FOR DINNER, PERHAPS SUGGEST HIS HOME IN THE PACIFIC PALISADES AS A VENUE.
HIS MANSION IS REMOTE, AND I'M RELATIVELY CERTAIN I CAN HACK THROUGH HIS SECURITY SYSTEMS TO GET US INSIDE.
WHAT DO YOU NEED FROM US?
US?
YEAH, *US.*
I THOUG WE WER SISTERS THIS THIN
WE NEED NEW WEAPONS, A VEHICLE WITH A CLONED *VIN,* AND CLOTHING TO HIDE OUR IDENTITIES.
NOTHING THAT WAS PRESENT AT THE PENN SITE CAN BE USED FOR A SECOND KILL.
EXCEPT FOR THE LIPSTICK THING, RIGHT? BECAU THAT SHOULD BE LIK OUR TRADEMARK.
I'LL HANDLE THE GUNS AND THE CAR.
MISHA? YOU OKAY?
I'M GOING OUT FOR A WA I NEED SOME AIR.

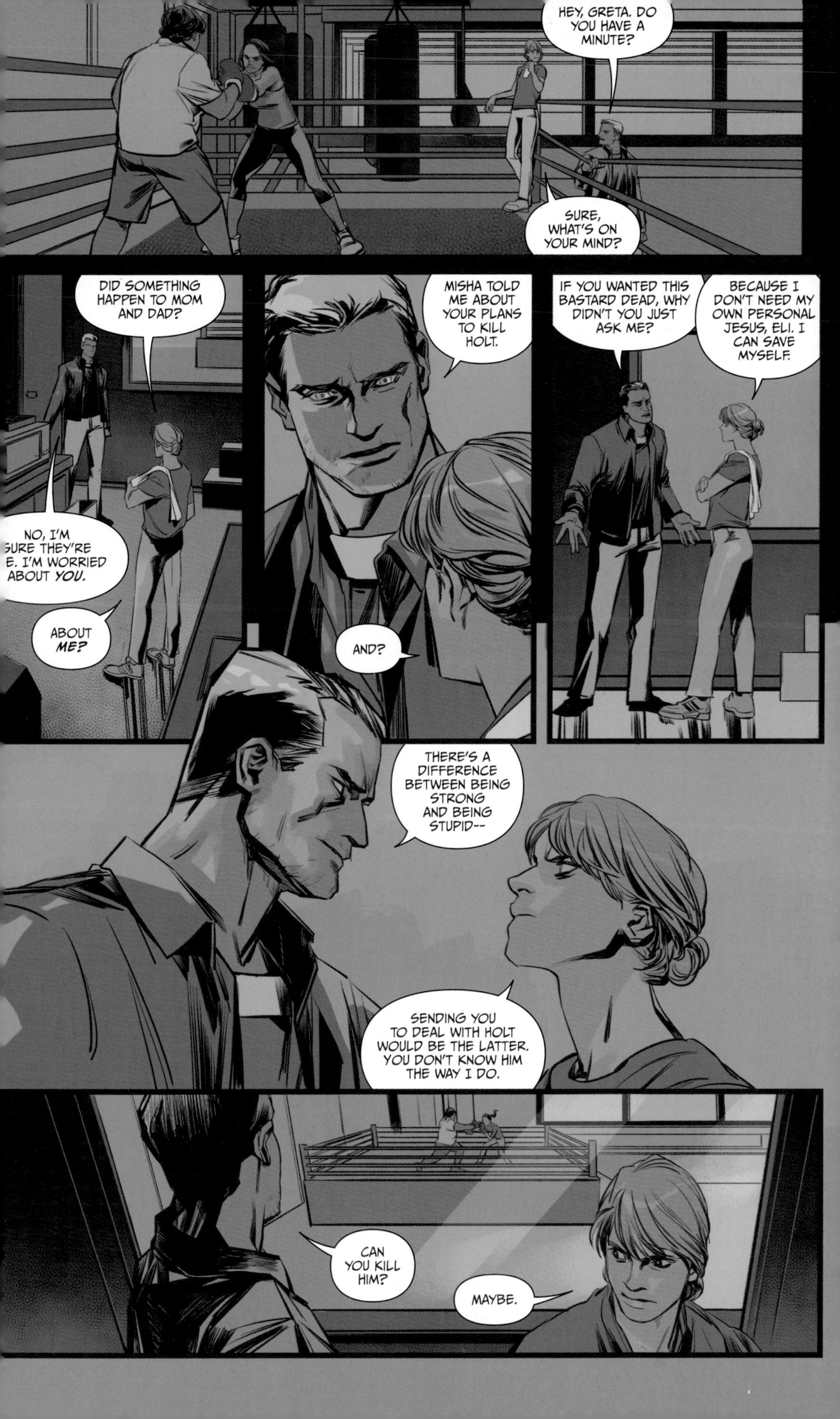

HEY, GRETA. DO YOU HAVE A MINUTE?
SURE, WHAT'S ON YOUR MIND?
DID SOMETHING HAPPEN TO MOM AND DAD?
NO, I'M
SURE THEY'RE
E. I'M WORRIED ABOUT *YOU.*
ABOUT *ME?*
MISHA TOLD ME ABOUT YOUR PLANS TO KILL HOLT.
AND?
IF YOU WANTED THIS BASTARD DEAD, WHY DIDN'T YOU JUST ASK ME?
BECAUSE I DON'T NEED MY OWN PERSONAL JESUS, ELI. I CAN SAVE MYSELF.
THERE'S A DIFFERENCE BETWEEN BEING STRONG AND BEING STUPID--
SENDING YOU TO DEAL WITH HOLT WOULD BE THE LATTER. YOU DON'T KNOW HIM THE WAY I DO.
CAN YOU KILL HIM?
MAYBE.

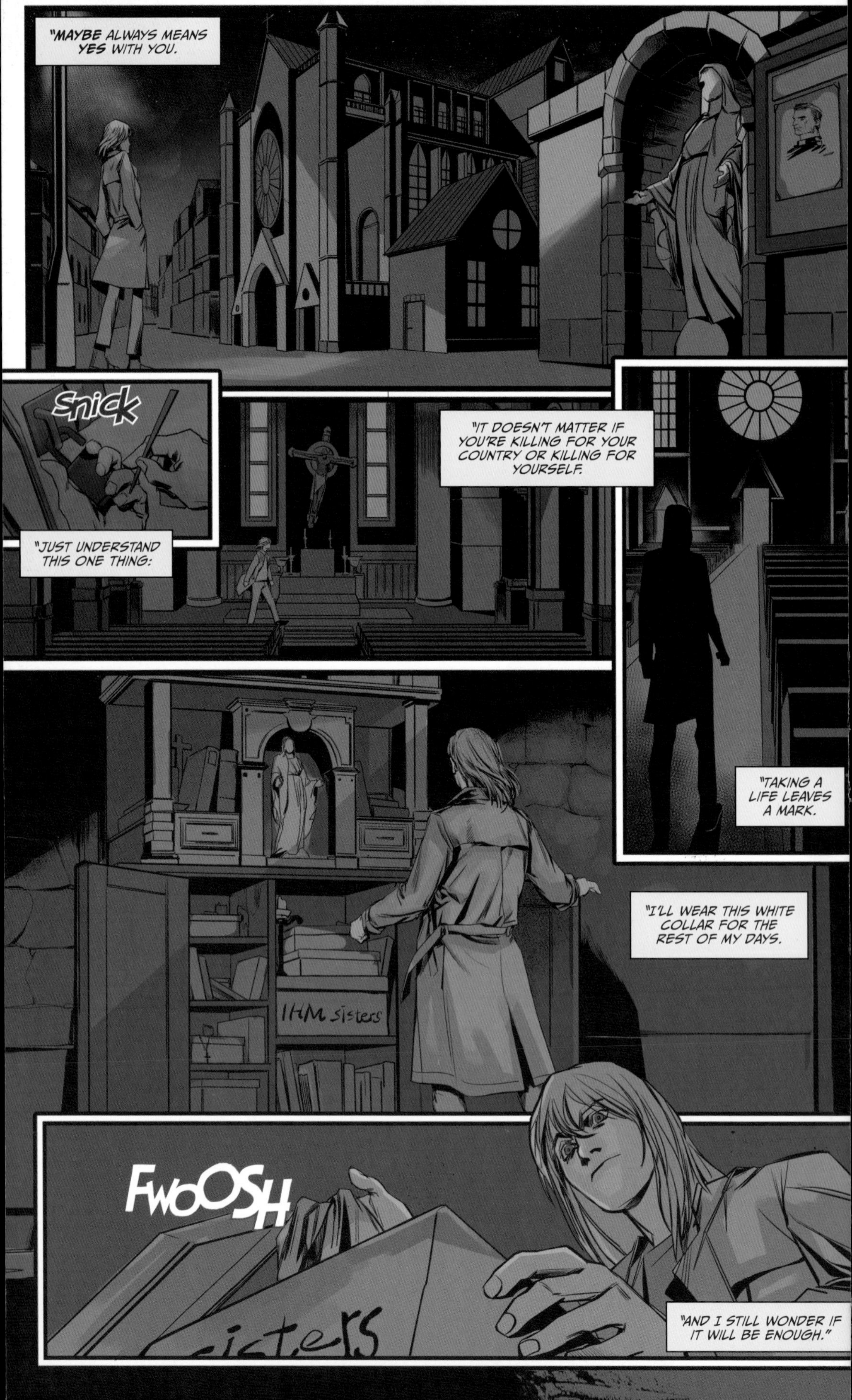
"MAYBE ALWAYS MEANS YES WITH YOU.
SNICK
"JUST UNDERSTAND THIS ONE THING:
"IT DOESN'T MATTER IF YOU'RE KILLING FOR YOUR COUNTRY OR KILLING FOR YOURSELF.
"TAKING A LIFE LEAVES A MARK.
IHM sisters
"I'LL WEAR THIS WHITE COLLAR FOR THE REST OF MY DAYS.
FWOOSH
sisters
"AND I STILL WONDER IF IT WILL BE ENOUGH."

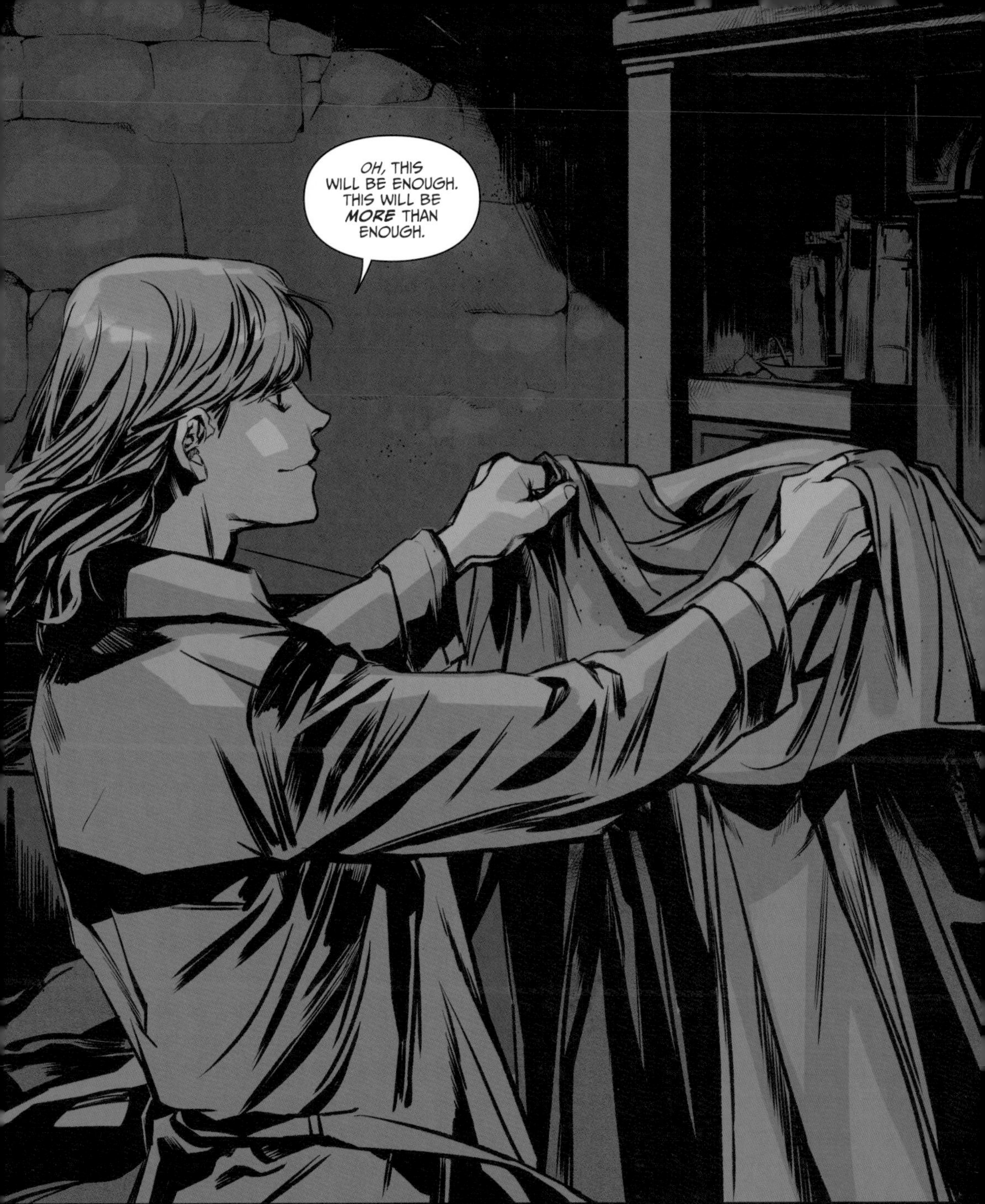
OH, THIS WILL BE ENOUGH. THIS WILL BE MORE THAN ENOUGH.

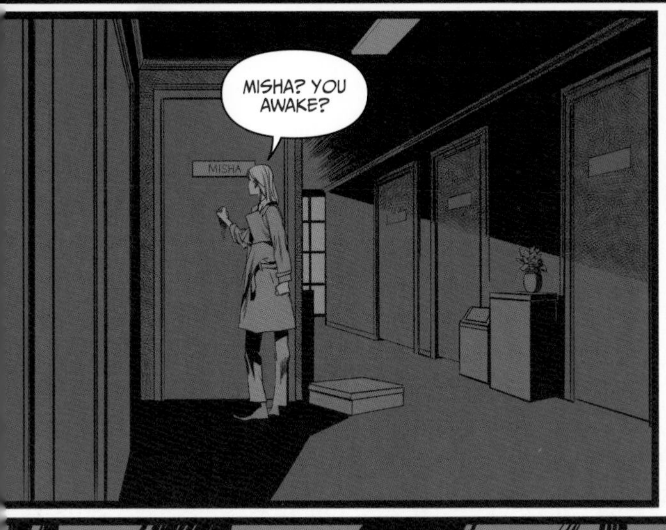
MISHA? YOU AWAKE?
MISHA

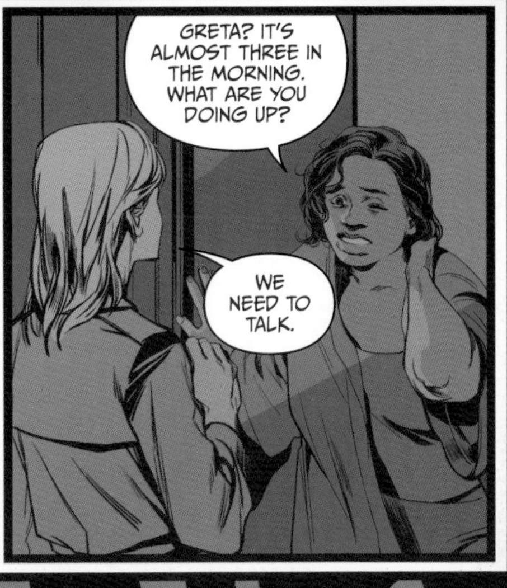
GRETA? IT'S ALMOST THREE IN THE MORNING. WHAT ARE YOU DOING UP?
WE NEED TO TALK.

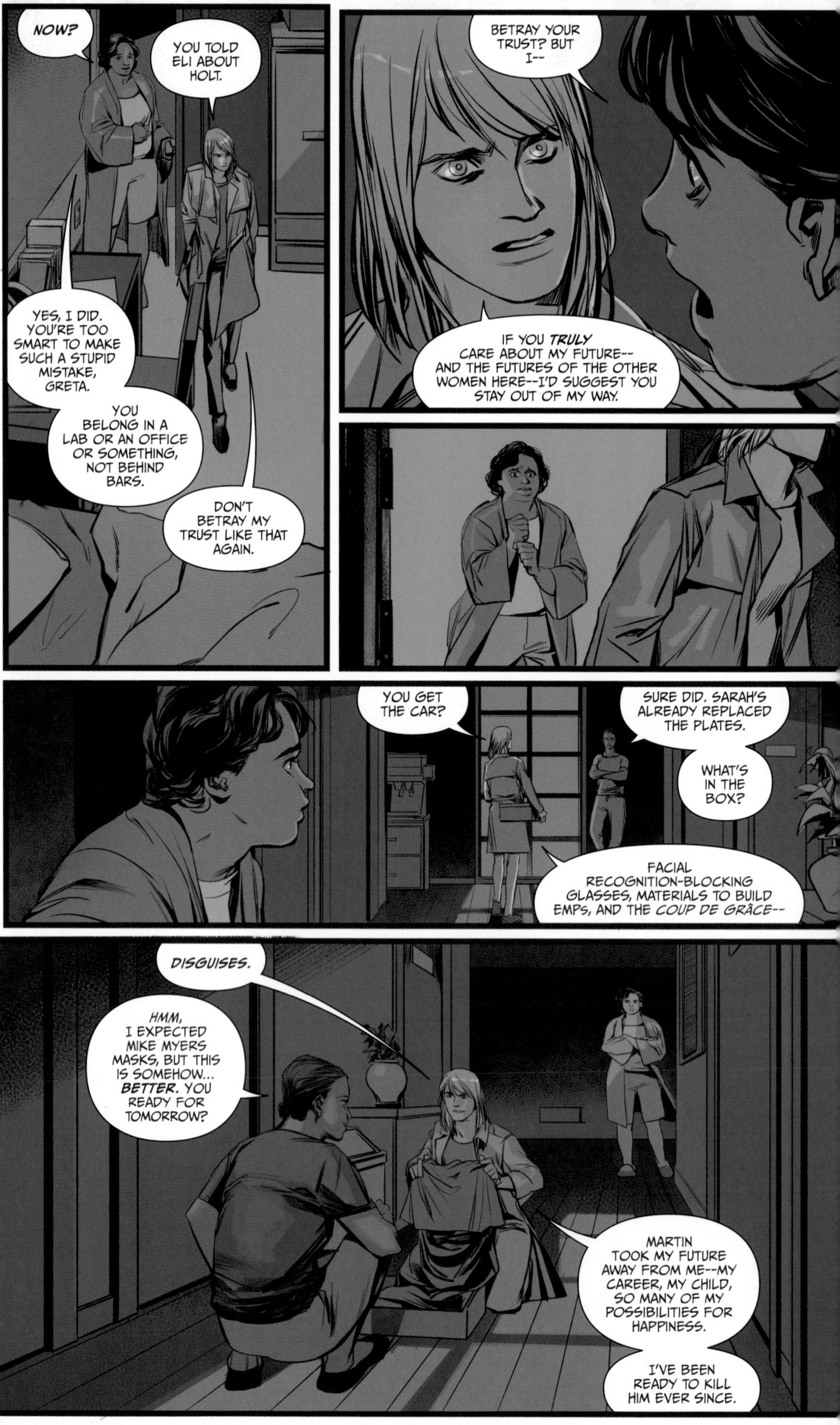
NOW?
YOU TOLD ELI ABOUT HOLT.
YES, I DID. YOU'RE TOO SMART TO MAKE SUCH A STUPID MISTAKE, GRETA.
YOU BELONG IN A LAB OR AN OFFICE OR SOMETHING, NOT BEHIND BARS.
DON'T BETRAY MY TRUST LIKE THAT AGAIN.
BETRAY YOUR TRUST? BUT I--
IF YOU *TRULY* CARE ABOUT MY FUTURE-- AND THE FUTURES OF THE OTHER WOMEN HERE--I'D SUGGEST YOU STAY OUT OF MY WAY.
YOU GET THE CAR?
SURE DID. SARAH'S ALREADY REPLACED THE PLATES.
WHAT'S IN THE BOX?
FACIAL RECOGNITION-BLOCKING GLASSES, MATERIALS TO BUILD EMPS, AND THE *COUP DE GRÂCE*--
DISGUISES.
HMM, I EXPECTED MIKE MYERS MASKS, BUT THIS IS SOMEHOW... *BETTER.* YOU READY FOR TOMORROW?
MARTIN TOOK MY FUTURE AWAY FROM ME--MY CAREER, MY CHILD, SO MANY OF MY POSSIBILITIES FOR HAPPINESS.
I'VE BEEN READY TO KILL HIM EVER SINCE.

OH, YES. I'VE FOUND IT TO BE VERY... *EMPOWERING.*

I SUPPOSE THAT'S ONE WAY TO PUT IT.

MEANING?

GRETA! HOW I'VE MISSED YOU, DARLING. IT'S GOOD TO SEE YOU LOOKING SO LUMINOUS. SO...*HAPPY.*

THE HAVEN HOUSE SEEMS TO HAVE AGREED WITH YOU?

YOU HAVE BEEN A *VERY* BUSY GIRL, GRETA.

TWO WET JOBS IN ONE MONTH? AND HERE I WAS, THINKING YOU WERE TOO RELIGIOUS TO SULLY YOUR HANDS WITH BLOOD.

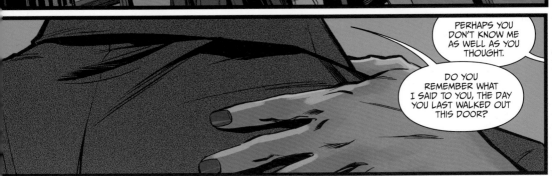

PERHAPS YOU DON'T KNOW ME AS WELL AS YOU THOUGHT.

DO YOU REMEMBER WHAT I SAID TO YOU, THE DAY YOU LAST WALKED OUT THIS DOOR?

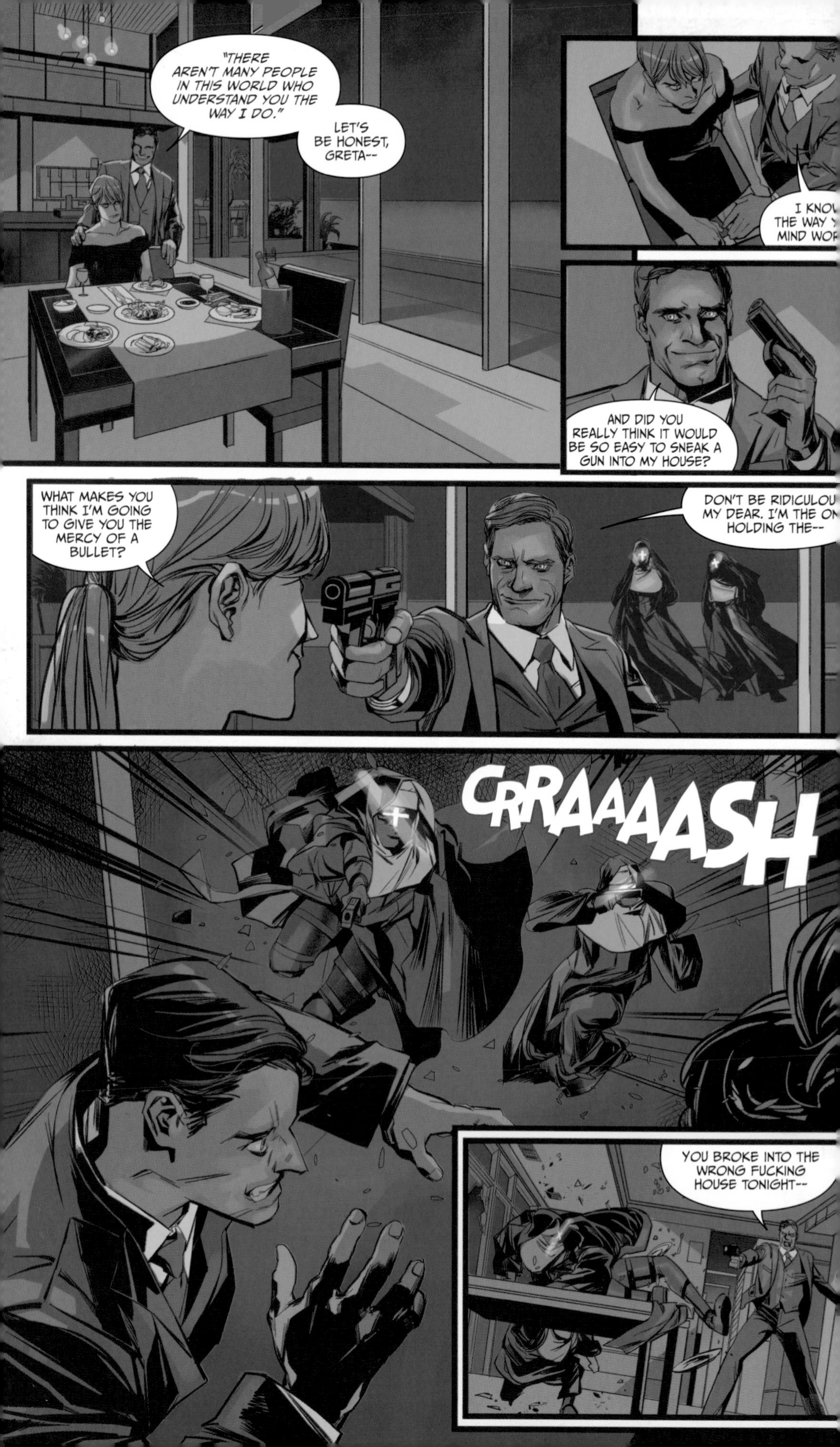
"THERE AREN'T MANY PEOPLE IN THIS WORLD WHO UNDERSTAND YOU THE WAY I DO."
LET'S BE HONEST, GRETA--
I KNOW THE WAY Y MIND WOR
AND DID YOU REALLY THINK IT WOULD BE SO EASY TO SNEAK A GUN INTO MY HOUSE?
WHAT MAKES YOU THINK I'M GOING TO GIVE YOU THE MERCY OF A BULLET?
DON'T BE RIDICULOU MY DEAR. I'M THE ON HOLDING THE--
CRRAAAASH
YOU BROKE INTO THE WRONG FUCKING HOUSE TONIGHT--

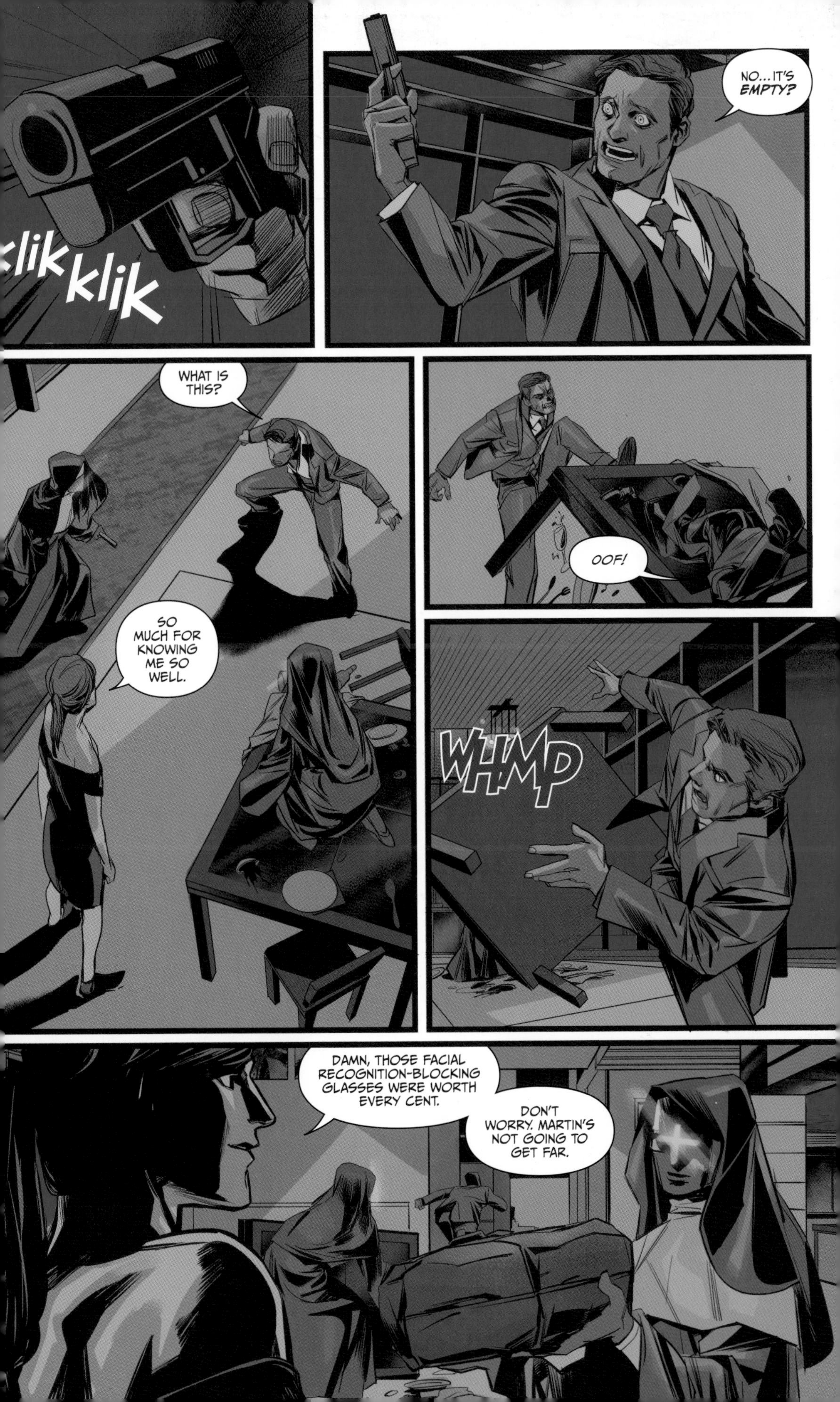
klik klik
NO... IT'S EMPTY?
WHAT IS THIS?
OOF!
SO MUCH FOR KNOWING ME SO WELL.
WHMP
DAMN, THOSE FACIAL RECOGNITION-BLOCKING GLASSES WERE WORTH EVERY CENT.
DON'T WORRY. MARTIN'S NOT GOING TO GET FAR.

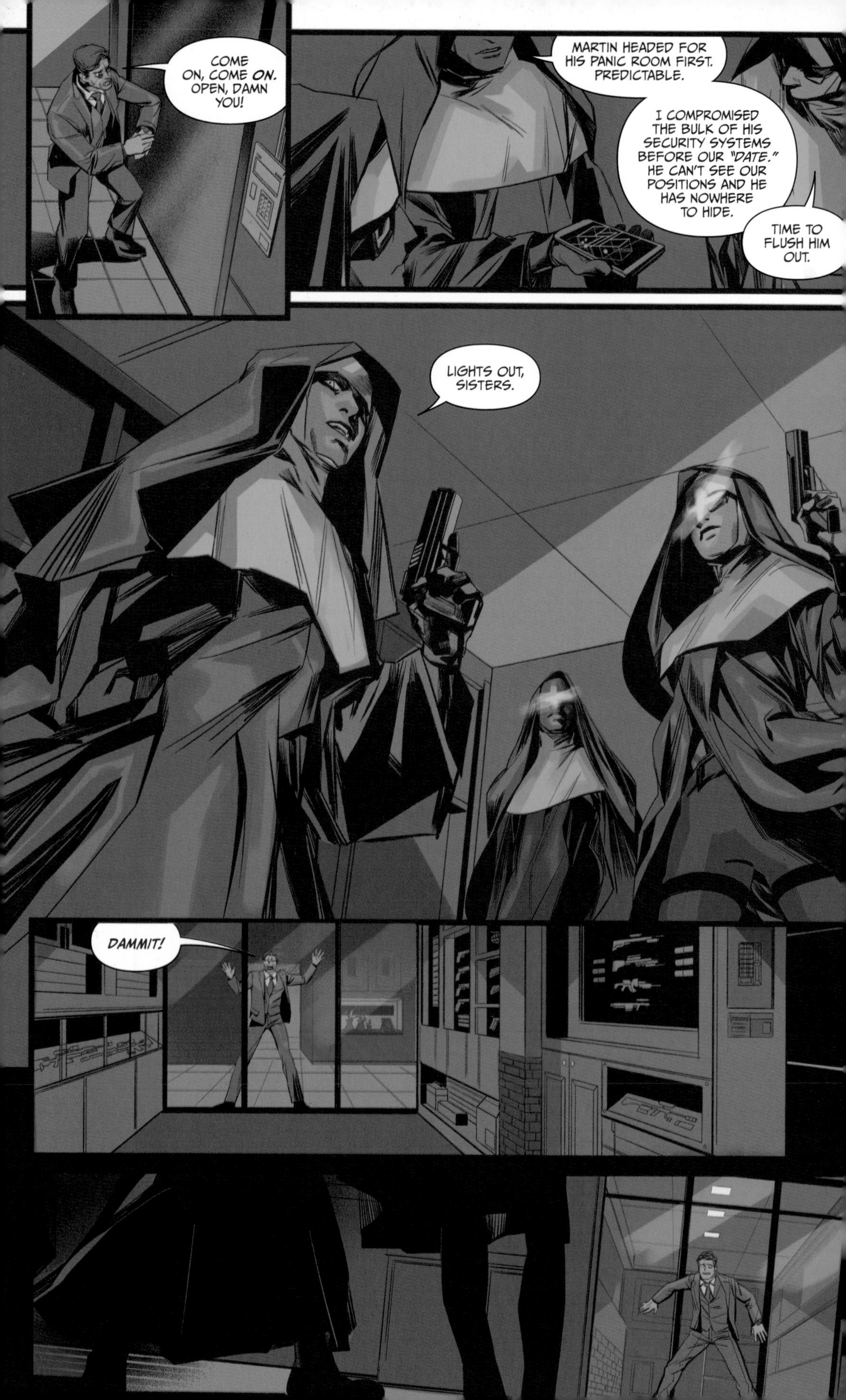
COME ON, COME ON. OPEN, DAMN YOU!
MARTIN HEADED FOR HIS PANIC ROOM FIRST. PREDICTABLE.
I COMPROMISED THE BULK OF HIS SECURITY SYSTEMS BEFORE OUR "DATE." HE CAN'T SEE OUR POSITIONS AND HE HAS NOWHERE TO HIDE.
TIME TO FLUSH HIM OUT.
LIGHTS OUT, SISTERS.
DAMMIT!

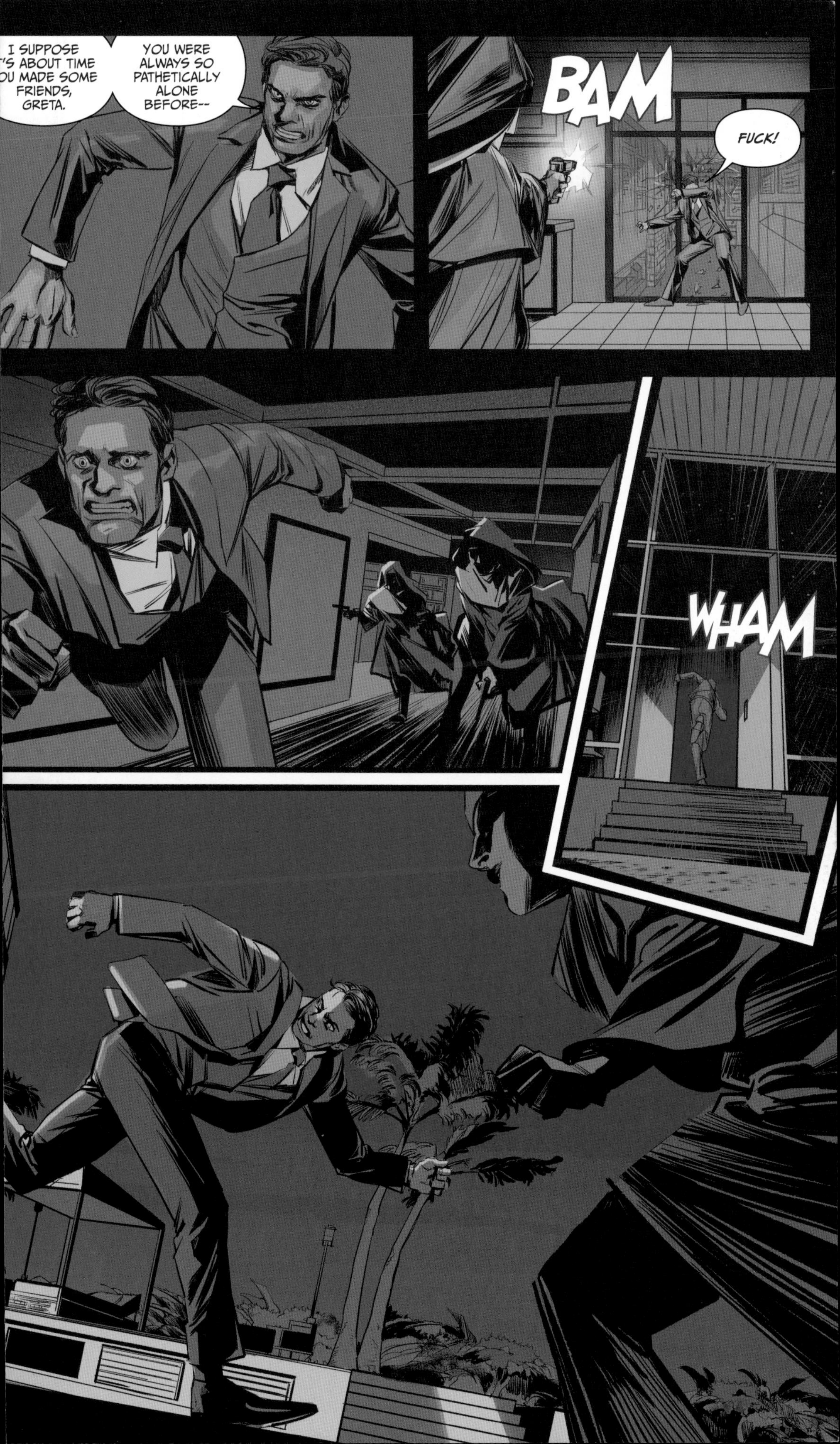
I SUPPOSE IT'S ABOUT TIME YOU MADE SOME FRIENDS, GRETA.
YOU WERE ALWAYS SO PATHETICALLY ALONE BEFORE--
BAM
FUCK!
WHAM

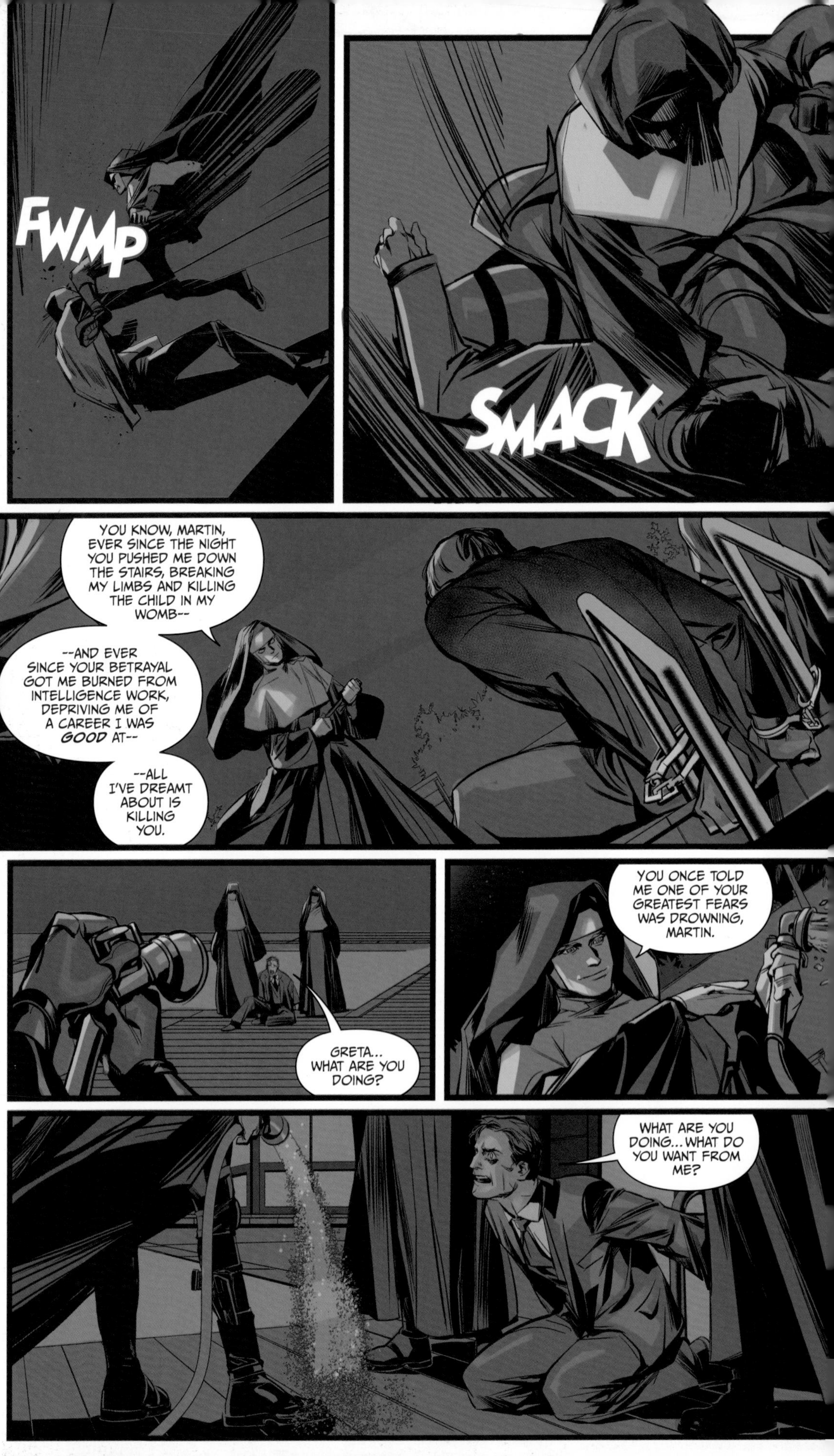
FWMP
SMACK
YOU KNOW, MARTIN, EVER SINCE THE NIGHT YOU PUSHED ME DOWN THE STAIRS, BREAKING MY LIMBS AND KILLING THE CHILD IN MY WOMB--
--AND EVER SINCE YOUR BETRAYAL GOT ME BURNED FROM INTELLIGENCE WORK, DEPRIVING ME OF A CAREER I WAS *GOOD* AT--
--ALL I'VE DREAMT ABOUT IS KILLING YOU.
GRETA... WHAT ARE YOU DOING?
YOU ONCE TOLD ME ONE OF YOUR GREATEST FEARS WAS DROWNING, MARTIN.
WHAT ARE YOU DOING... WHAT DO YOU WANT FROM ME?

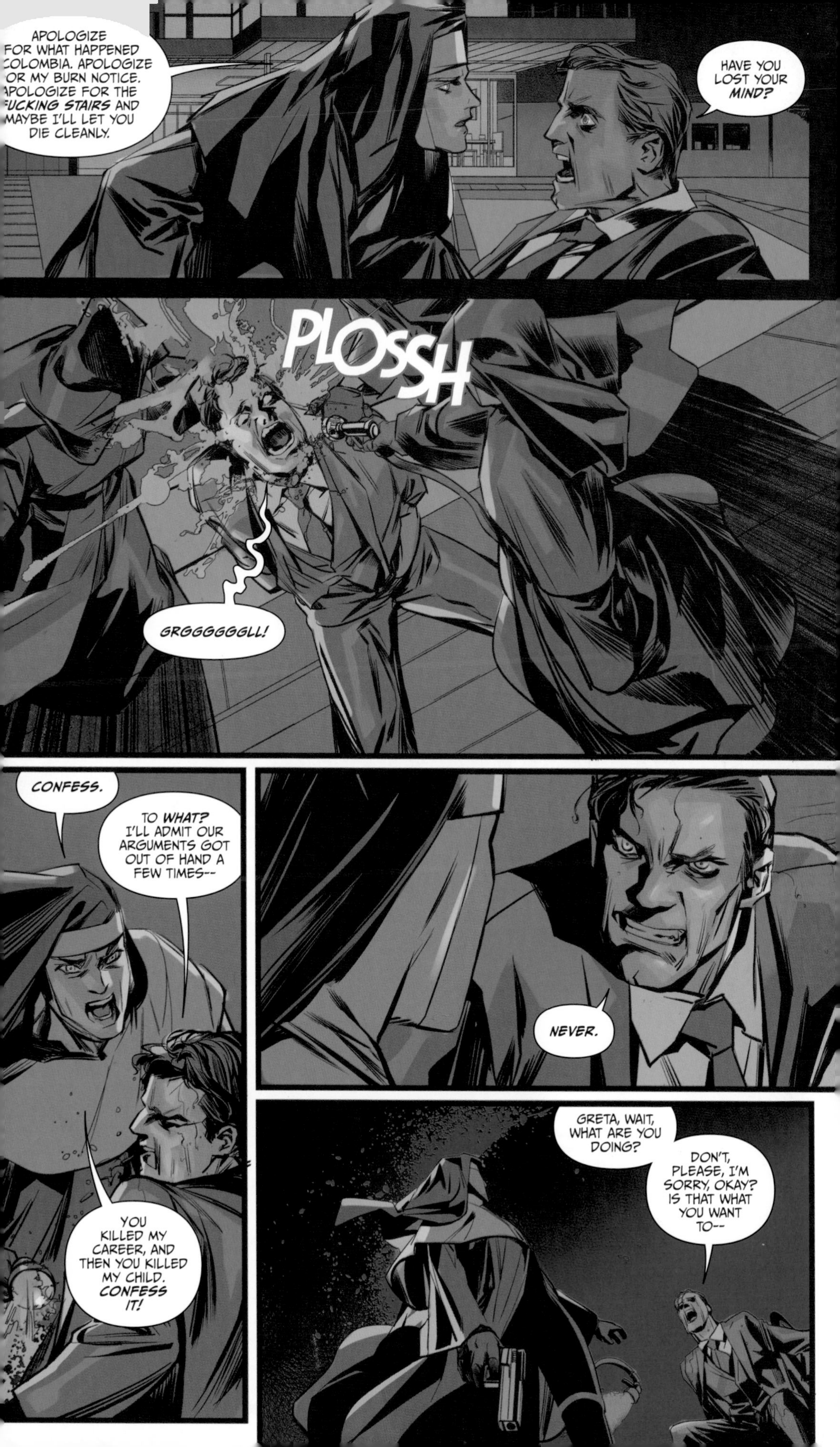
APOLOGIZE FOR WHAT HAPPENED COLOMBIA. APOLOGIZE OR MY BURN NOTICE. APOLOGIZE FOR THE FUCKING STAIRS AND MAYBE I'LL LET YOU DIE CLEANLY.
HAVE YOU LOST YOUR MIND?
PLOSSH
GRGGGGGGLL!
CONFESS.
TO WHAT? I'LL ADMIT OUR ARGUMENTS GOT OUT OF HAND A FEW TIMES--
YOU KILLED MY CAREER, AND THEN YOU KILLED MY CHILD. CONFESS IT!
NEVER.
GRETA, WAIT, WHAT ARE YOU DOING?
DON'T, PLEASE, I'M SORRY, OKAY? IS THAT WHAT YOU WANT TO--

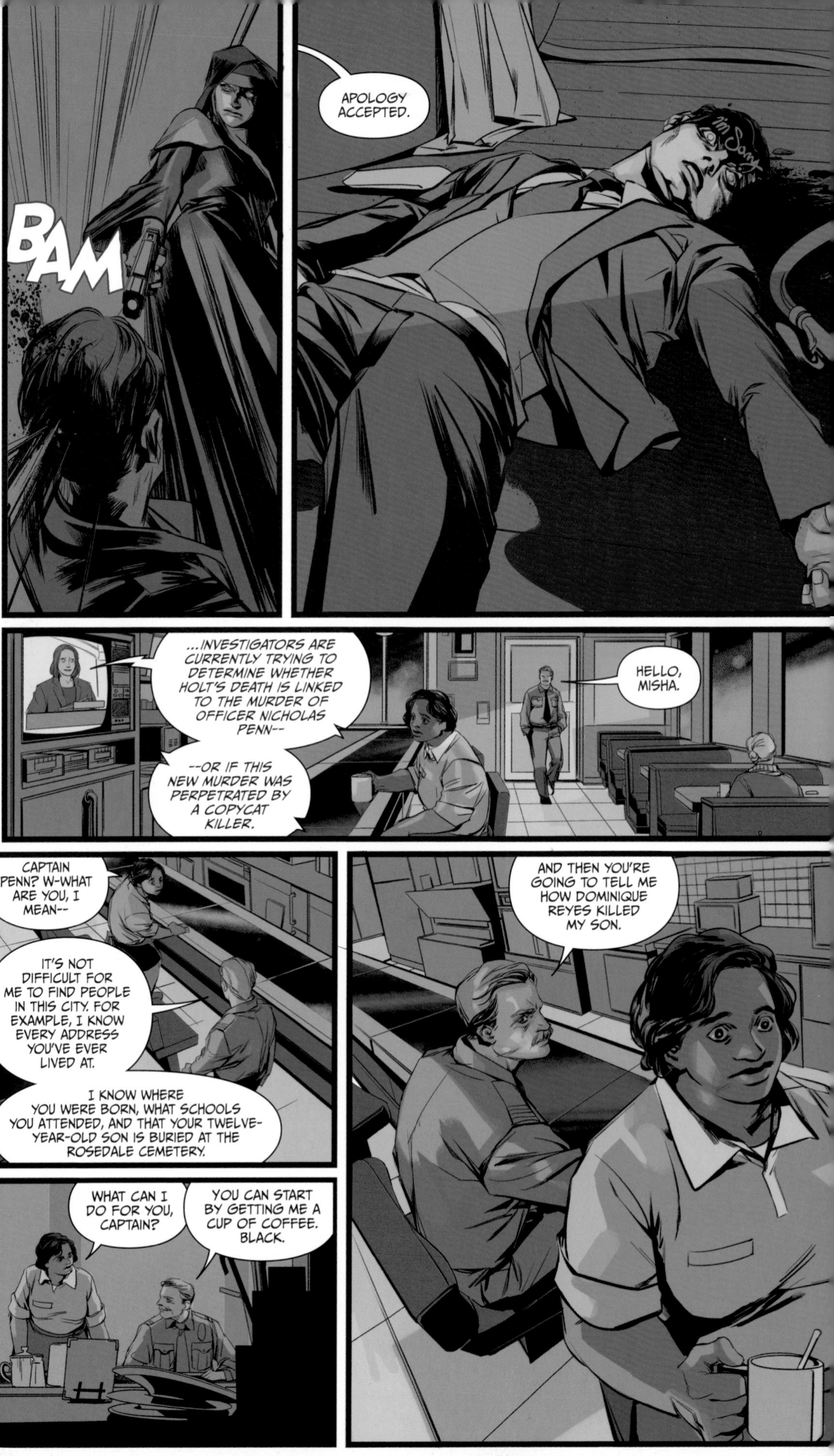
BAM
APOLOGY ACCEPTED.
i'm Sorry
...INVESTIGATORS ARE CURRENTLY TRYING TO DETERMINE WHETHER HOLT'S DEATH IS LINKED TO THE MURDER OF OFFICER NICHOLAS PENN--
--OR IF THIS NEW MURDER WAS PERPETRATED BY A COPYCAT KILLER.
HELLO, MISHA.
CAPTAIN PENN? W-WHAT ARE YOU, I MEAN--
IT'S NOT DIFFICULT FOR ME TO FIND PEOPLE IN THIS CITY. FOR EXAMPLE, I KNOW EVERY ADDRESS YOU'VE EVER LIVED AT.
I KNOW WHERE YOU WERE BORN, WHAT SCHOOLS YOU ATTENDED, AND THAT YOUR TWELVE-YEAR-OLD SON IS BURIED AT THE ROSEDALE CEMETERY.
WHAT CAN I DO FOR YOU, CAPTAIN?
YOU CAN START BY GETTING ME A CUP OF COFFEE. BLACK.
AND THEN YOU'RE GOING TO TELL ME HOW DOMINIQUE REYES KILLED MY SON.

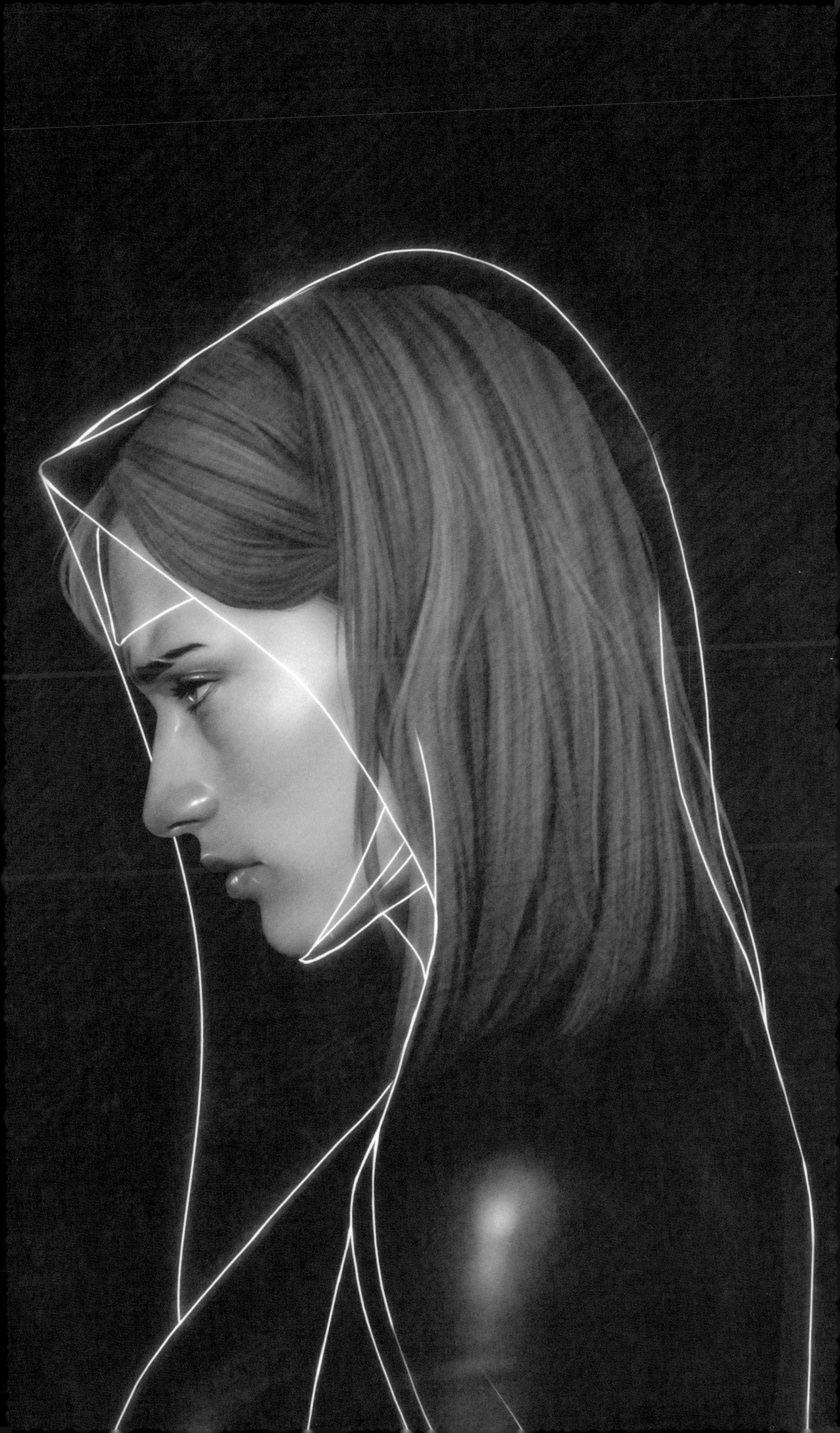

CHAPTER THREE

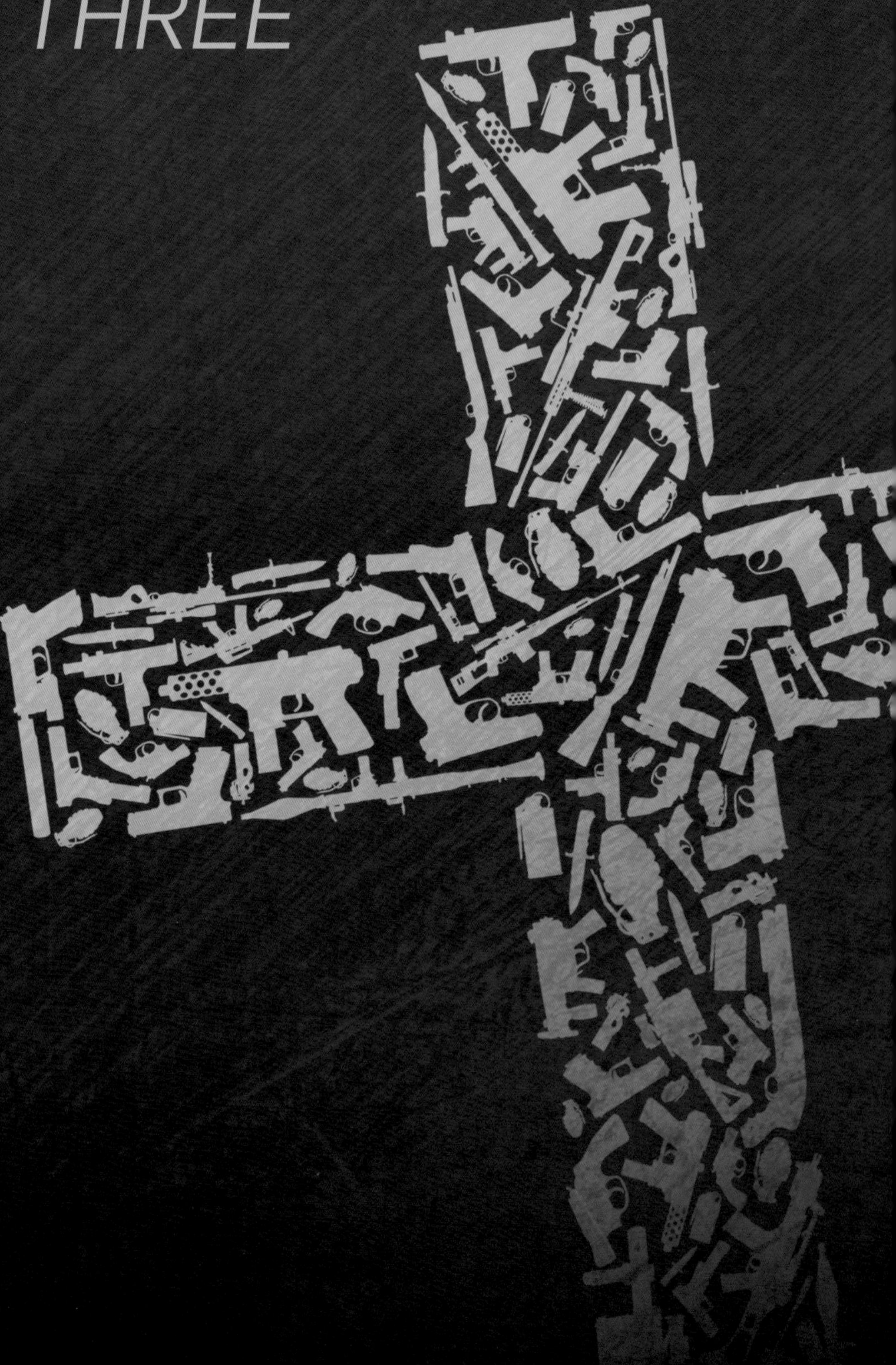

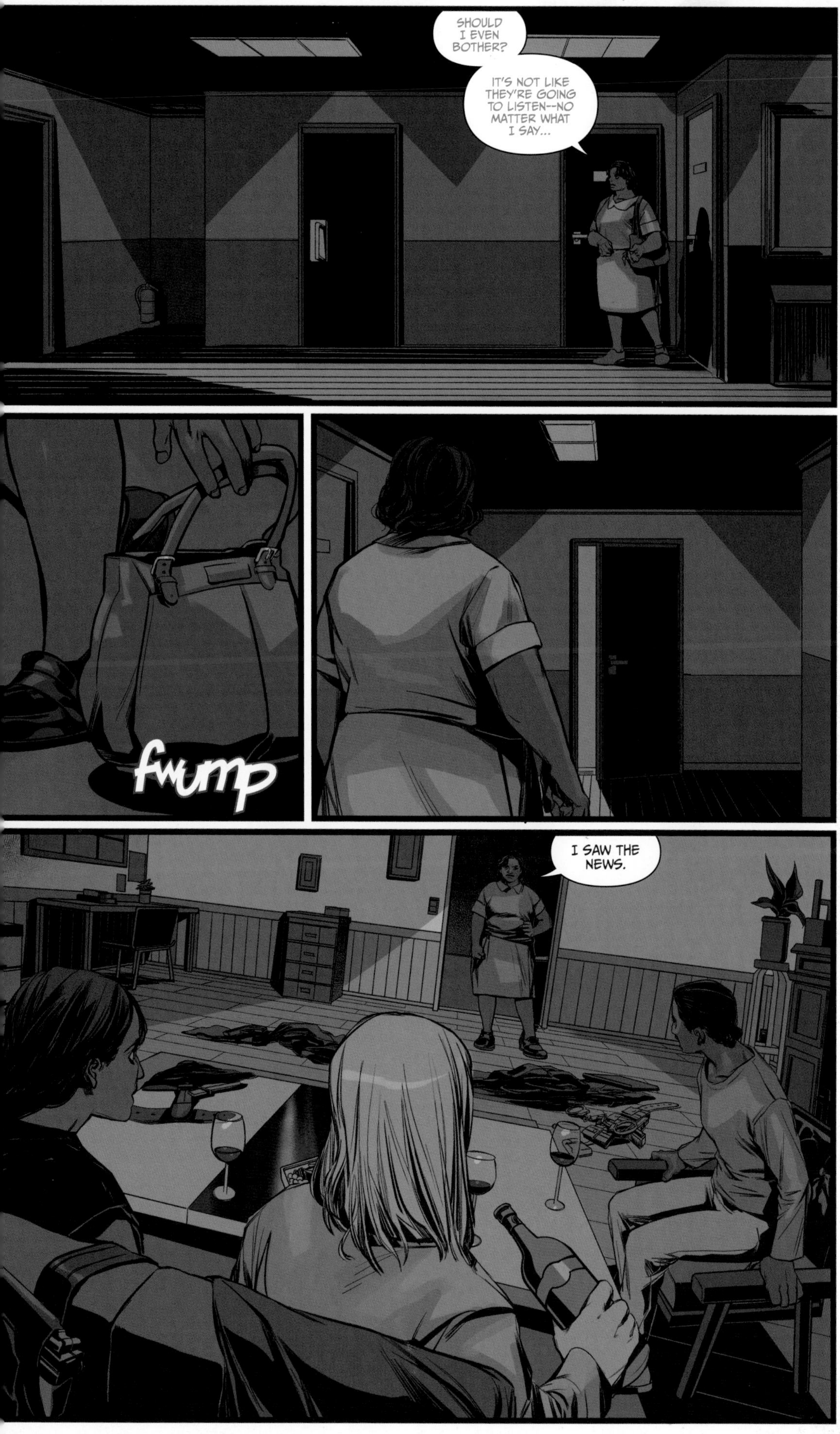
SHOULD I EVEN BOTHER?
IT'S NOT LIKE THEY'RE GOING TO LISTEN--NO MATTER WHAT I SAY...
fwump
I SAW THE NEWS.

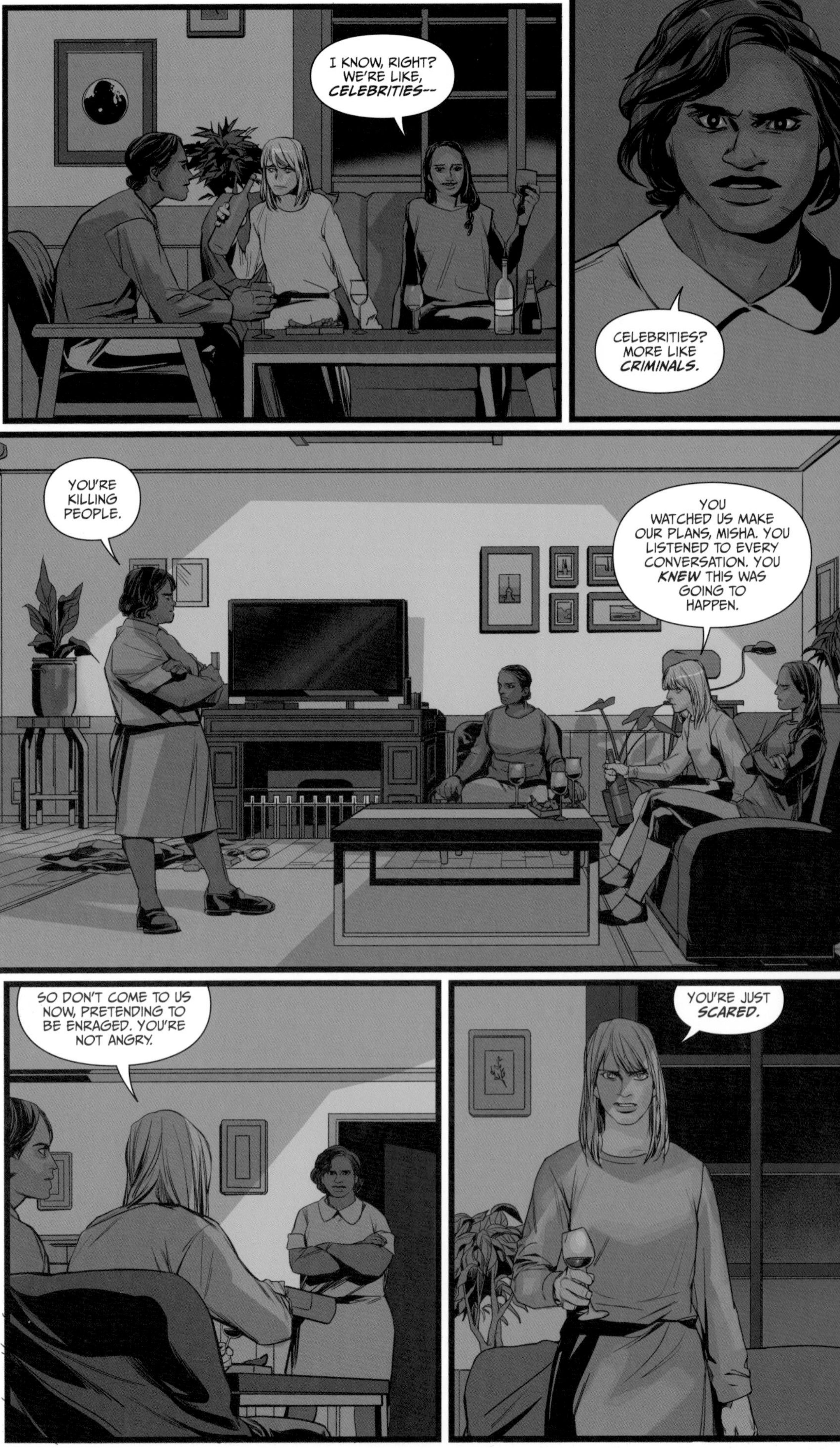
I KNOW, RIGHT? WE'RE LIKE, CELEBRITIES--
CELEBRITIES? MORE LIKE CRIMINALS.
YOU'RE KILLING PEOPLE.
YOU WATCHED US MAKE OUR PLANS, MISHA. YOU LISTENED TO EVERY CONVERSATION. YOU KNEW THIS WAS GOING TO HAPPEN.
SO DON'T COME TO US NOW, PRETENDING TO BE ENRAGED. YOU'RE NOT ANGRY.
YOU'RE JUST SCARED.

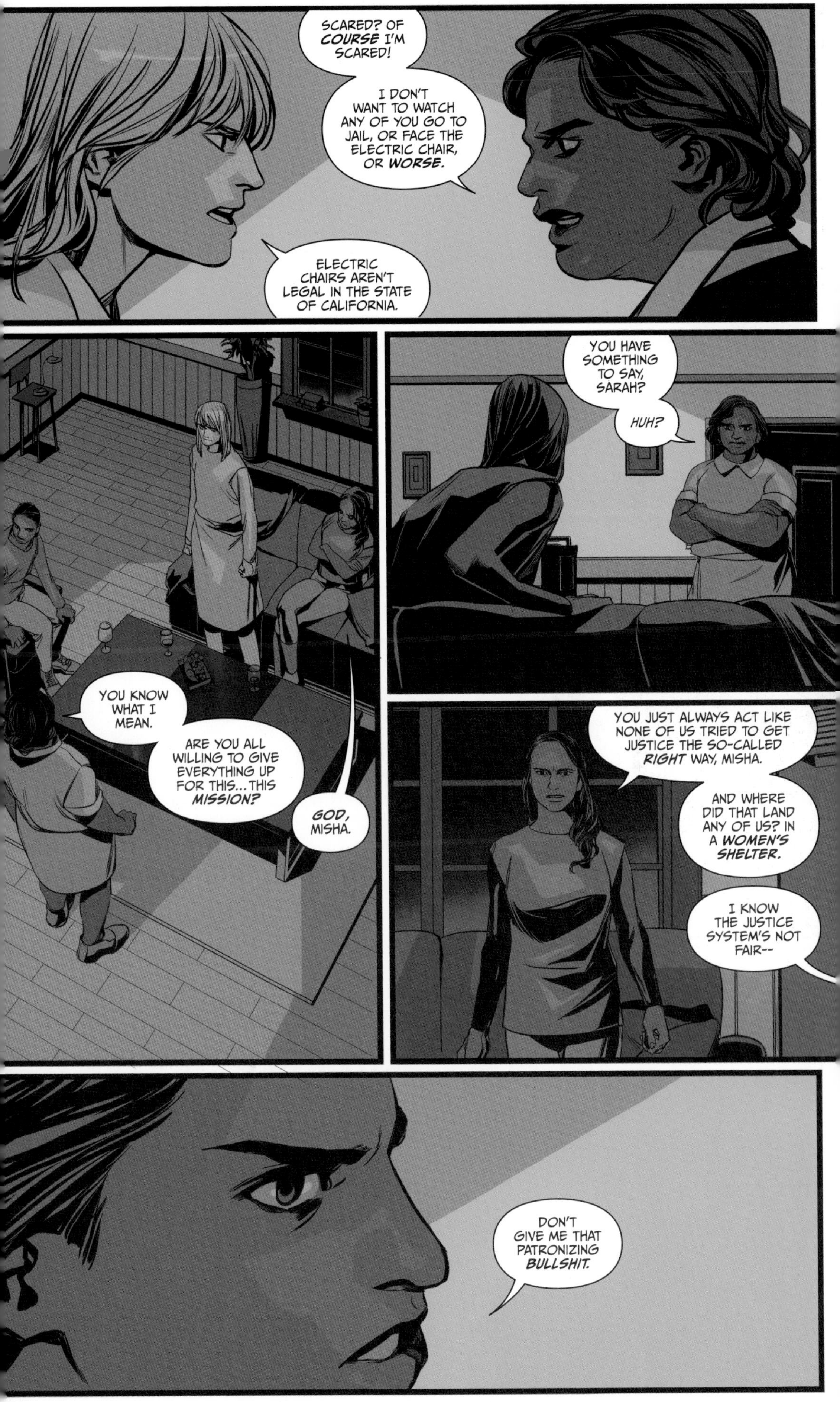
SCARED? OF COURSE I'M SCARED!
I DON'T WANT TO WATCH ANY OF YOU GO TO JAIL, OR FACE THE ELECTRIC CHAIR, OR WORSE.
ELECTRIC CHAIRS AREN'T LEGAL IN THE STATE OF CALIFORNIA.
YOU KNOW WHAT I MEAN.
ARE YOU ALL WILLING TO GIVE EVERYTHING UP FOR THIS... THIS MISSION?
GOD, MISHA.
YOU HAVE SOMETHING TO SAY, SARAH?
HUH?
YOU JUST ALWAYS ACT LIKE NONE OF US TRIED TO GET JUSTICE THE SO-CALLED RIGHT WAY, MISHA.
AND WHERE DID THAT LAND ANY OF US? IN A WOMEN'S SHELTER.
I KNOW THE JUSTICE SYSTEM'S NOT FAIR--
DON'T GIVE ME THAT PATRONIZING BULLSHIT.

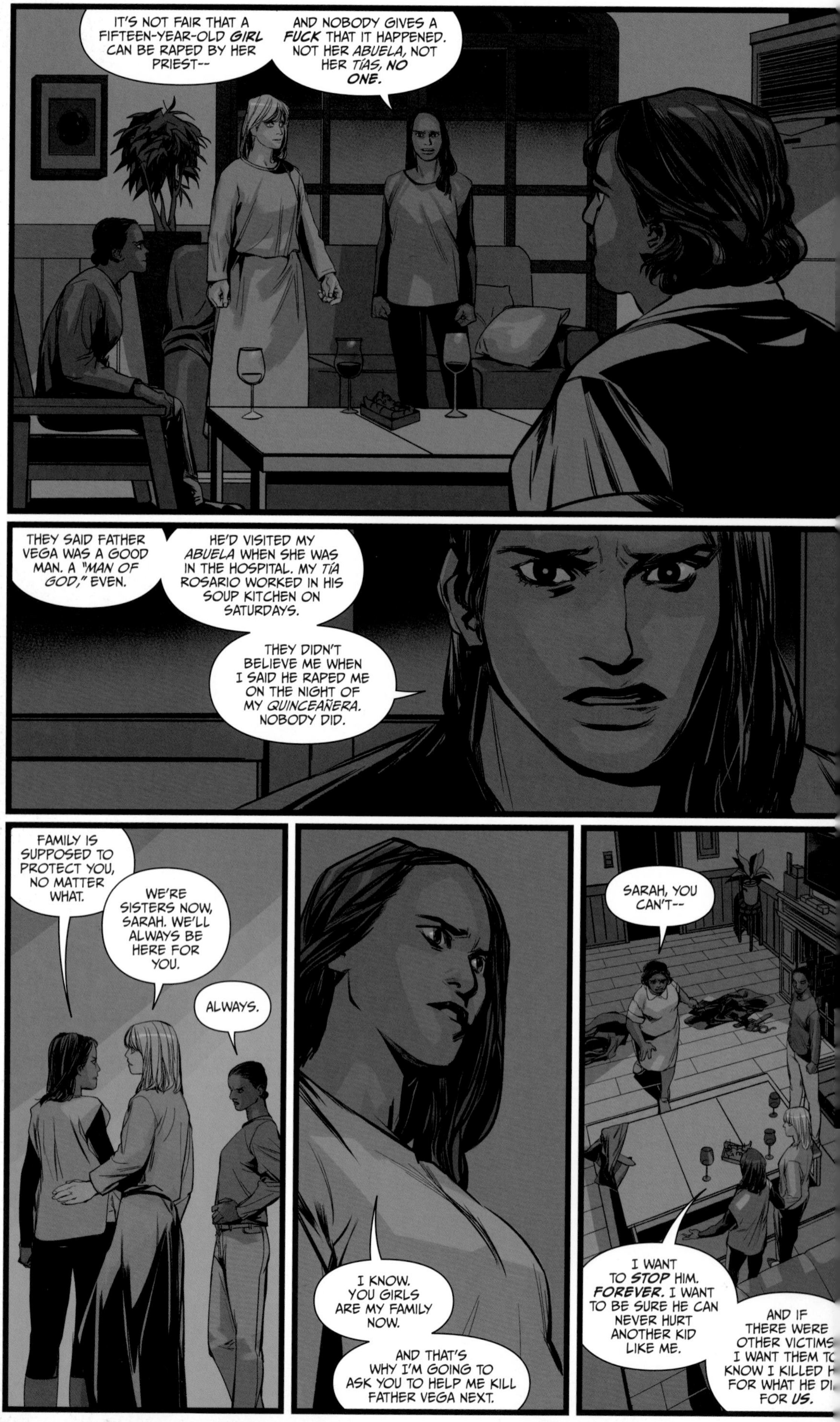
IT'S NOT FAIR THAT A FIFTEEN-YEAR-OLD *GIRL* CAN BE RAPED BY HER PRIEST--
AND NOBODY GIVES A *FUCK* THAT IT HAPPENED. NOT HER *ABUELA,* NOT HER *TÍAS, NO ONE.*
THEY SAID FATHER VEGA WAS A GOOD MAN. A *"MAN OF GOD,"* EVEN.
HE'D VISITED MY *ABUELA* WHEN SHE WAS IN THE HOSPITAL. MY *TÍA* ROSARIO WORKED IN HIS SOUP KITCHEN ON SATURDAYS.
THEY DIDN'T BELIEVE ME WHEN I SAID HE RAPED ME ON THE NIGHT OF MY *QUINCEAÑERA.* NOBODY DID.
FAMILY IS SUPPOSED TO PROTECT YOU, NO MATTER WHAT.
WE'RE SISTERS NOW, SARAH. WE'LL ALWAYS BE HERE FOR YOU.
ALWAYS.
I KNOW. YOU GIRLS ARE MY FAMILY NOW.
AND THAT'S WHY I'M GOING TO ASK YOU TO HELP ME KILL FATHER VEGA NEXT.
SARAH, YOU CAN'T--
I WANT TO *STOP* HIM. *FOREVER.* I WANT TO BE SURE HE CAN NEVER HURT ANOTHER KID LIKE ME.
AND IF THERE WERE OTHER VICTIMS I WANT THEM T KNOW I KILLED H FOR WHAT HE DI FOR *US.*

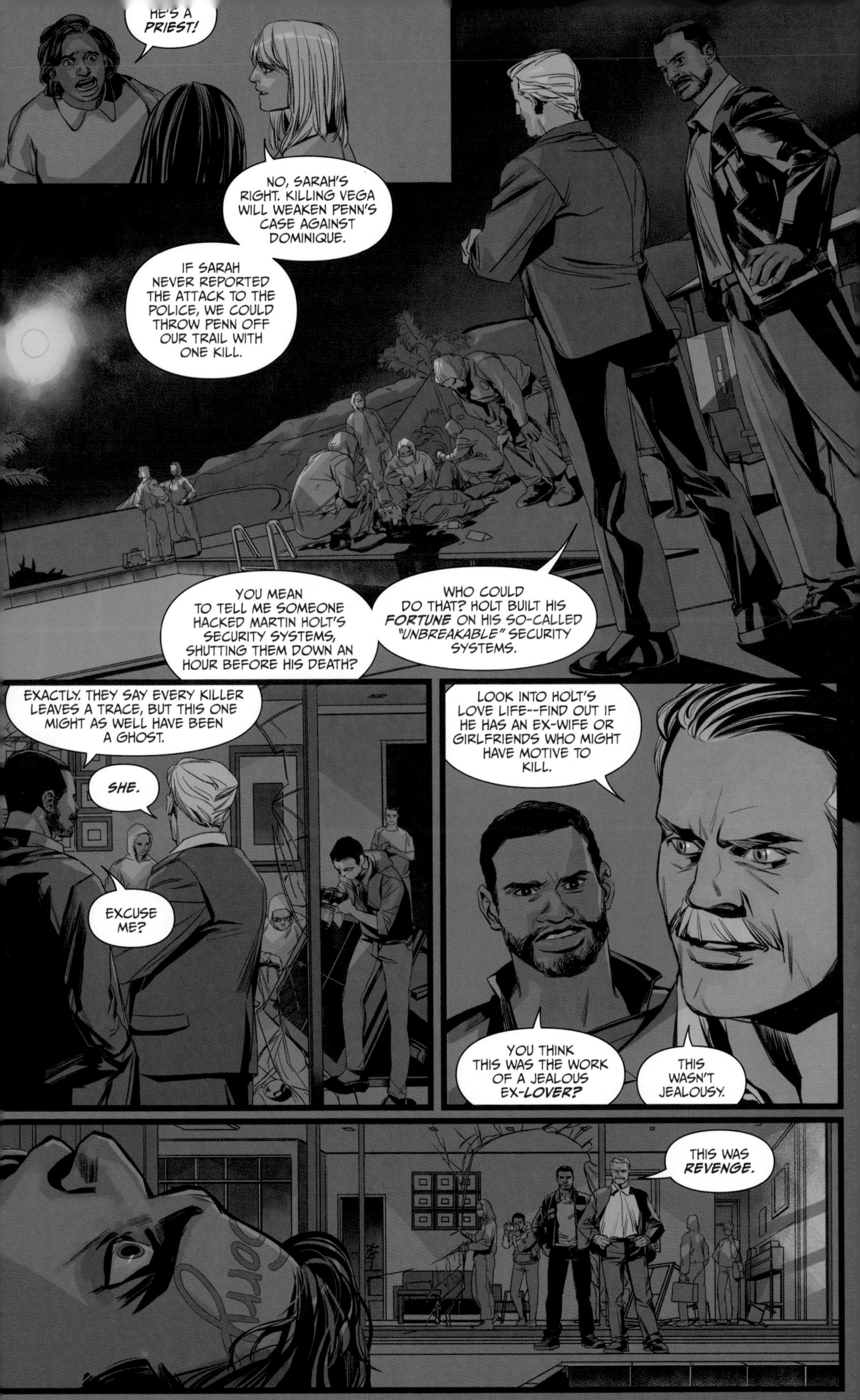
HE'S A PRIEST!
NO, SARAH'S RIGHT. KILLING VEGA WILL WEAKEN PENN'S CASE AGAINST DOMINIQUE.
IF SARAH NEVER REPORTED THE ATTACK TO THE POLICE, WE COULD THROW PENN OFF OUR TRAIL WITH ONE KILL.
YOU MEAN TO TELL ME SOMEONE HACKED MARTIN HOLT'S SECURITY SYSTEMS, SHUTTING THEM DOWN AN HOUR BEFORE HIS DEATH?
WHO COULD DO THAT? HOLT BUILT HIS FORTUNE ON HIS SO-CALLED "UNBREAKABLE" SECURITY SYSTEMS.
EXACTLY. THEY SAY EVERY KILLER LEAVES A TRACE, BUT THIS ONE MIGHT AS WELL HAVE BEEN A GHOST.
SHE.
EXCUSE ME?
LOOK INTO HOLT'S LOVE LIFE--FIND OUT IF HE HAS AN EX-WIFE OR GIRLFRIENDS WHO MIGHT HAVE MOTIVE TO KILL.
YOU THINK THIS WAS THE WORK OF A JEALOUS EX-LOVER?
THIS WASN'T JEALOUSY.
THIS WAS REVENGE.
SORRY

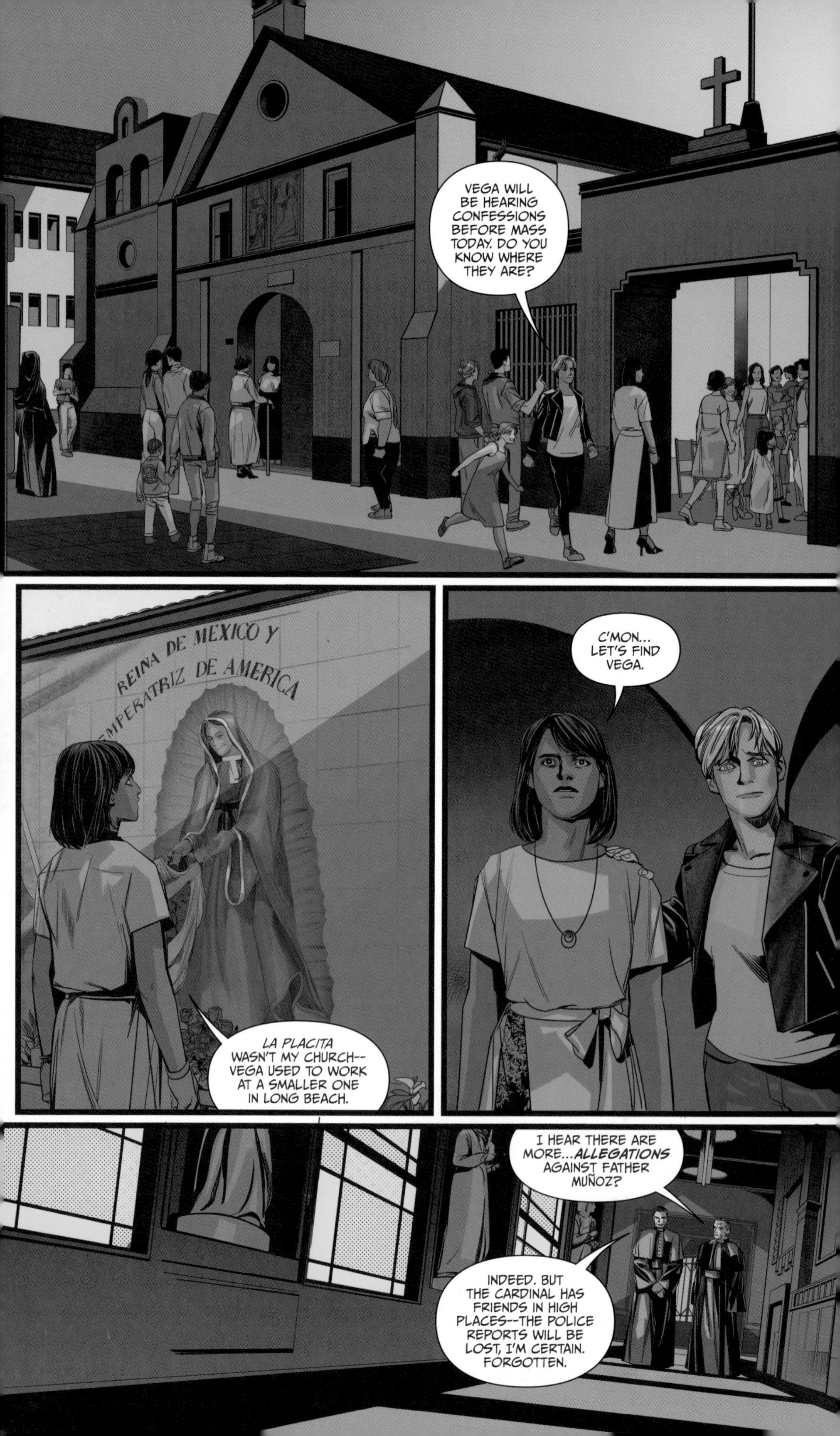
VEGA WILL BE HEARING CONFESSIONS BEFORE MASS TODAY. DO YOU KNOW WHERE THEY ARE?
REINA DE MEXICO Y EMPERATRIZ DE AMERICA
LA PLACITA WASN'T MY CHURCH-- VEGA USED TO WORK AT A SMALLER ONE IN LONG BEACH.
C'MON... LET'S FIND VEGA.
I HEAR THERE ARE MORE... ***ALLEGATIONS*** AGAINST FATHER MUÑOZ?
INDEED. BUT THE CARDINAL HAS FRIENDS IN HIGH PLACES--THE POLICE REPORTS WILL BE LOST, I'M CERTAIN. FORGOTTEN.

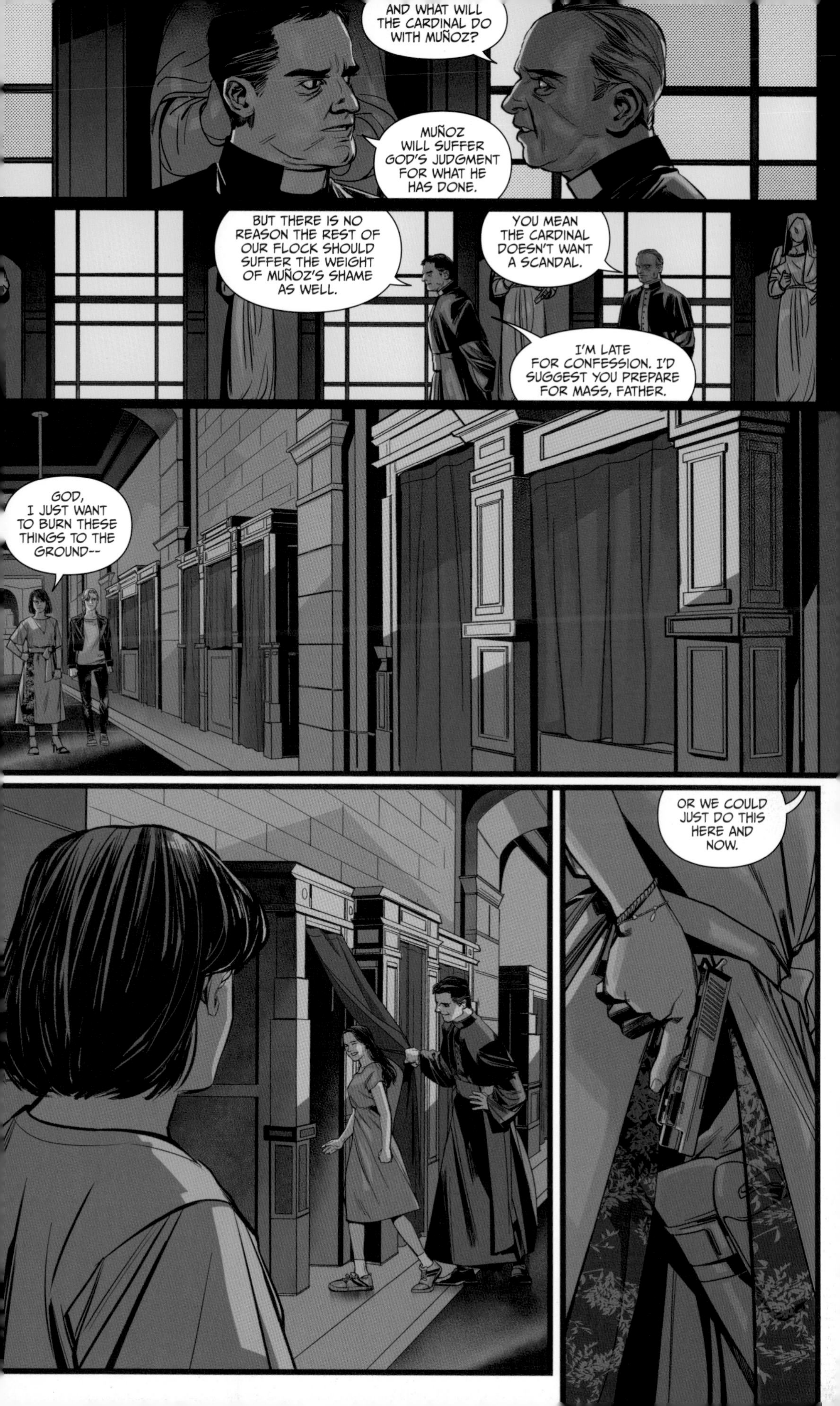
AND WHAT WILL THE CARDINAL DO WITH MUÑOZ?
MUÑOZ WILL SUFFER GOD'S JUDGMENT FOR WHAT HE HAS DONE.
BUT THERE IS NO REASON THE REST OF OUR FLOCK SHOULD SUFFER THE WEIGHT OF MUÑOZ'S SHAME AS WELL.
YOU MEAN THE CARDINAL DOESN'T WANT A SCANDAL.
I'M LATE FOR CONFESSION. I'D SUGGEST YOU PREPARE FOR MASS, FATHER.
GOD, I JUST WANT TO BURN THESE THINGS TO THE GROUND--
OR WE COULD JUST DO THIS HERE AND NOW.

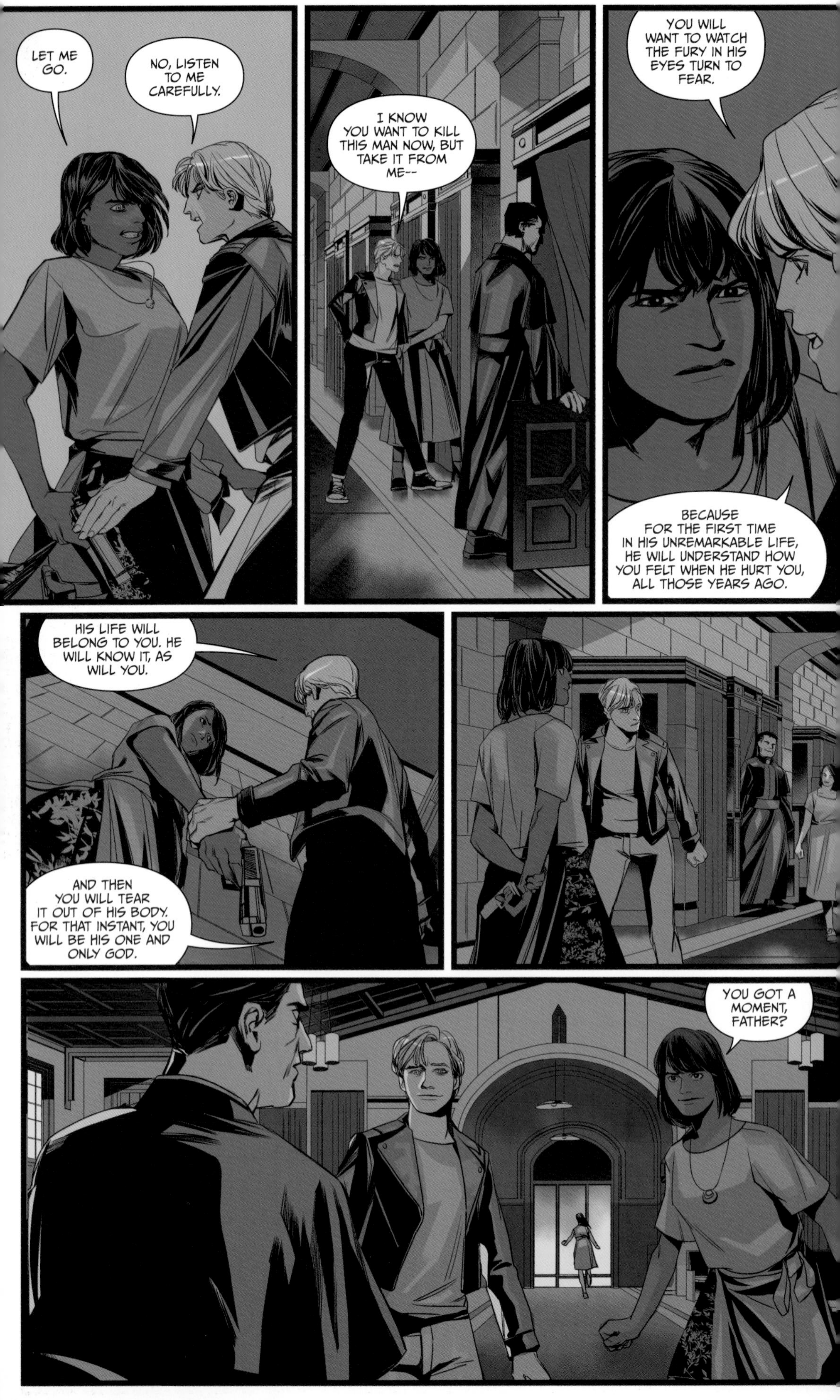
LET ME GO.
NO, LISTEN TO ME CAREFULLY.
I KNOW YOU WANT TO KILL THIS MAN NOW, BUT TAKE IT FROM ME--
YOU WILL WANT TO WATCH THE FURY IN HIS EYES TURN TO FEAR.
BECAUSE FOR THE FIRST TIME IN HIS UNREMARKABLE LIFE, HE WILL UNDERSTAND HOW YOU FELT WHEN HE HURT YOU, ALL THOSE YEARS AGO.
HIS LIFE WILL BELONG TO YOU. HE WILL KNOW IT, AS WILL YOU.
AND THEN YOU WILL TEAR IT OUT OF HIS BODY. FOR THAT INSTANT, YOU WILL BE HIS ONE AND ONLY GOD.
YOU GOT A MOMENT, FATHER?

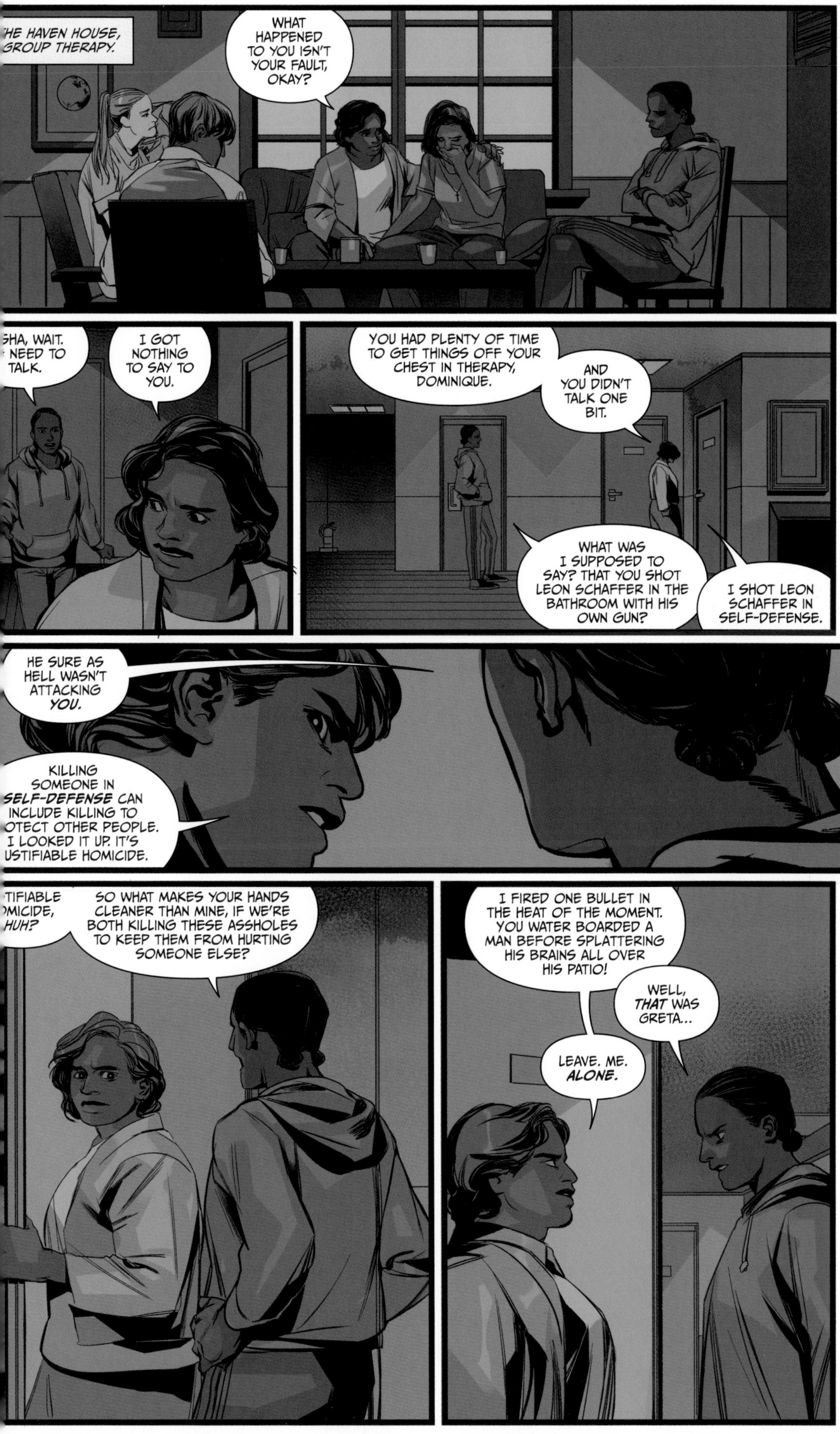

HE HAVEN HOUSE, GROUP THERAPY.
WHAT HAPPENED TO YOU ISN'T YOUR FAULT, OKAY?
SHA, WAIT. NEED TO TALK.
I GOT NOTHING TO SAY TO YOU.
YOU HAD PLENTY OF TIME TO GET THINGS OFF YOUR CHEST IN THERAPY, DOMINIQUE.
AND YOU DIDN'T TALK ONE BIT.
WHAT WAS I SUPPOSED TO SAY? THAT YOU SHOT LEON SCHAFFER IN THE BATHROOM WITH HIS OWN GUN?
I SHOT LEON SCHAFFER IN SELF-DEFENSE.
HE SURE AS HELL WASN'T ATTACKING YOU.
KILLING SOMEONE IN SELF-DEFENSE CAN INCLUDE KILLING TO OTECT OTHER PEOPLE. I LOOKED IT UP. IT'S USTIFIABLE HOMICIDE.
TIFIABLE MICIDE, HUH?
SO WHAT MAKES YOUR HANDS CLEANER THAN MINE, IF WE'RE BOTH KILLING THESE ASSHOLES TO KEEP THEM FROM HURTING SOMEONE ELSE?
I FIRED ONE BULLET IN THE HEAT OF THE MOMENT. YOU WATER BOARDED A MAN BEFORE SPLATTERING HIS BRAINS ALL OVER HIS PATIO!
WELL, THAT WAS GRETA...
LEAVE. ME. ALONE.

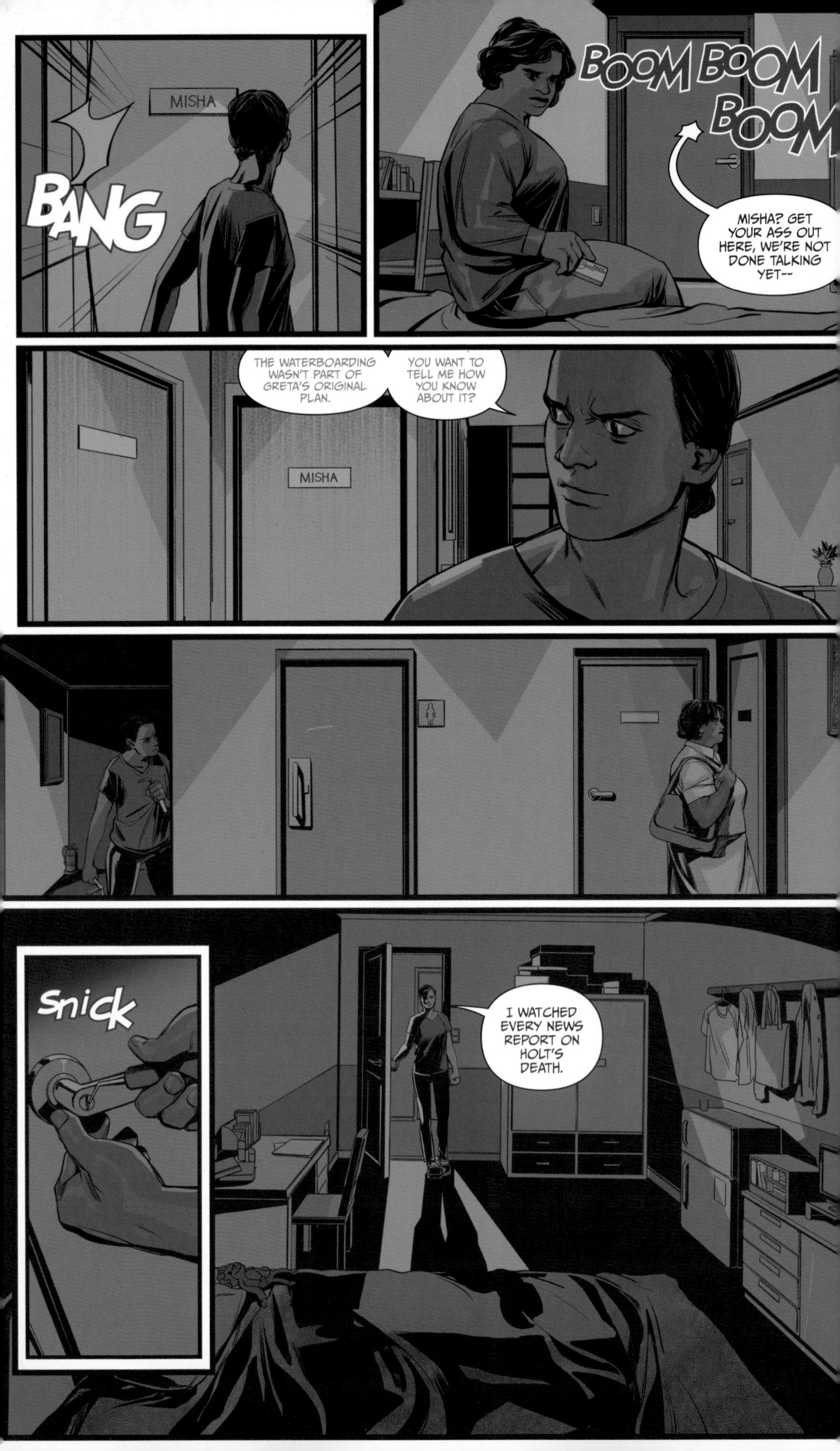
MISHA
BANG
BOOM BOOM
BOOM
MISHA? GET YOUR ASS OUT HERE, WE'RE NOT DONE TALKING YET--
THE WATERBOARDING WASN'T PART OF GRETA'S ORIGINAL PLAN.
YOU WANT TO TELL ME HOW YOU KNOW ABOUT IT?
MISHA
Snick
I WATCHED EVERY NEWS REPORT ON HOLT'S DEATH.

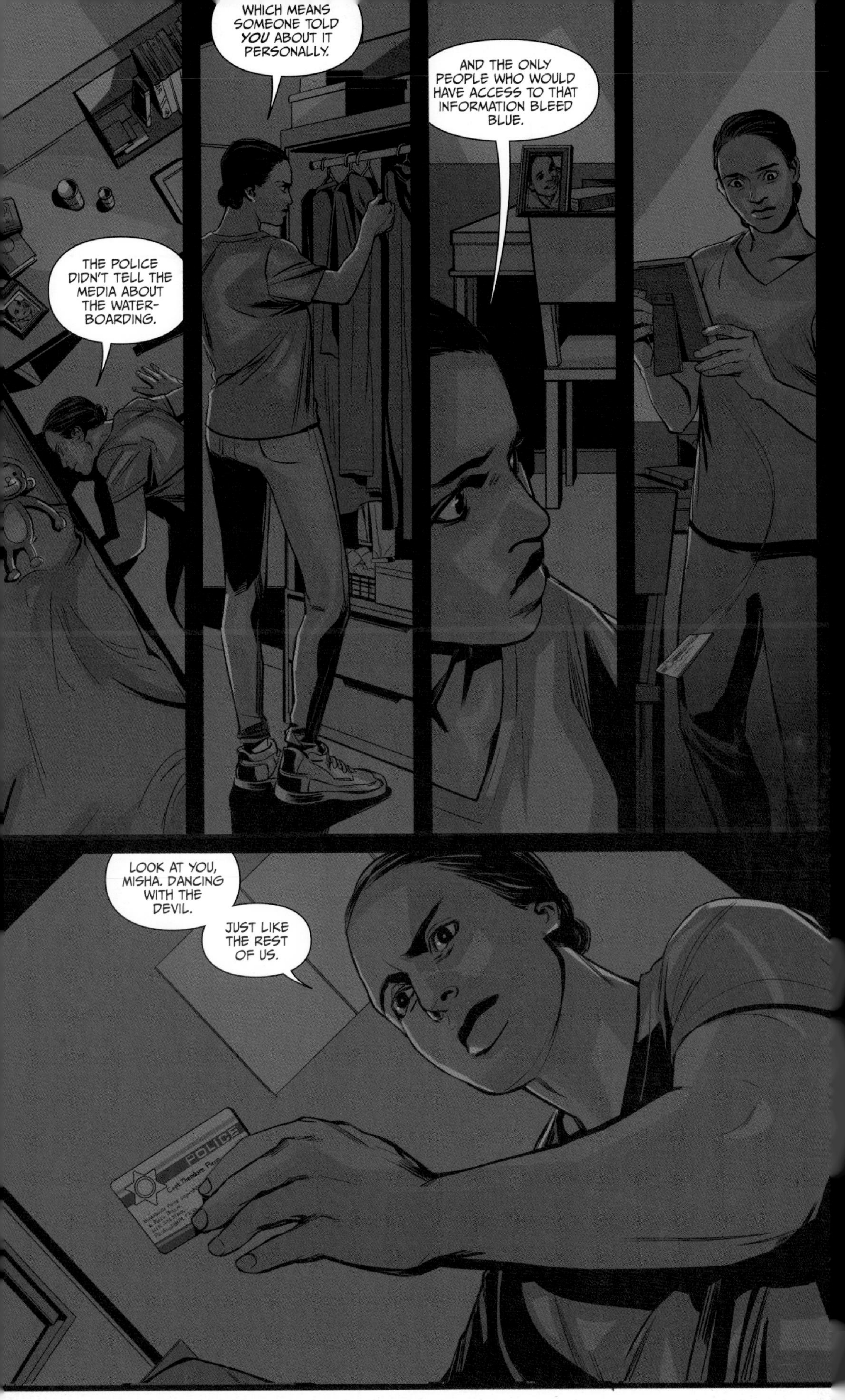
THE POLICE DIDN'T TELL THE MEDIA ABOUT THE WATER-BOARDING.
WHICH MEANS SOMEONE TOLD *YOU* ABOUT IT PERSONALLY.
AND THE ONLY PEOPLE WHO WOULD HAVE ACCESS TO THAT INFORMATION BLEED BLUE.
LOOK AT YOU, MISHA. DANCING WITH THE DEVIL.
JUST LIKE THE REST OF US.
POLICE

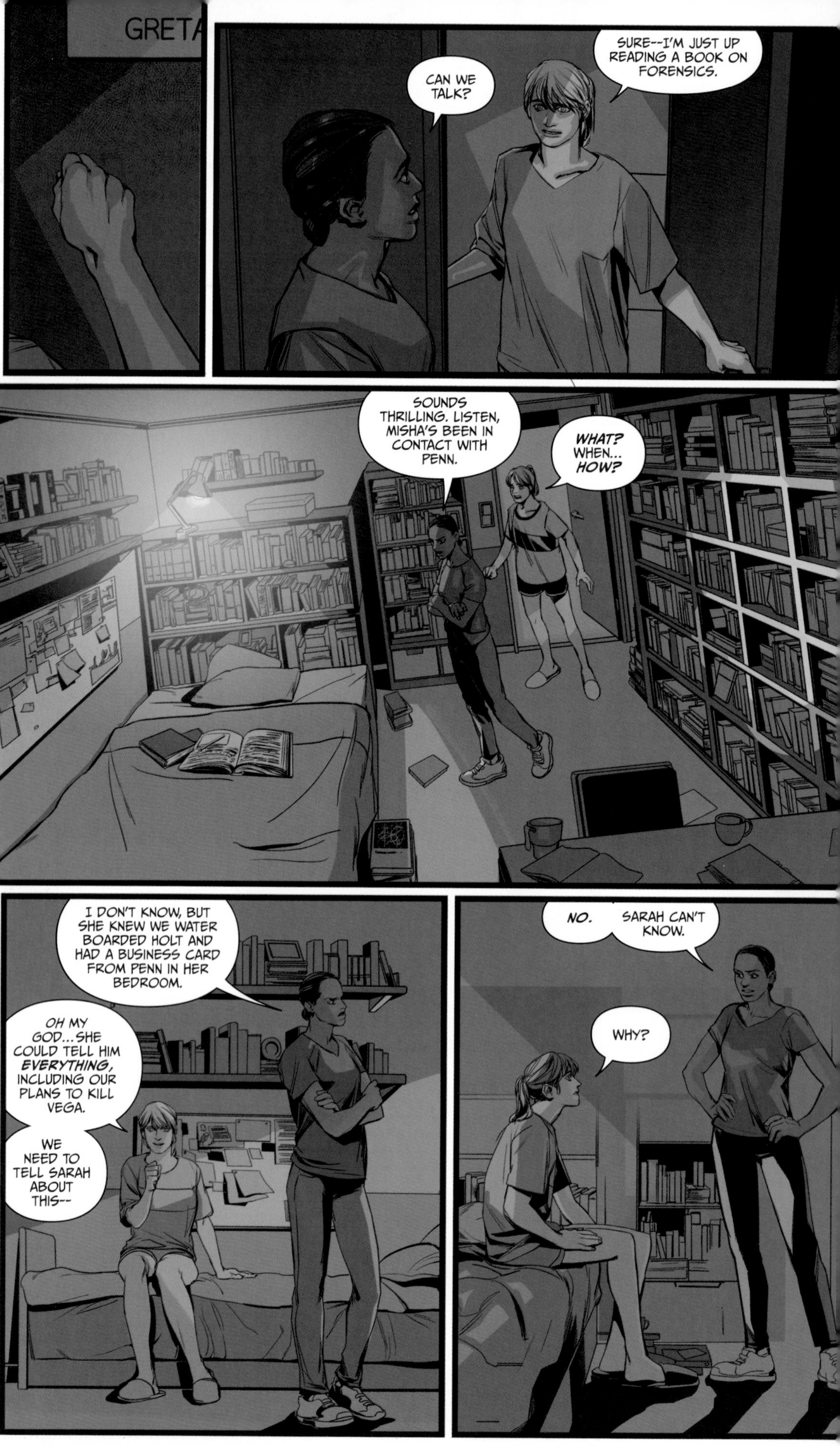
GRETA
CAN WE TALK?
SURE--I'M JUST UP READING A BOOK ON FORENSICS.
SOUNDS THRILLING. LISTEN, MISHA'S BEEN IN CONTACT WITH PENN.
WHAT? WHEN... HOW?
I DON'T KNOW, BUT SHE KNEW WE WATER BOARDED HOLT AND HAD A BUSINESS CARD FROM PENN IN HER BEDROOM.
OH MY GOD... SHE COULD TELL HIM EVERYTHING, INCLUDING OUR PLANS TO KILL VEGA.
WE NEED TO TELL SARAH ABOUT THIS--
NO.
SARAH CAN'T KNOW.
WHY?

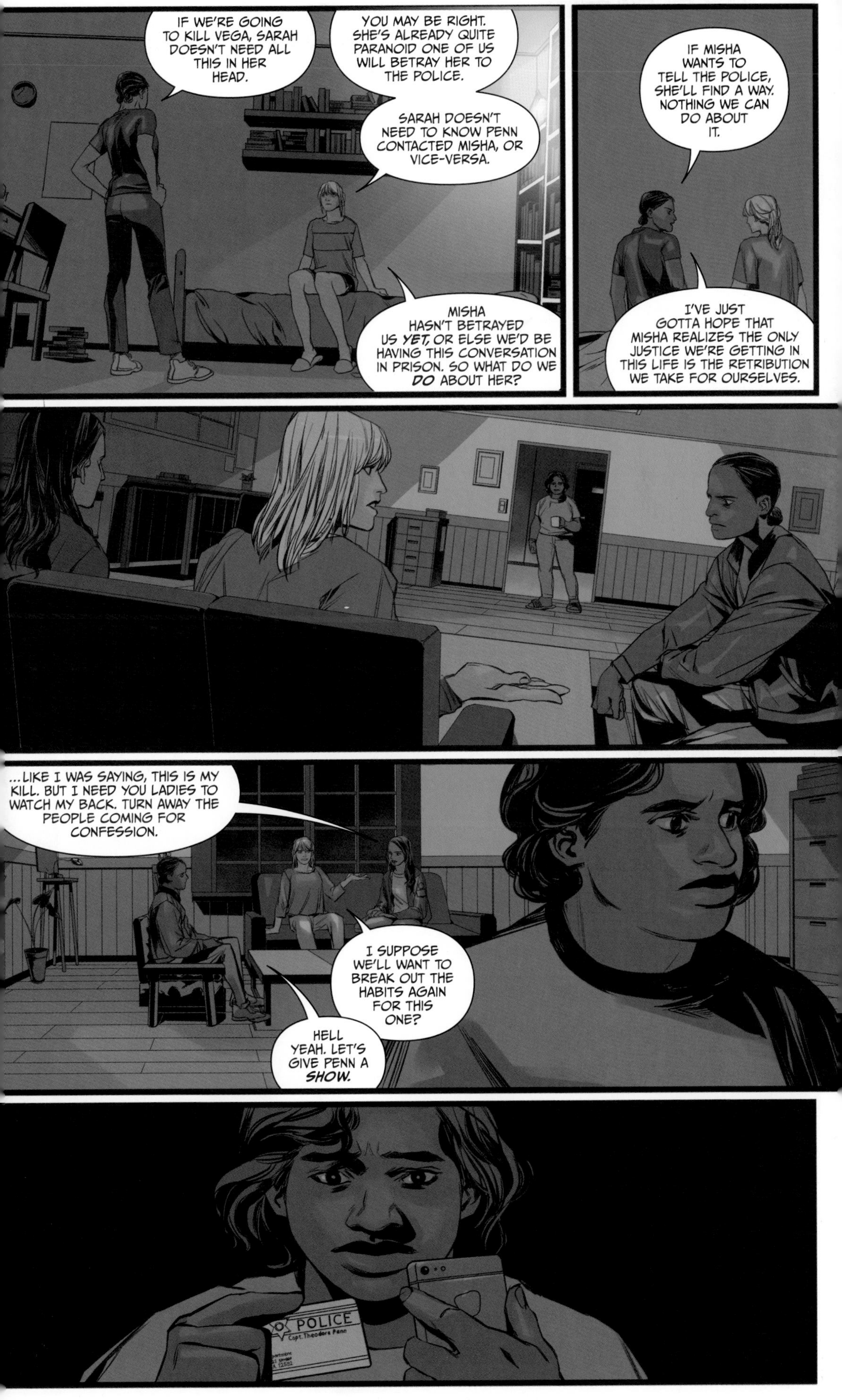
IF WE'RE GOING TO KILL VEGA, SARAH DOESN'T NEED ALL THIS IN HER HEAD.
YOU MAY BE RIGHT. SHE'S ALREADY QUITE PARANOID ONE OF US WILL BETRAY HER TO THE POLICE.
SARAH DOESN'T NEED TO KNOW PENN CONTACTED MISHA, OR VICE-VERSA.
MISHA HASN'T BETRAYED US *YET*, OR ELSE WE'D BE HAVING THIS CONVERSATION IN PRISON. SO WHAT DO WE *DO* ABOUT HER?
IF MISHA WANTS TO TELL THE POLICE, SHE'LL FIND A WAY. NOTHING WE CAN DO ABOUT IT.
I'VE JUST GOTTA HOPE THAT MISHA REALIZES THE ONLY JUSTICE WE'RE GETTING IN THIS LIFE IS THE RETRIBUTION WE TAKE FOR OURSELVES.
...LIKE I WAS SAYING, THIS IS MY KILL. BUT I NEED YOU LADIES TO WATCH MY BACK. TURN AWAY THE PEOPLE COMING FOR CONFESSION.
I SUPPOSE WE'LL WANT TO BREAK OUT THE HABITS AGAIN FOR THIS ONE?
HELL YEAH. LET'S GIVE PENN A *SHOW*.
POLICE
Capt. Theodore Penn

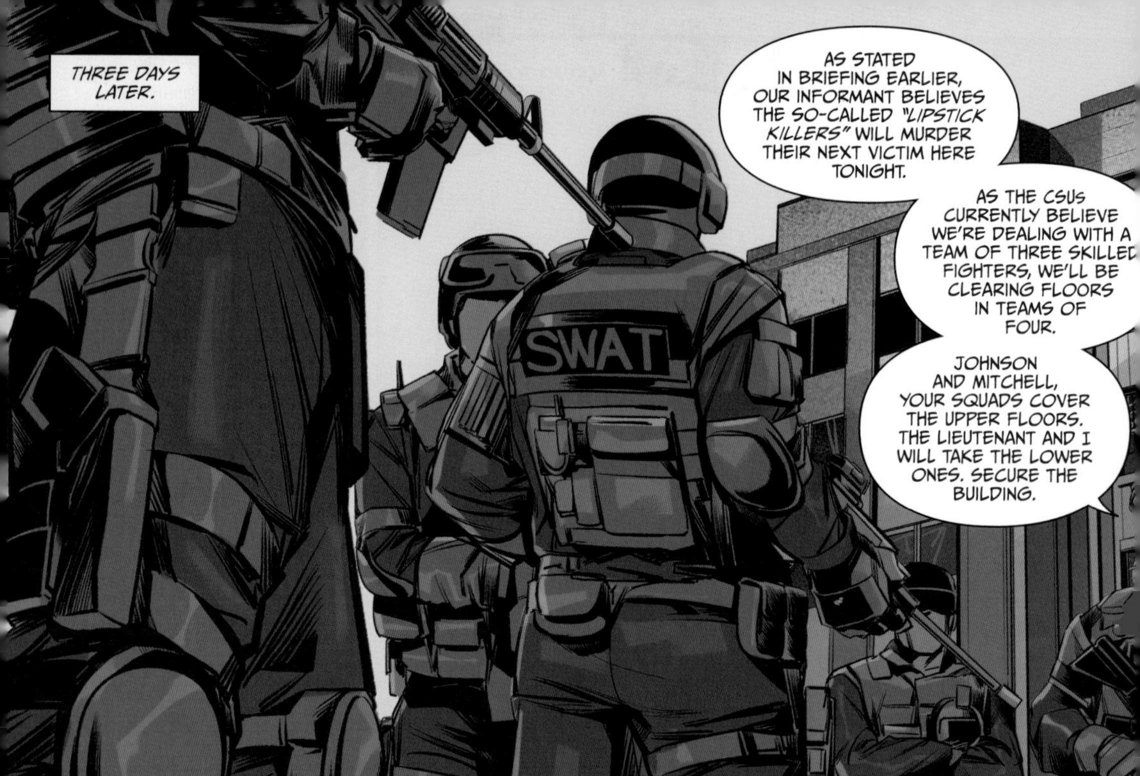
THREE DAYS LATER.
AS STATED IN BRIEFING EARLIER, OUR INFORMANT BELIEVES THE SO-CALLED "LIPSTICK KILLERS" WILL MURDER THEIR NEXT VICTIM HERE TONIGHT.
AS THE CSUs CURRENTLY BELIEVE WE'RE DEALING WITH A TEAM OF THREE SKILLED FIGHTERS, WE'LL BE CLEARING FLOORS IN TEAMS OF FOUR.
JOHNSON AND MITCHELL, YOUR SQUADS COVER THE UPPER FLOORS. THE LIEUTENANT AND I WILL TAKE THE LOWER ONES. SECURE THE BUILDING.
SWAT
SWAT

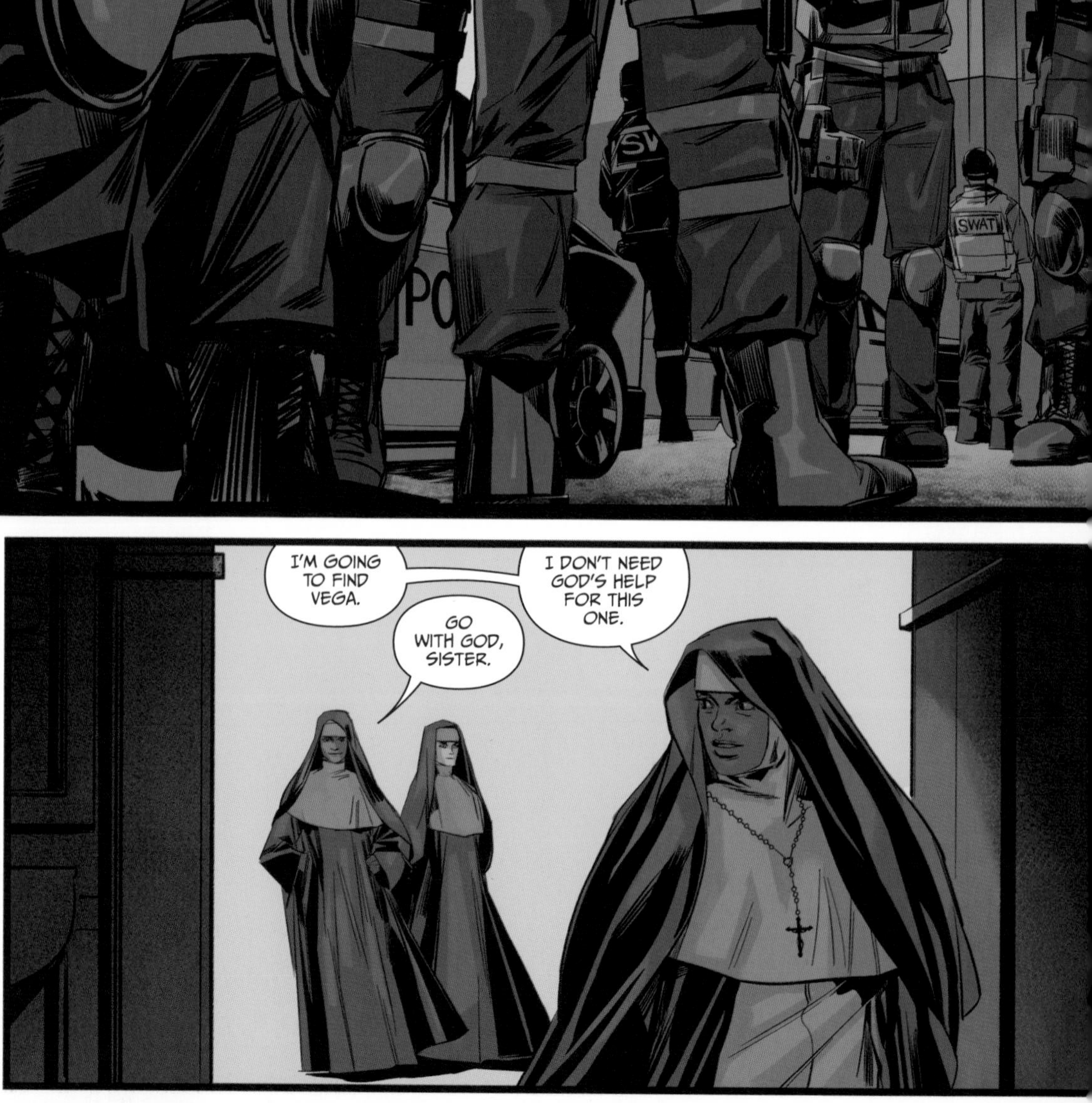
I'M GOING TO FIND VEGA.
I DON'T NEED GOD'S HELP FOR THIS ONE.
GO WITH GOD, SISTER.

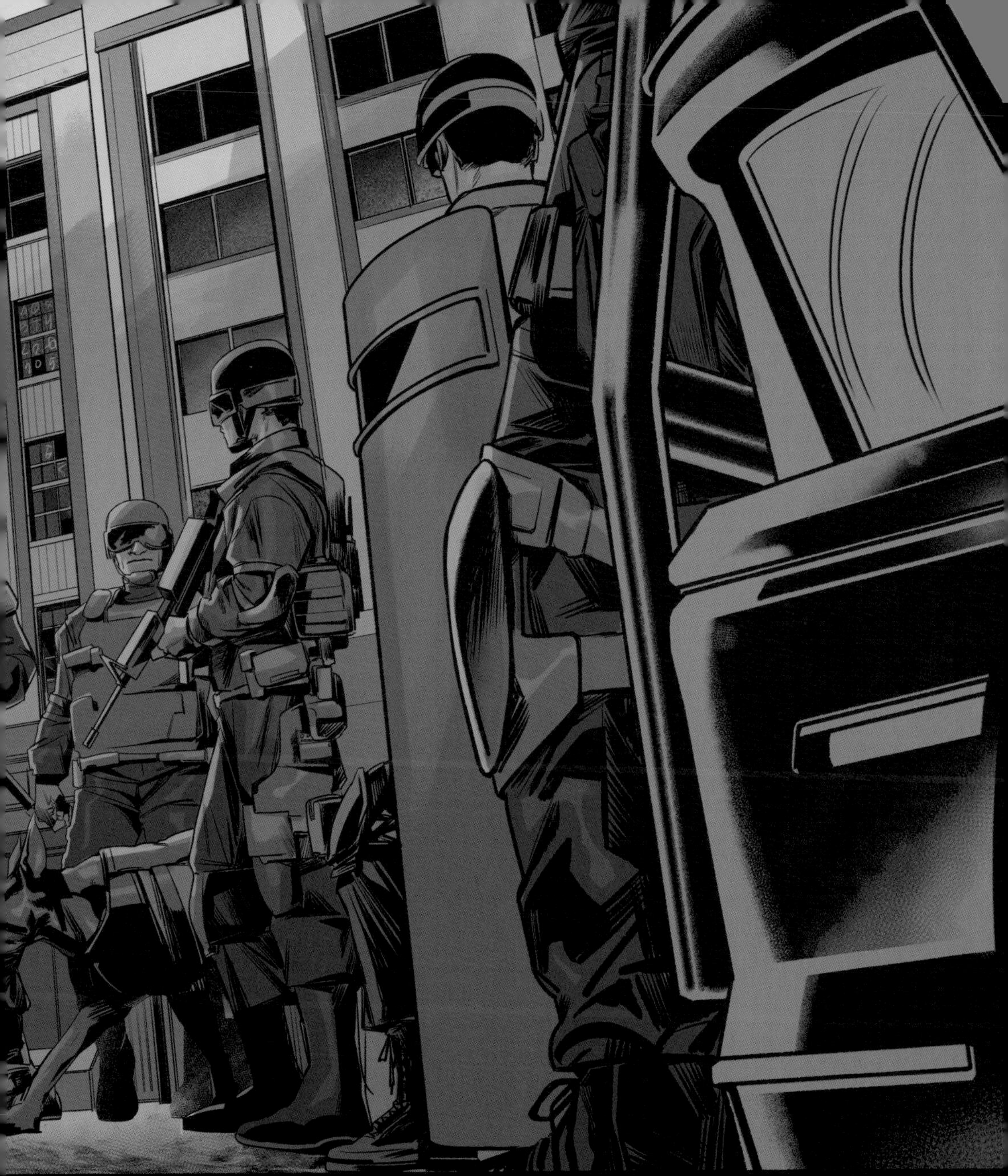

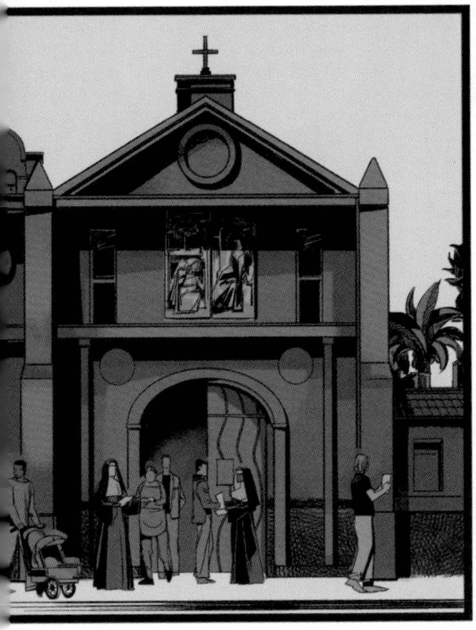

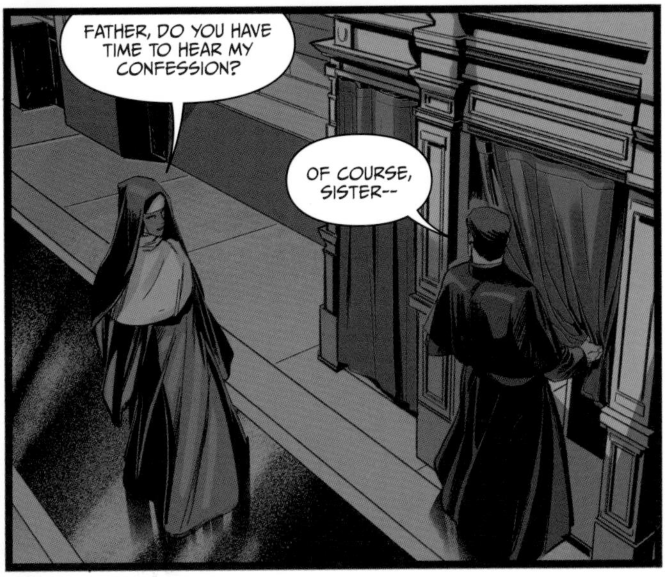
FATHER, DO YOU HAVE TIME TO HEAR MY CONFESSION?
OF COURSE, SISTER--

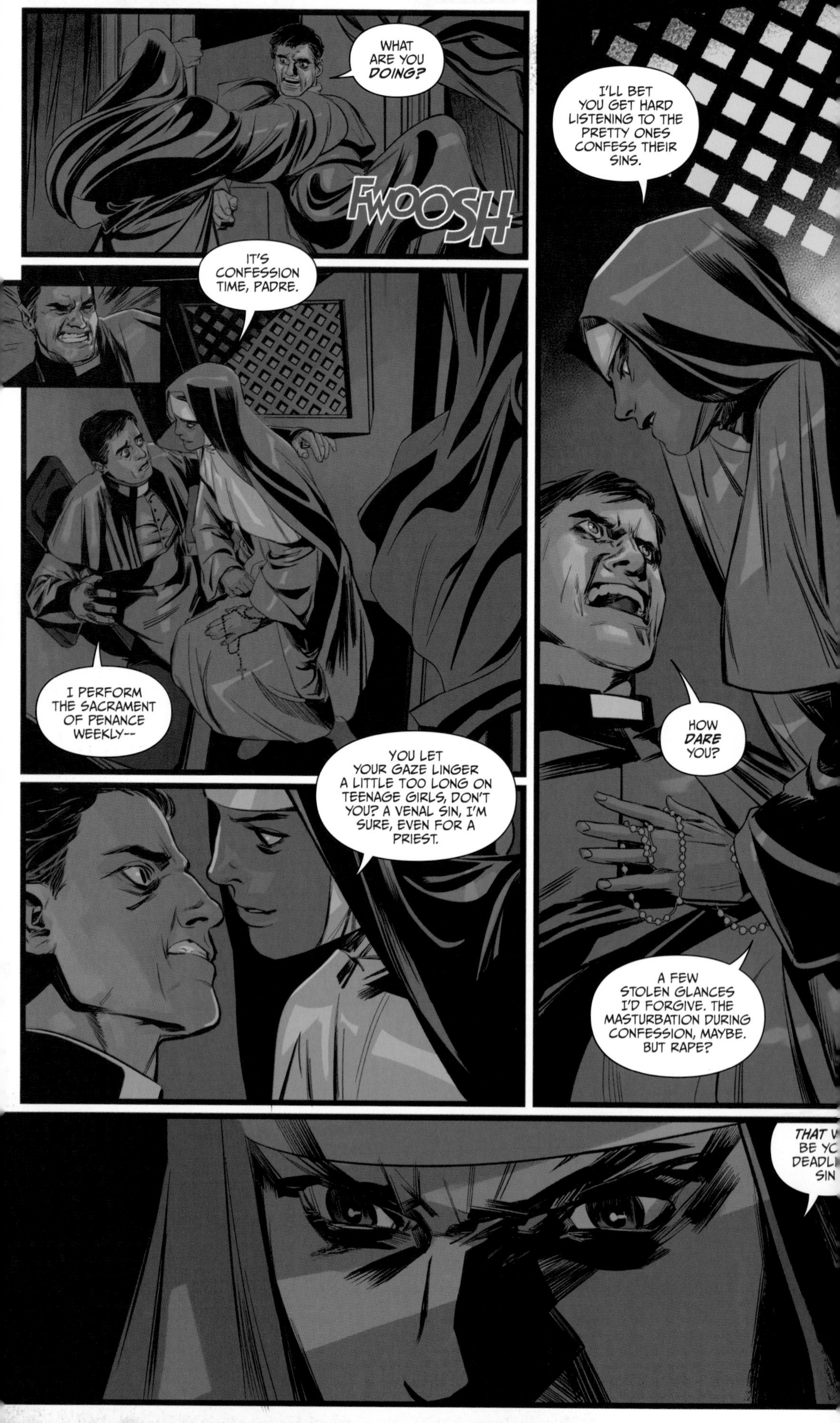
WHAT ARE YOU *DOING?*
FWOOSH
IT'S CONFESSION TIME, PADRE.
I PERFORM THE SACRAMENT OF PENANCE WEEKLY--
YOU LET YOUR GAZE LINGER A LITTLE TOO LONG ON TEENAGE GIRLS, DON'T YOU? A VENAL SIN, I'M SURE, EVEN FOR A PRIEST.
I'LL BET YOU GET HARD LISTENING TO THE PRETTY ONES CONFESS THEIR SINS.
HOW *DARE* YOU?
A FEW STOLEN GLANCES I'D FORGIVE. THE MASTURBATION DURING CONFESSION, MAYBE. BUT RAPE?

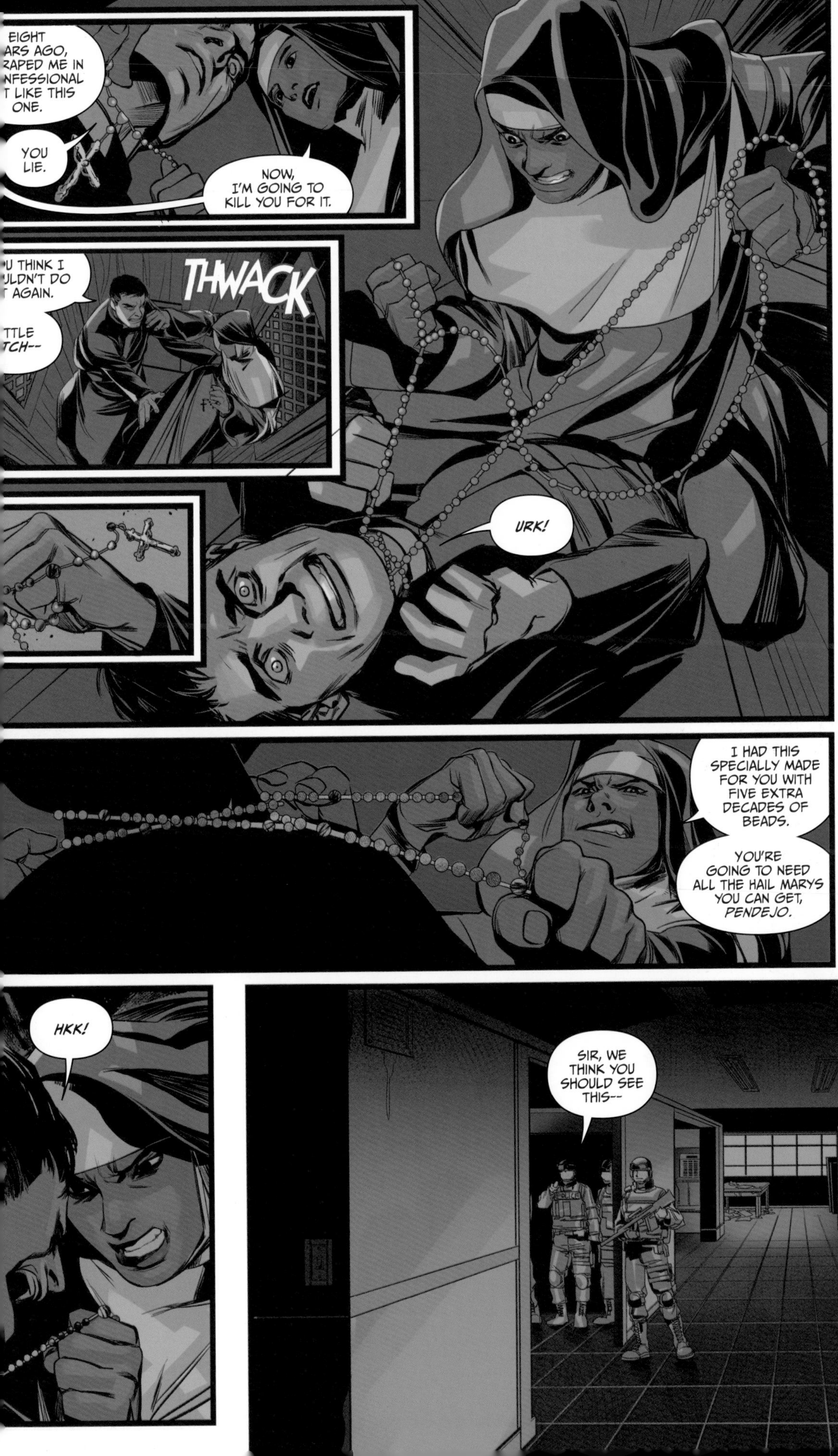

EIGHT ARS AGO, RAPED ME IN NFESSIONAL T LIKE THIS ONE.
YOU LIE.
NOW, I'M GOING TO KILL YOU FOR IT.
U THINK I ULDN'T DO T AGAIN.
TTLE TCH--
THWACK
URK!
I HAD THIS SPECIALLY MADE FOR YOU WITH FIVE EXTRA DECADES OF BEADS.
YOU'RE GOING TO NEED ALL THE HAIL MARYS YOU CAN GET, *PENDEJO.*
HKK!
SIR, WE THINK YOU SHOULD SEE THIS--

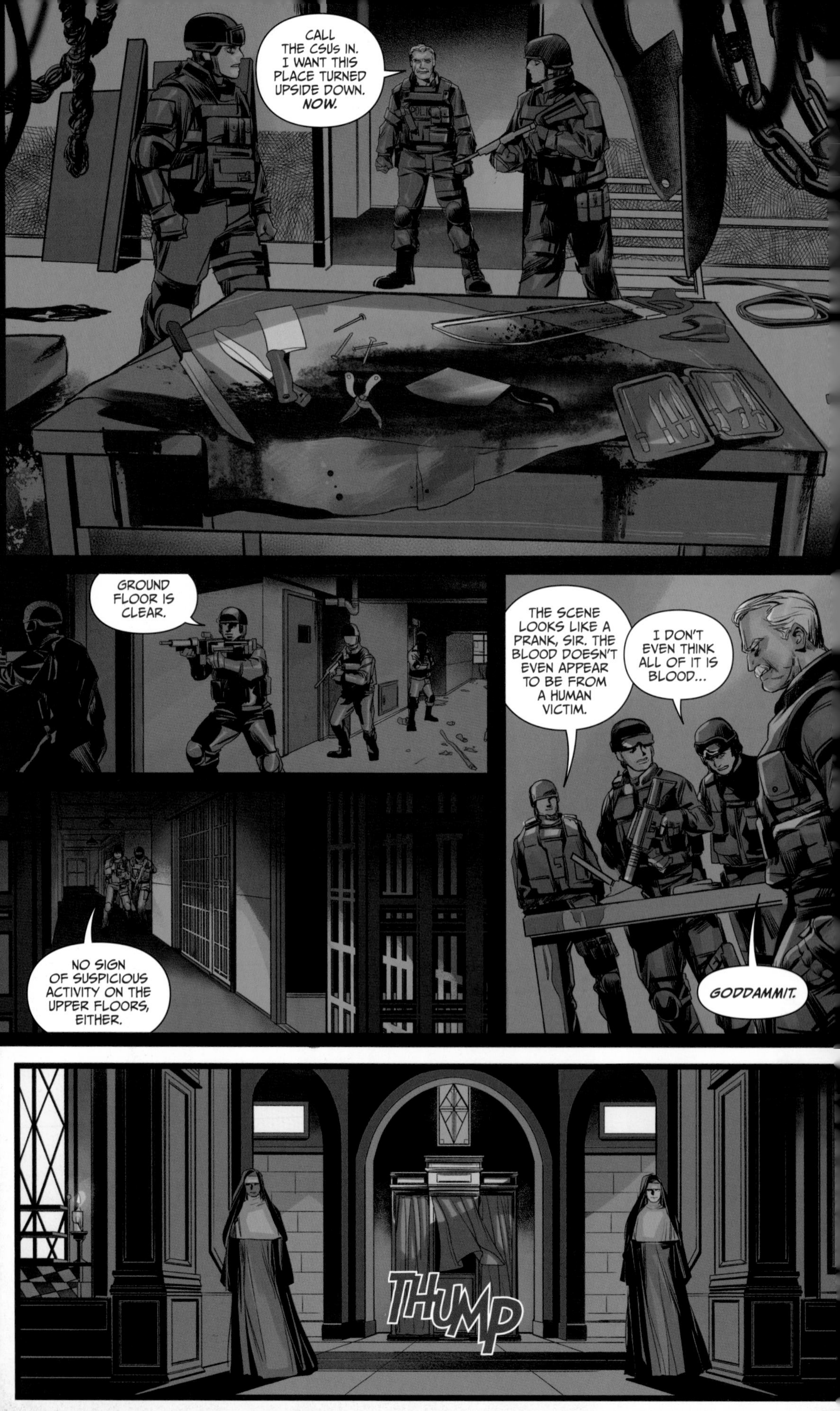
CALL THE CSUs IN. I WANT THIS PLACE TURNED UPSIDE DOWN. *NOW.*
GROUND FLOOR IS CLEAR.
NO SIGN OF SUSPICIOUS ACTIVITY ON THE UPPER FLOORS, EITHER.
THE SCENE LOOKS LIKE A PRANK, SIR. THE BLOOD DOESN'T EVEN APPEAR TO BE FROM A HUMAN VICTIM.
I DON'T EVEN THINK ALL OF IT IS BLOOD...
GODDAMMIT.
THUMP

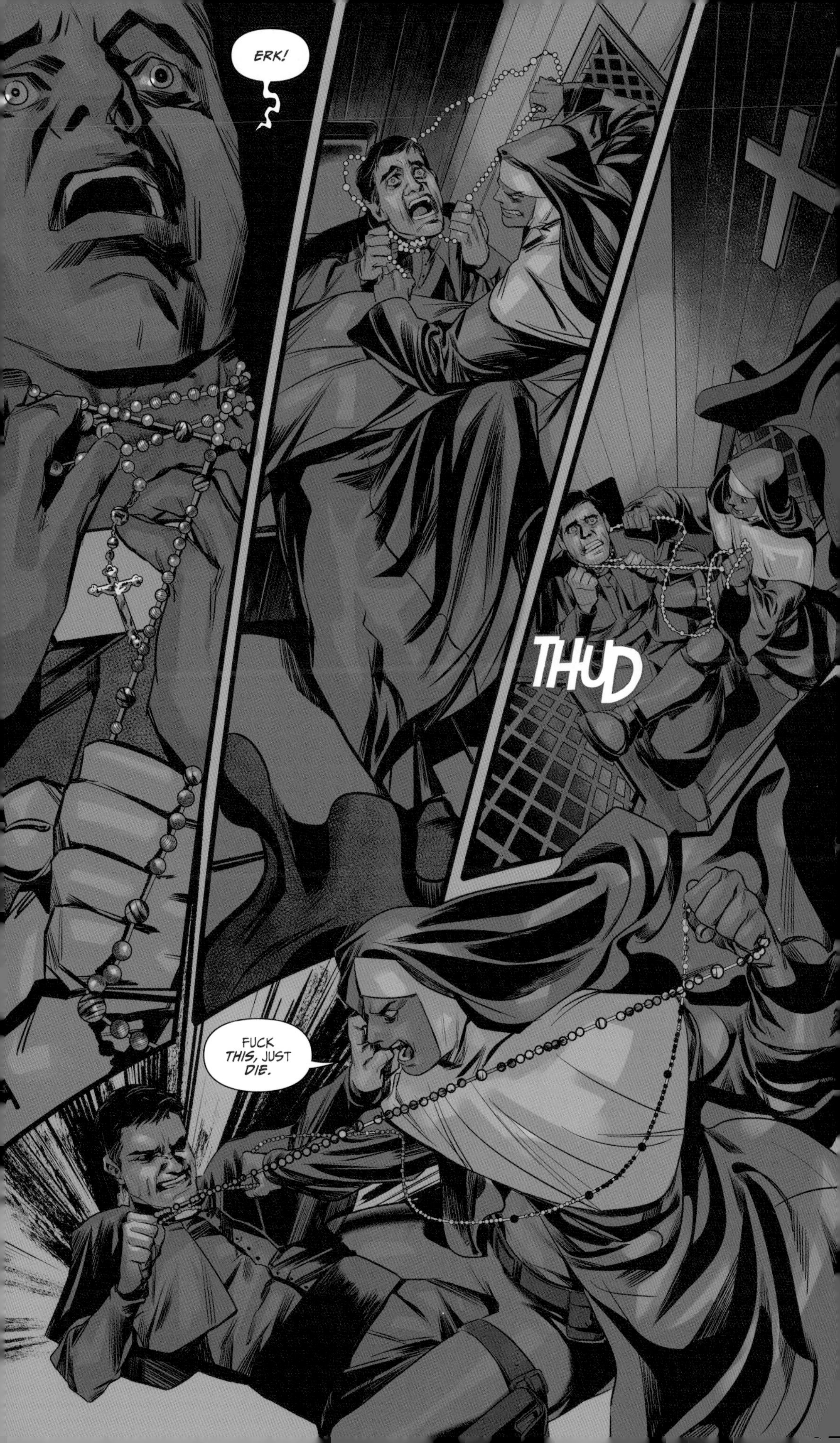
ERK!
THUD
FUCK THIS, JUST DIE.

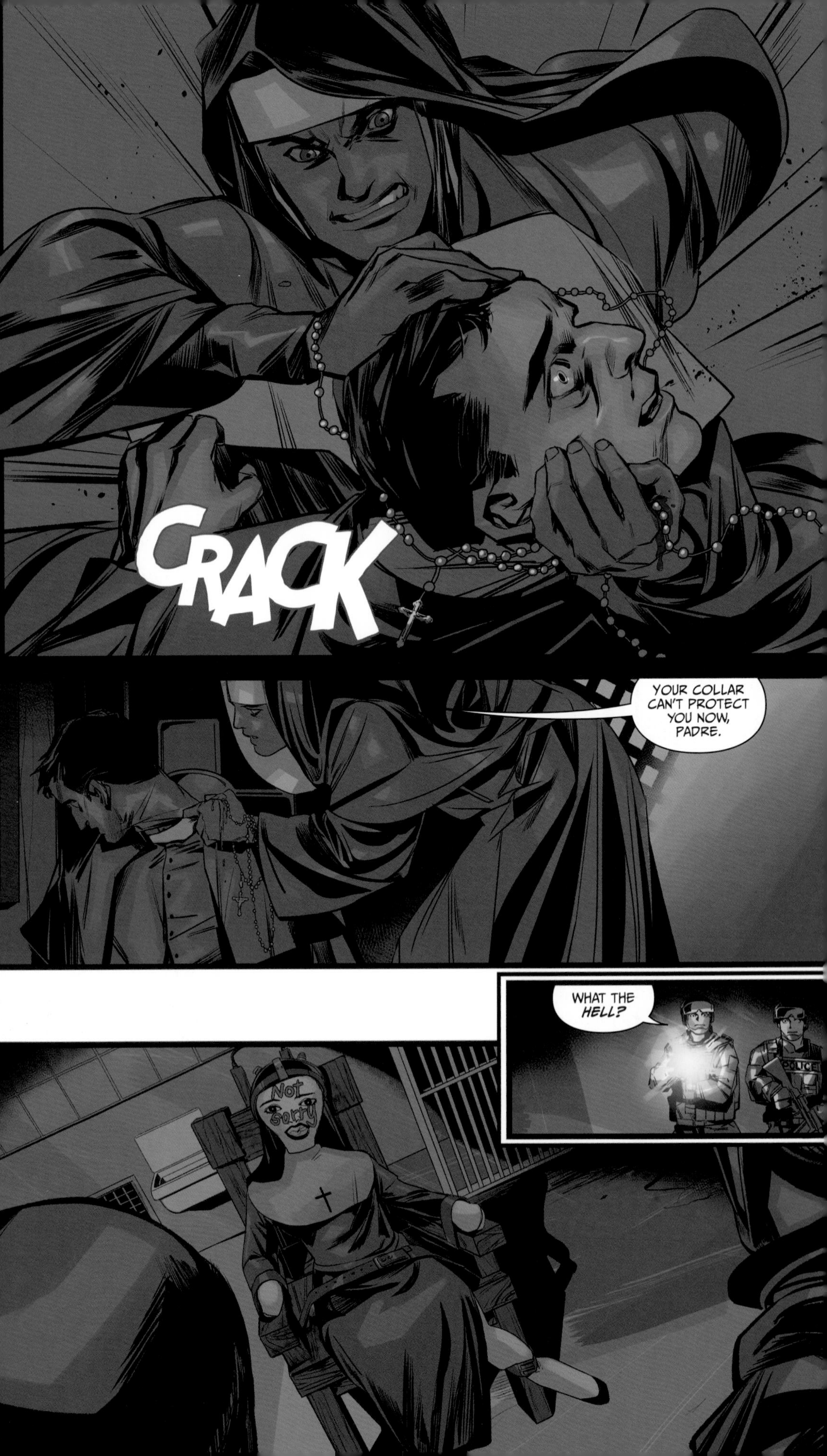
CRACK
YOUR COLLAR CAN'T PROTECT YOU NOW, PADRE.
WHAT THE *HELL?*
Not sorry
POLICE

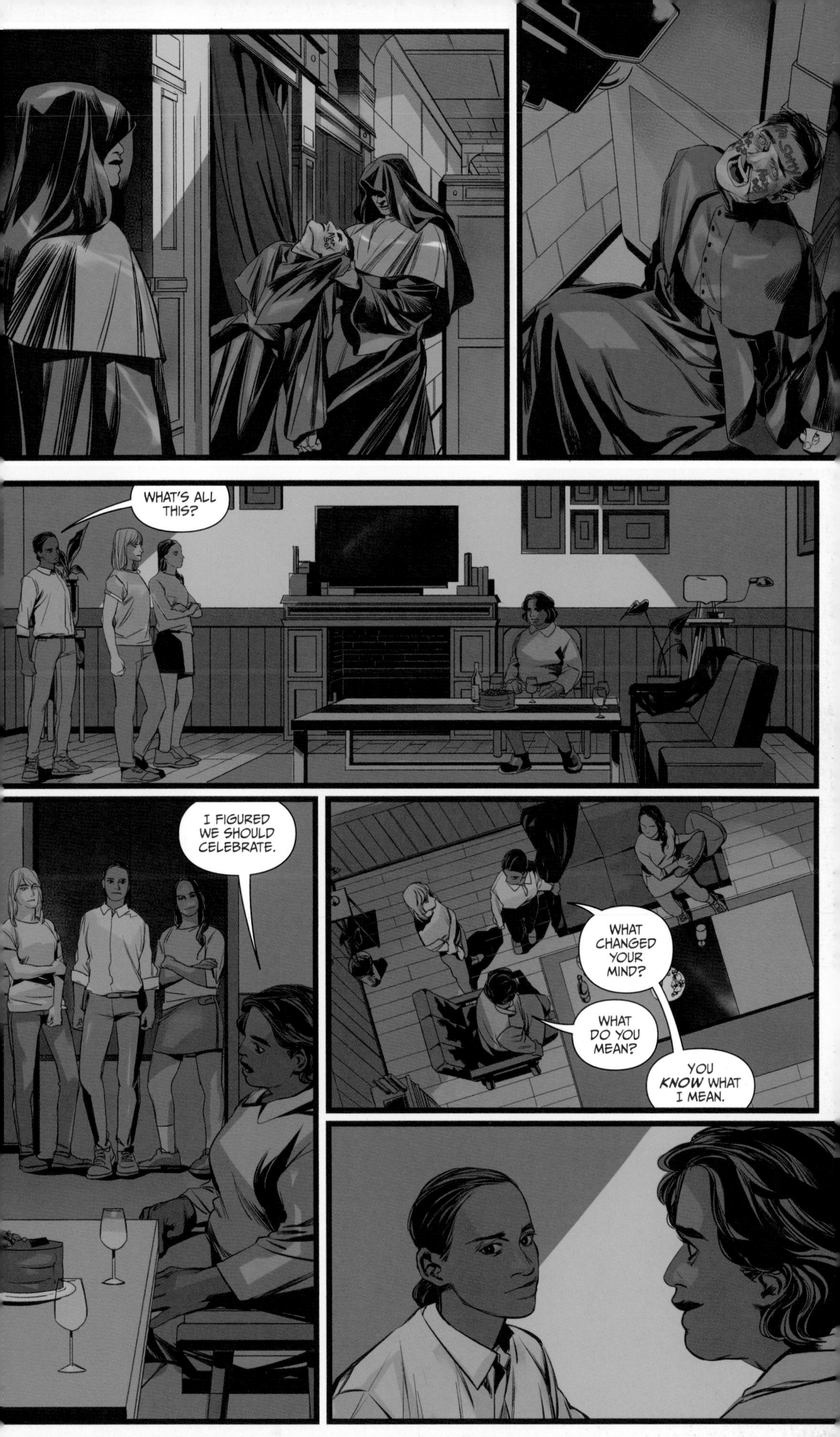

WHAT'S ALL THIS?
I FIGURED WE SHOULD CELEBRATE.
WHAT CHANGED YOUR MIND?
WHAT DO YOU MEAN?
YOU KNOW WHAT I MEAN.

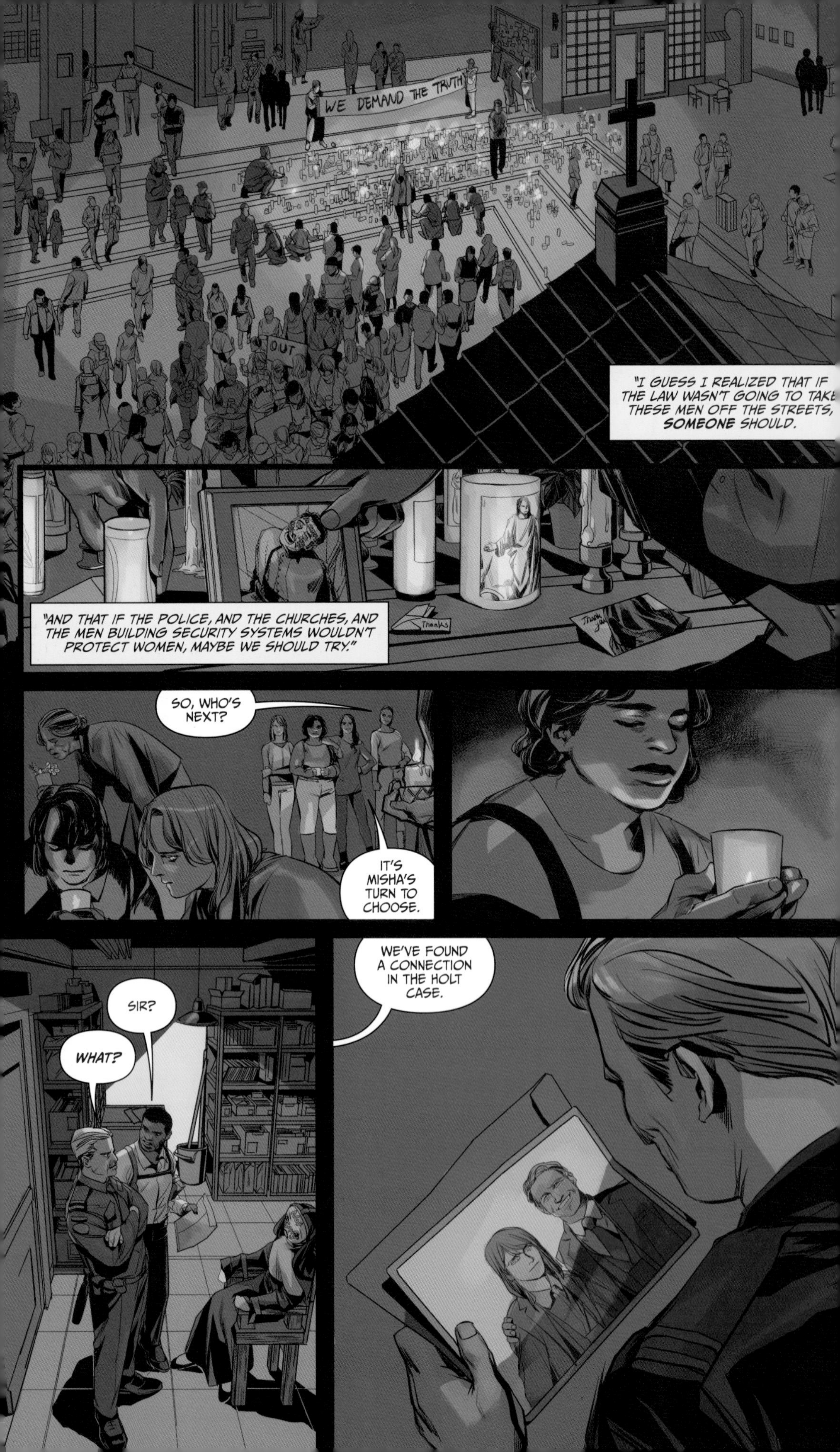
WE DEMAND THE TRUTH
OUT
"I GUESS I REALIZED THAT IF THE LAW WASN'T GOING TO TAKE THESE MEN OFF THE STREETS, SOMEONE SHOULD.
"AND THAT IF THE POLICE, AND THE CHURCHES, AND THE MEN BUILDING SECURITY SYSTEMS WOULDN'T PROTECT WOMEN, MAYBE WE SHOULD TRY."
Thanks
SO, WHO'S NEXT?
IT'S MISHA'S TURN TO CHOOSE.
SIR?
WHAT?
WE'VE FOUND A CONNECTION IN THE HOLT CASE.

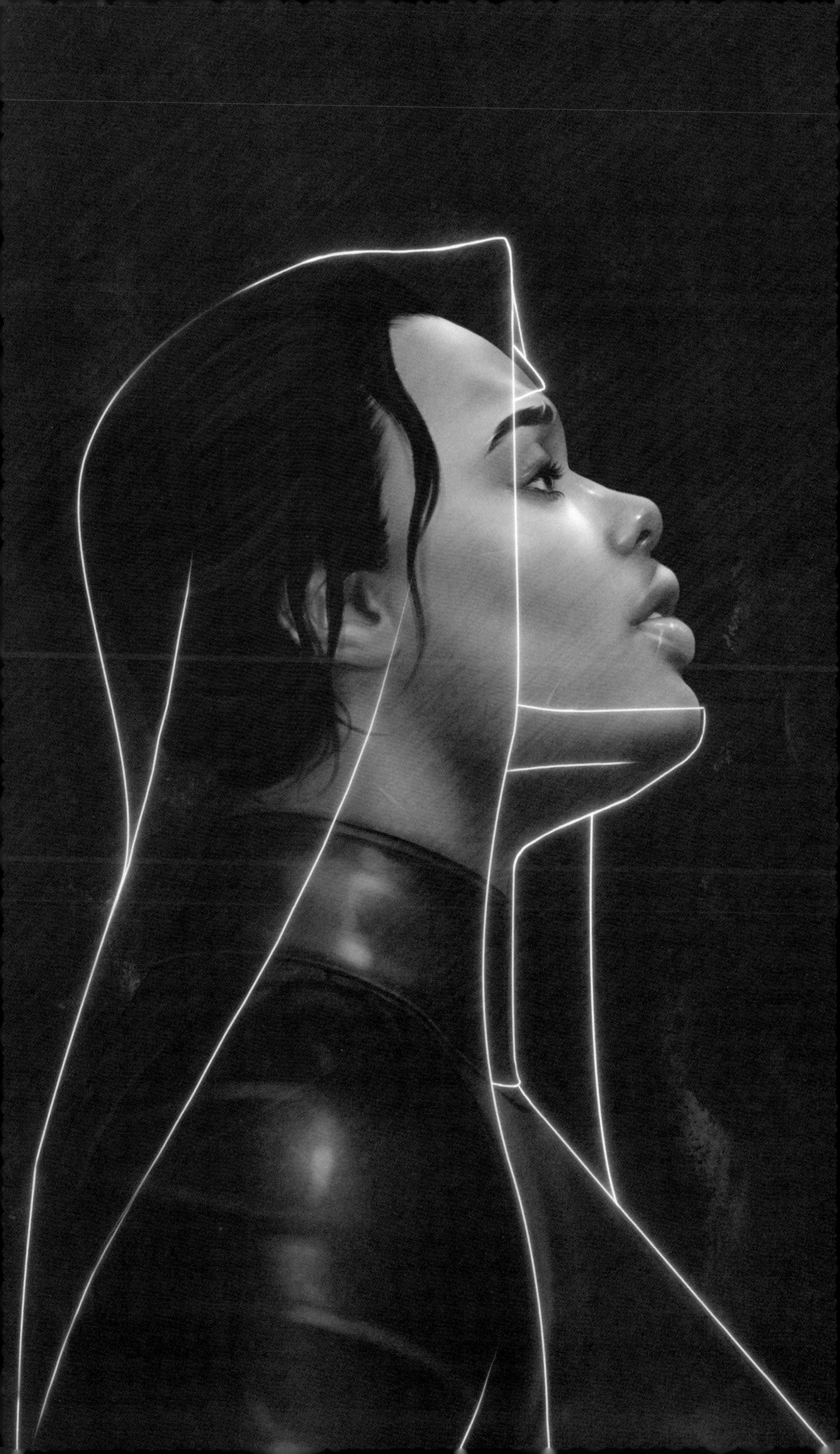

CHAPTER FOUR

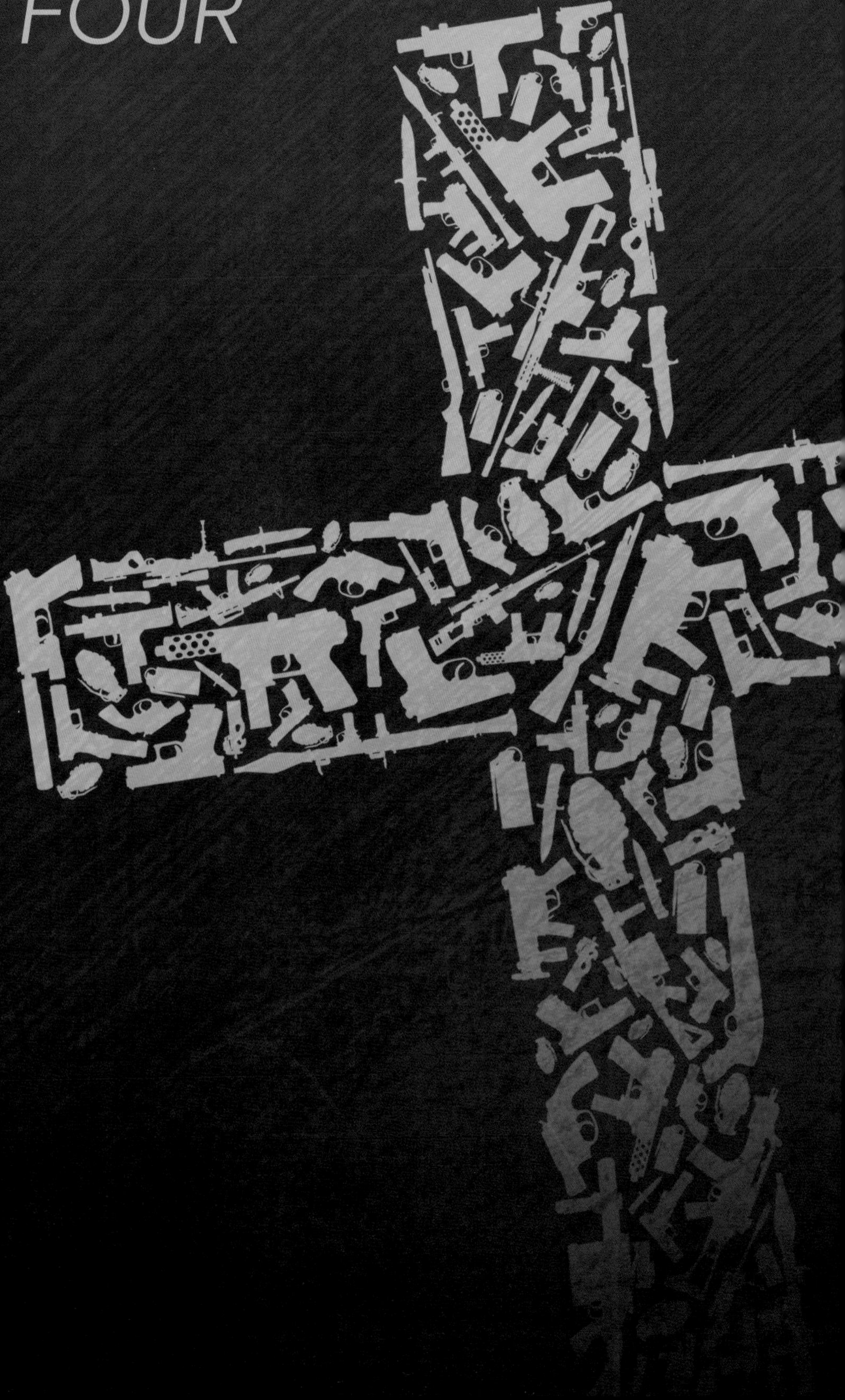

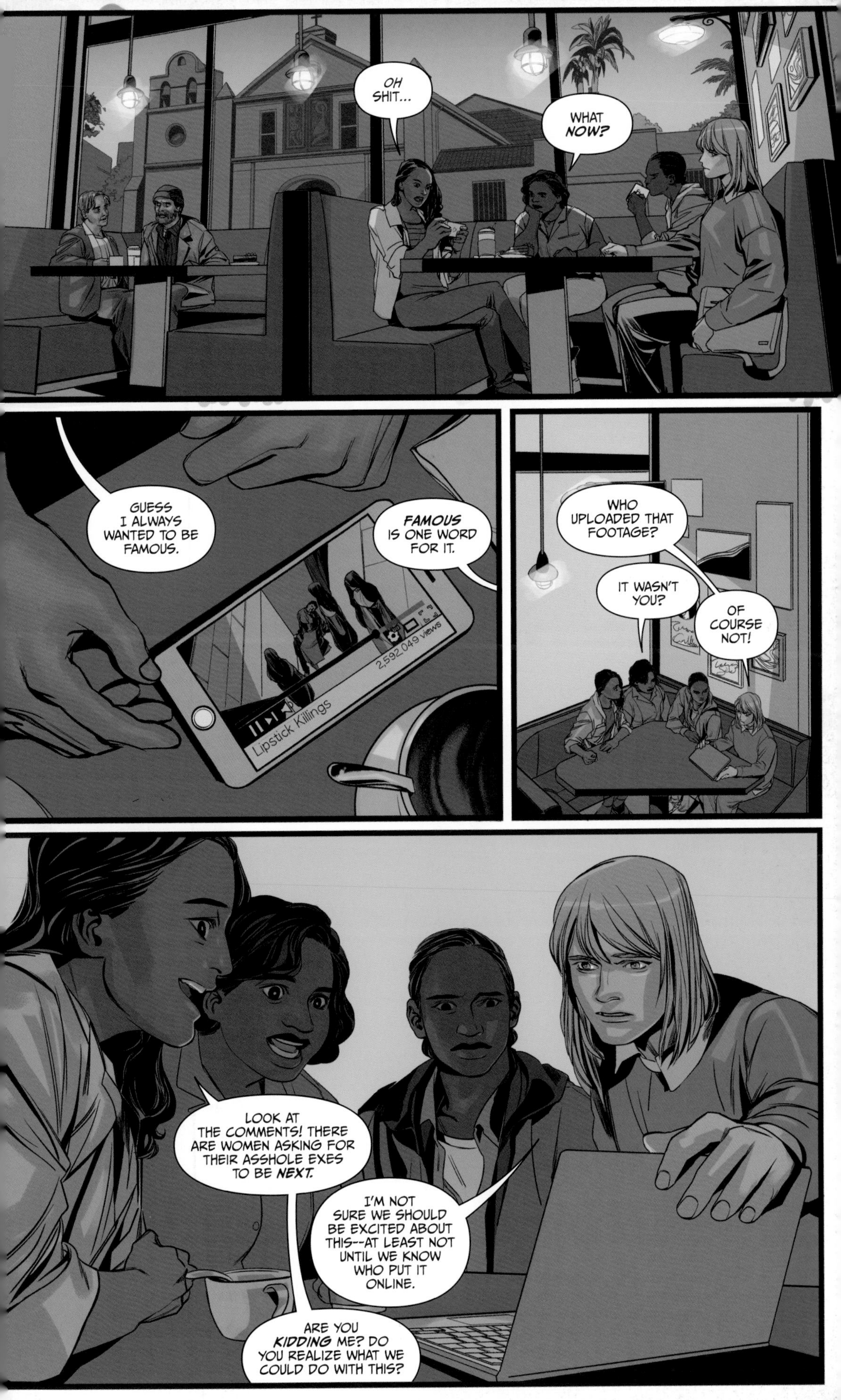
OH SHIT...
WHAT *NOW?*
GUESS I ALWAYS WANTED TO BE FAMOUS.
FAMOUS IS ONE WORD FOR IT.
Lipstick Killings
2,592,049 views
WHO UPLOADED THAT FOOTAGE?
IT WASN'T YOU?
OF COURSE NOT!
LOOK AT THE COMMENTS! THERE ARE WOMEN ASKING FOR THEIR ASSHOLE EXES TO BE *NEXT.*
I'M NOT SURE WE SHOULD BE EXCITED ABOUT THIS--AT LEAST NOT UNTIL WE KNOW WHO PUT IT ONLINE.
ARE YOU *KIDDING* ME? DO YOU REALIZE WHAT WE COULD DO WITH THIS?

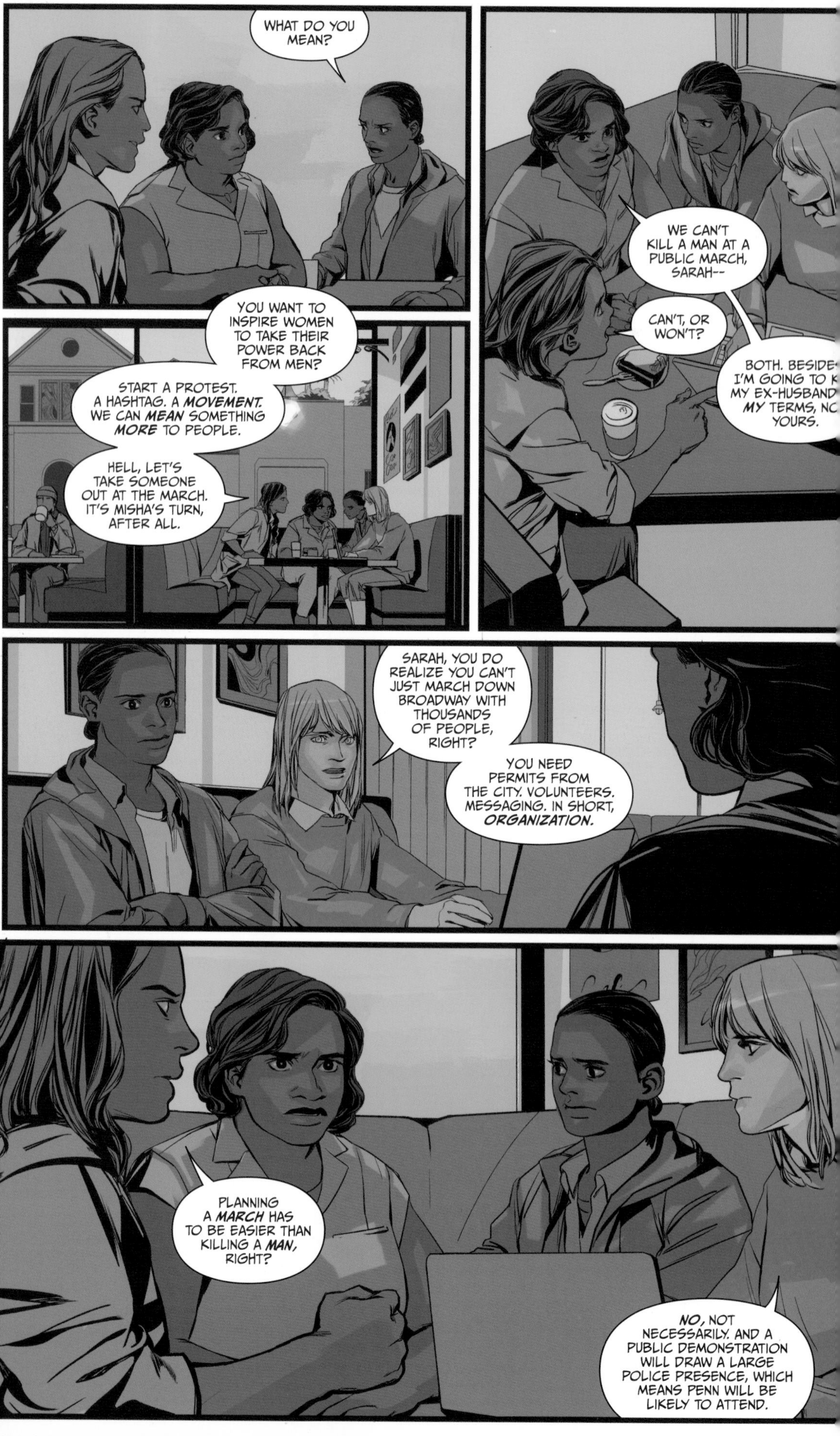
WHAT DO YOU MEAN?
YOU WANT TO INSPIRE WOMEN TO TAKE THEIR POWER BACK FROM MEN?
START A PROTEST. A HASHTAG. A *MOVEMENT.* WE CAN *MEAN* SOMETHING *MORE* TO PEOPLE.
HELL, LET'S TAKE SOMEONE OUT AT THE MARCH. IT'S MISHA'S TURN, AFTER ALL.
WE CAN'T KILL A MAN AT A PUBLIC MARCH, SARAH--
CAN'T, OR WON'T?
BOTH. BESIDE I'M GOING TO K MY EX-HUSBAND *MY* TERMS, NO YOURS.
SARAH, YOU DO REALIZE YOU CAN'T JUST MARCH DOWN BROADWAY WITH THOUSANDS OF PEOPLE, RIGHT?
YOU NEED PERMITS FROM THE CITY. VOLUNTEERS. MESSAGING. IN SHORT, *ORGANIZATION.*
PLANNING A *MARCH* HAS TO BE EASIER THAN KILLING A *MAN,* RIGHT?
NO, NOT NECESSARILY. AND A PUBLIC DEMONSTRATION WILL DRAW A LARGE POLICE PRESENCE, WHICH MEANS PENN WILL BE LIKELY TO ATTEND.

SO WHAT? IT'S NOT AGAINST THE LAW TO PROTEST PEACEFULLY.

I'M WORRIED ABOUT THAT *PEACEFUL* PART.

EXACTLY. TENSIONS SEEM TO BE RUNNING HIGH AT THE LAPD. PENN AND HIS MEN WILL ESCALATE ANY AND ALL HOSTILITIES.

AND THEN WE CATCH IT ALL ON FILM AND USE IT TO GET PENN FIRED.

WE SHOULDN'T GIVE THAT MAN ANY MORE AMMUNITION.

SAYS THE WOMAN WHO PLAYED HIM LIKE A FOOL.

I JUST THINK WE'VE GOT BETTER THINGS TO FOCUS ON, GIRLS.

LIKE KILLING YOUR ASSHOLE OF AN EX?

NO, THAT'S SOMETHING I'M GOING TO DO ALONE.

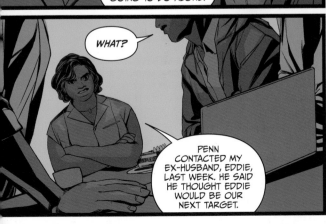

WHAT?

PENN CONTACTED MY EX-HUSBAND, EDDIE, LAST WEEK. HE SAID HE THOUGHT EDDIE WOULD BE OUR NEXT TARGET.

I DON'T WANT TO RISK OUR SISTERHOOD BY PLAYING RIGHT INTO PENN'S HANDS.

SO IF WE'RE GOING TO MURDER EDDIE FOR WHAT HE DID, WE'RE GOING TO DO IT *MY* WAY.

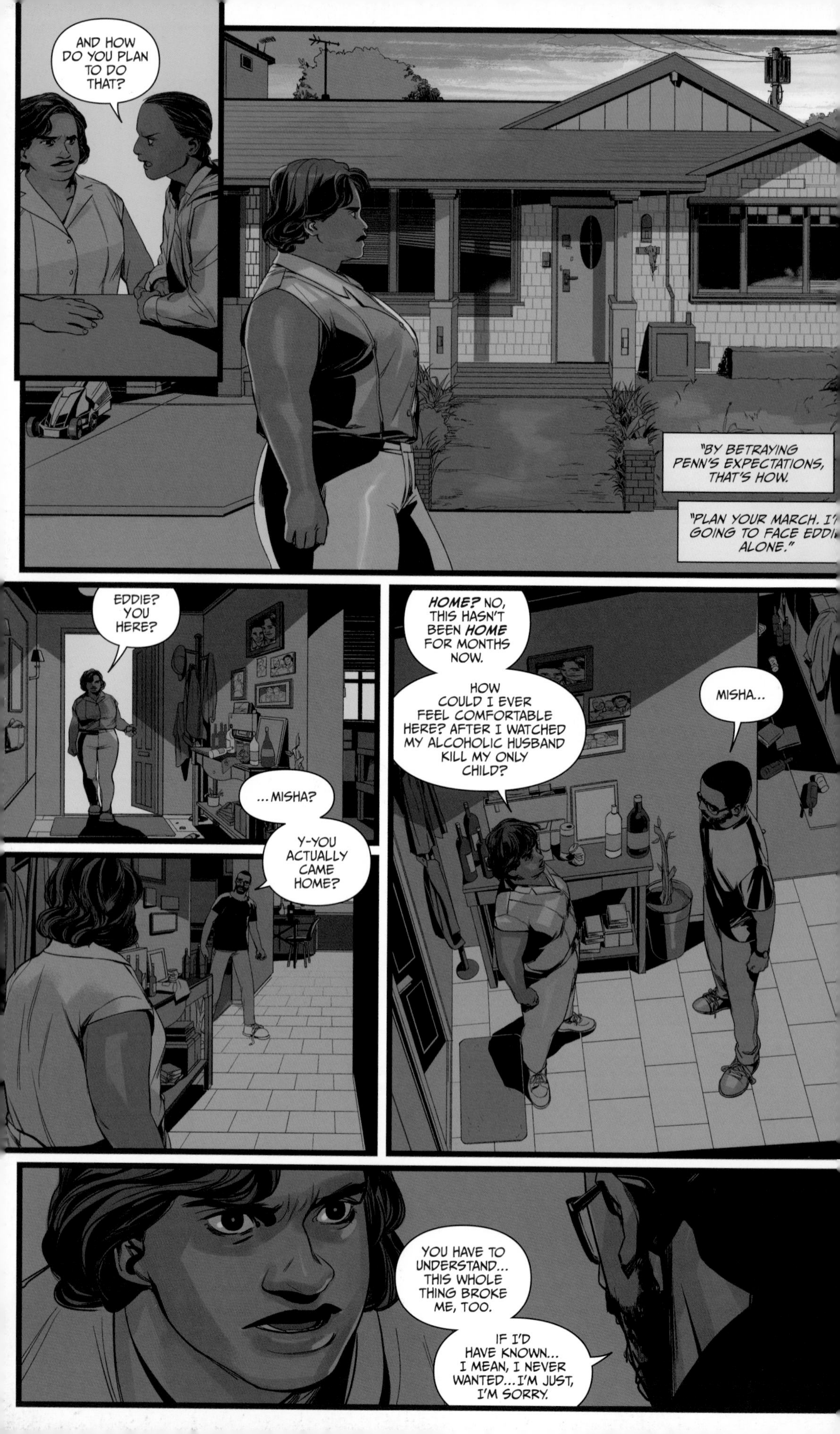
AND HOW DO YOU PLAN TO DO THAT?
"BY BETRAYING PENN'S EXPECTATIONS, THAT'S HOW.
"PLAN YOUR MARCH. I'M GOING TO FACE EDDIE ALONE."
EDDIE? YOU HERE?
...MISHA?
Y-YOU ACTUALLY CAME HOME?
HOME? NO, THIS HASN'T BEEN HOME FOR MONTHS NOW.
HOW COULD I EVER FEEL COMFORTABLE HERE? AFTER I WATCHED MY ALCOHOLIC HUSBAND KILL MY ONLY CHILD?
MISHA...
YOU HAVE TO UNDERSTAND... THIS WHOLE THING BROKE ME, TOO.
IF I'D HAVE KNOWN... I MEAN, I NEVER WANTED... I'M JUST, I'M SORRY.

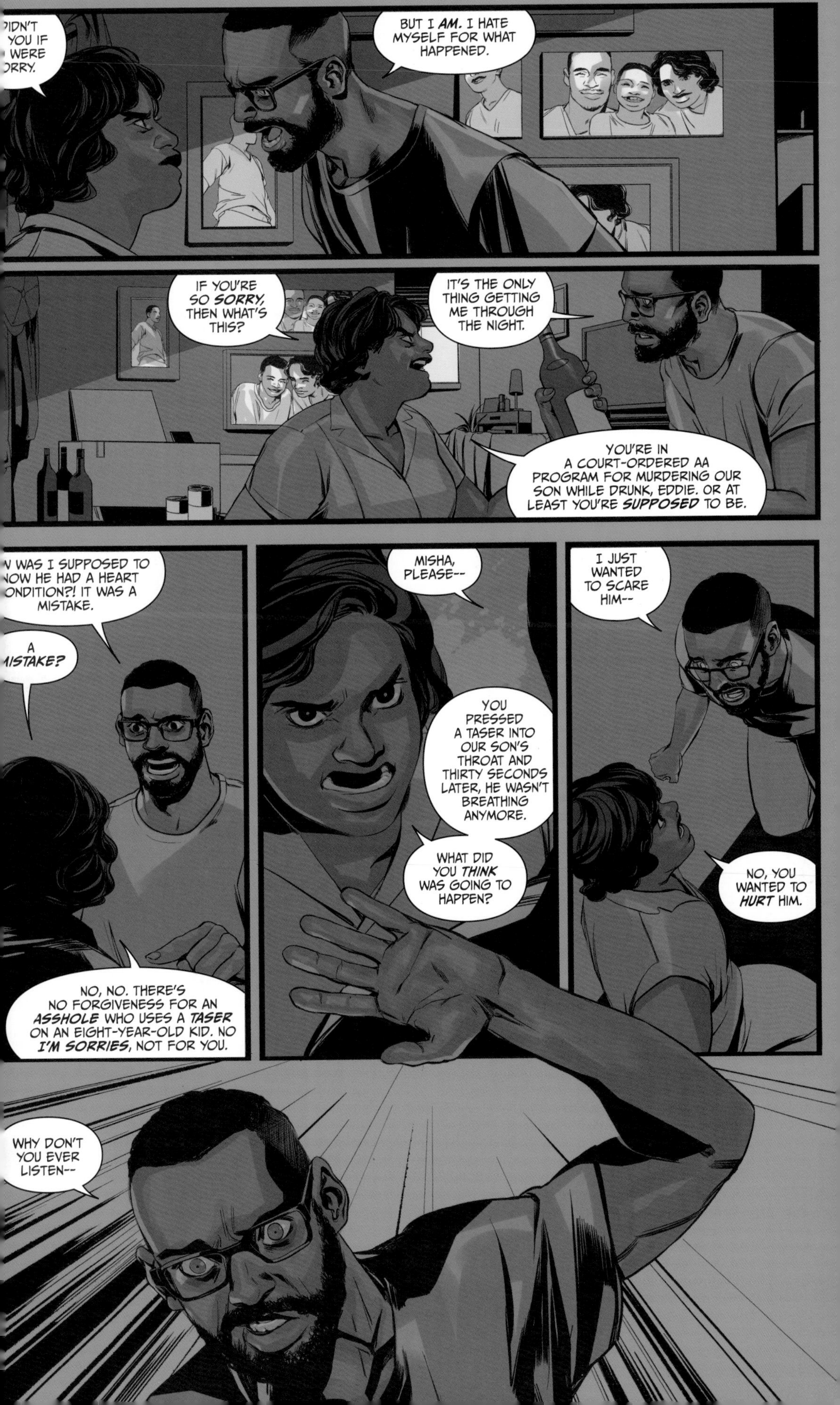

DIDN'T YOU IF WERE SORRY.
BUT I *AM.* I HATE MYSELF FOR WHAT HAPPENED.
IF YOU'RE SO *SORRY,* THEN WHAT'S THIS?
IT'S THE ONLY THING GETTING ME THROUGH THE NIGHT.
YOU'RE IN A COURT-ORDERED AA PROGRAM FOR MURDERING OUR SON WHILE DRUNK, EDDIE. OR AT LEAST YOU'RE *SUPPOSED* TO BE.
W WAS I SUPPOSED TO NOW HE HAD A HEART ONDITION?! IT WAS A MISTAKE.
A *MISTAKE?*
NO, NO. THERE'S NO FORGIVENESS FOR AN *ASSHOLE* WHO USES A *TASER* ON AN EIGHT-YEAR-OLD KID. NO *I'M SORRIES*, NOT FOR YOU.
MISHA, PLEASE--
YOU PRESSED A TASER INTO OUR SON'S THROAT AND THIRTY SECONDS LATER, HE WASN'T BREATHING ANYMORE.
WHAT DID YOU *THINK* WAS GOING TO HAPPEN?
I JUST WANTED TO SCARE HIM--
NO, YOU WANTED TO *HURT* HIM.
WHY DON'T YOU EVER LISTEN--

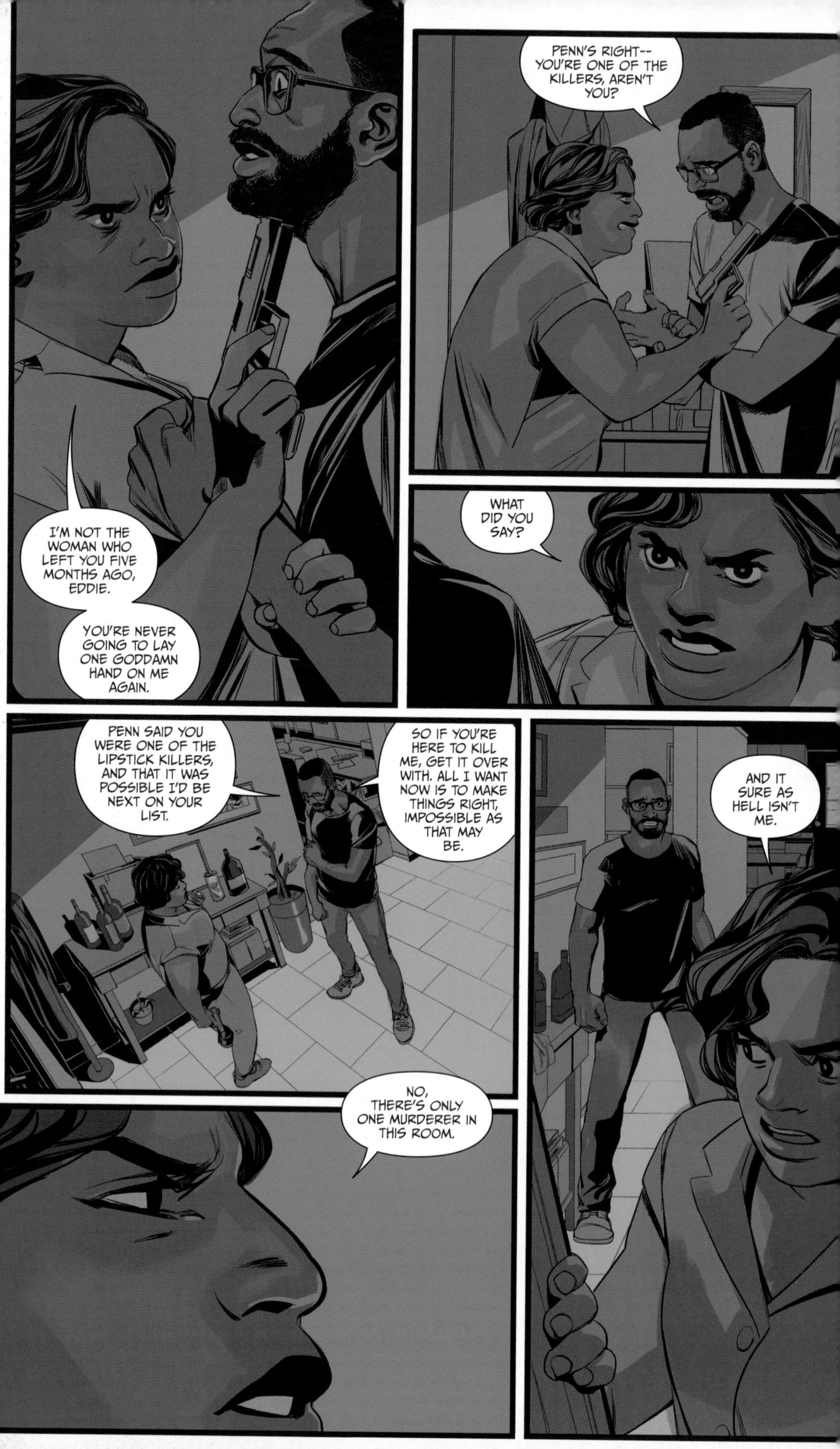
I'M NOT THE WOMAN WHO LEFT YOU FIVE MONTHS AGO, EDDIE.
YOU'RE NEVER GOING TO LAY ONE GODDAMN HAND ON ME AGAIN.
PENN'S RIGHT-- YOU'RE ONE OF THE KILLERS, AREN'T YOU?
WHAT DID YOU SAY?
PENN SAID YOU WERE ONE OF THE LIPSTICK KILLERS, AND THAT IT WAS POSSIBLE I'D BE NEXT ON YOUR LIST.
SO IF YOU'RE HERE TO KILL ME, GET IT OVER WITH. ALL I WANT NOW IS TO MAKE THINGS RIGHT, IMPOSSIBLE AS THAT MAY BE.
NO, THERE'S ONLY ONE MURDERER IN THIS ROOM.
AND IT SURE AS HELL ISN'T ME.

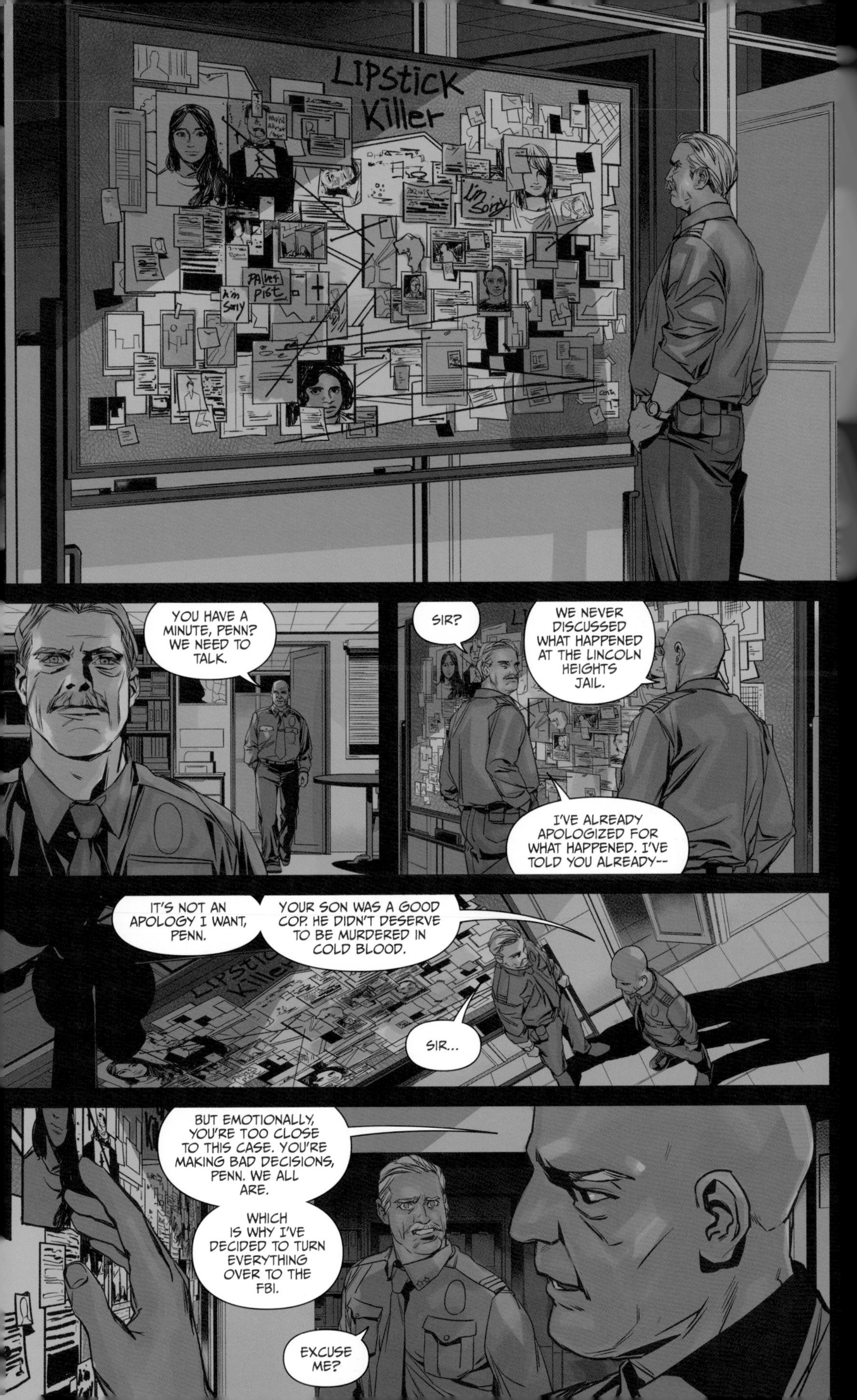
LIPStick Killer
I'm Sorry
I'm Sorry
YOU HAVE A MINUTE, PENN? WE NEED TO TALK.
SIR?
WE NEVER DISCUSSED WHAT HAPPENED AT THE LINCOLN HEIGHTS JAIL.
I'VE ALREADY APOLOGIZED FOR WHAT HAPPENED. I'VE TOLD YOU ALREADY--
IT'S NOT AN APOLOGY I WANT, PENN.
YOUR SON WAS A GOOD COP. HE DIDN'T DESERVE TO BE MURDERED IN COLD BLOOD.
SIR...
BUT EMOTIONALLY, YOU'RE TOO CLOSE TO THIS CASE. YOU'RE MAKING BAD DECISIONS, PENN. WE ALL ARE.
WHICH IS WHY I'VE DECIDED TO TURN EVERYTHING OVER TO THE FBI.
EXCUSE ME?

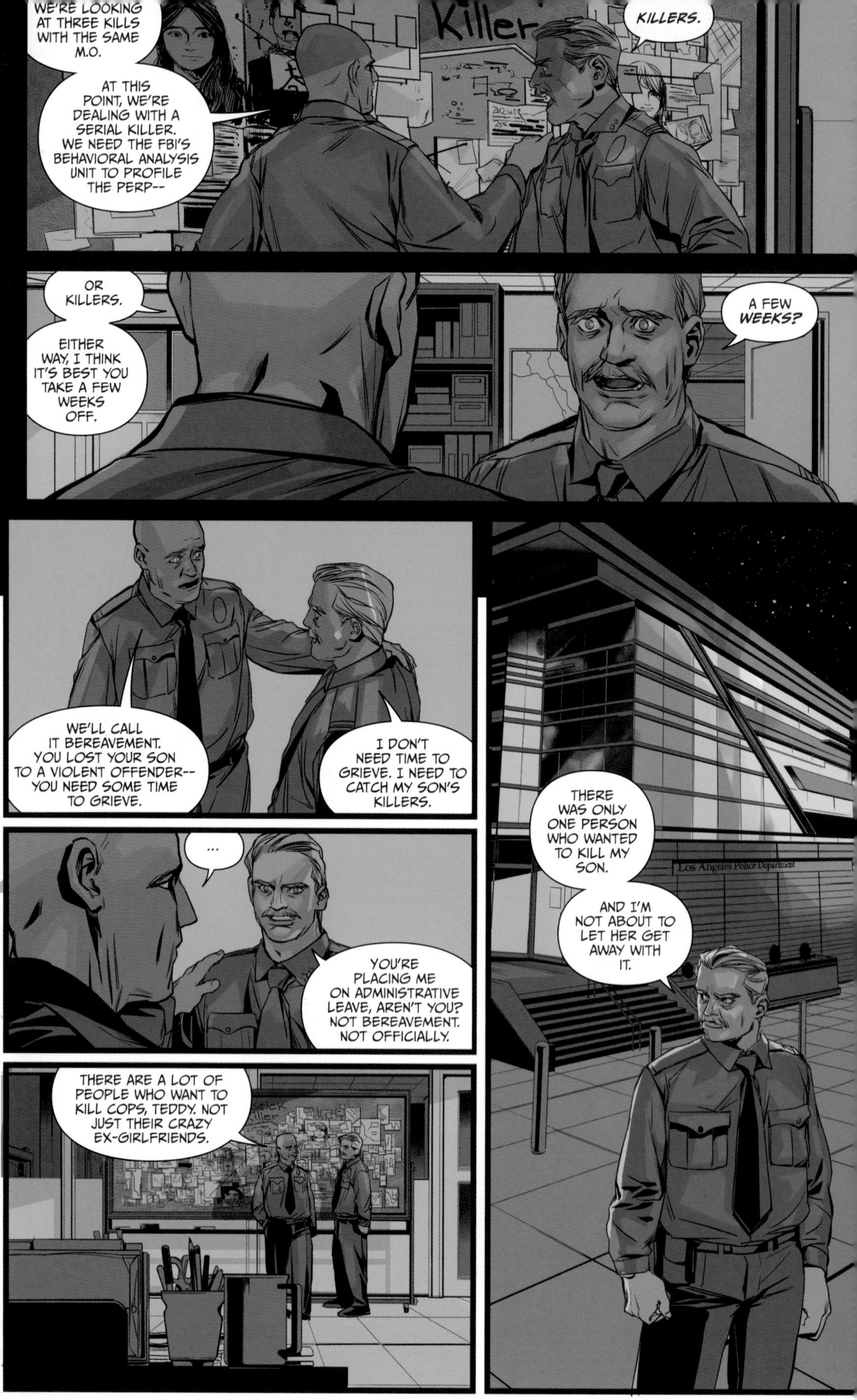
Killer
WE'RE LOOKING AT THREE KILLS WITH THE SAME M.O.
AT THIS POINT, WE'RE DEALING WITH A SERIAL KILLER. WE NEED THE FBI'S BEHAVIORAL ANALYSIS UNIT TO PROFILE THE PERP--
KILLERS.
OR KILLERS.
EITHER WAY, I THINK IT'S BEST YOU TAKE A FEW WEEKS OFF.
A FEW WEEKS?
WE'LL CALL IT BEREAVEMENT. YOU LOST YOUR SON TO A VIOLENT OFFENDER-- YOU NEED SOME TIME TO GRIEVE.
I DON'T NEED TIME TO GRIEVE. I NEED TO CATCH MY SON'S KILLERS.
...
YOU'RE PLACING ME ON ADMINISTRATIVE LEAVE, AREN'T YOU? NOT BEREAVEMENT. NOT OFFICIALLY.
THERE ARE A LOT OF PEOPLE WHO WANT TO KILL COPS, TEDDY. NOT JUST THEIR CRAZY EX-GIRLFRIENDS.
Los Angeles Police Department
THERE WAS ONLY ONE PERSON WHO WANTED TO KILL MY SON.
AND I'M NOT ABOUT TO LET HER GET AWAY WITH IT.

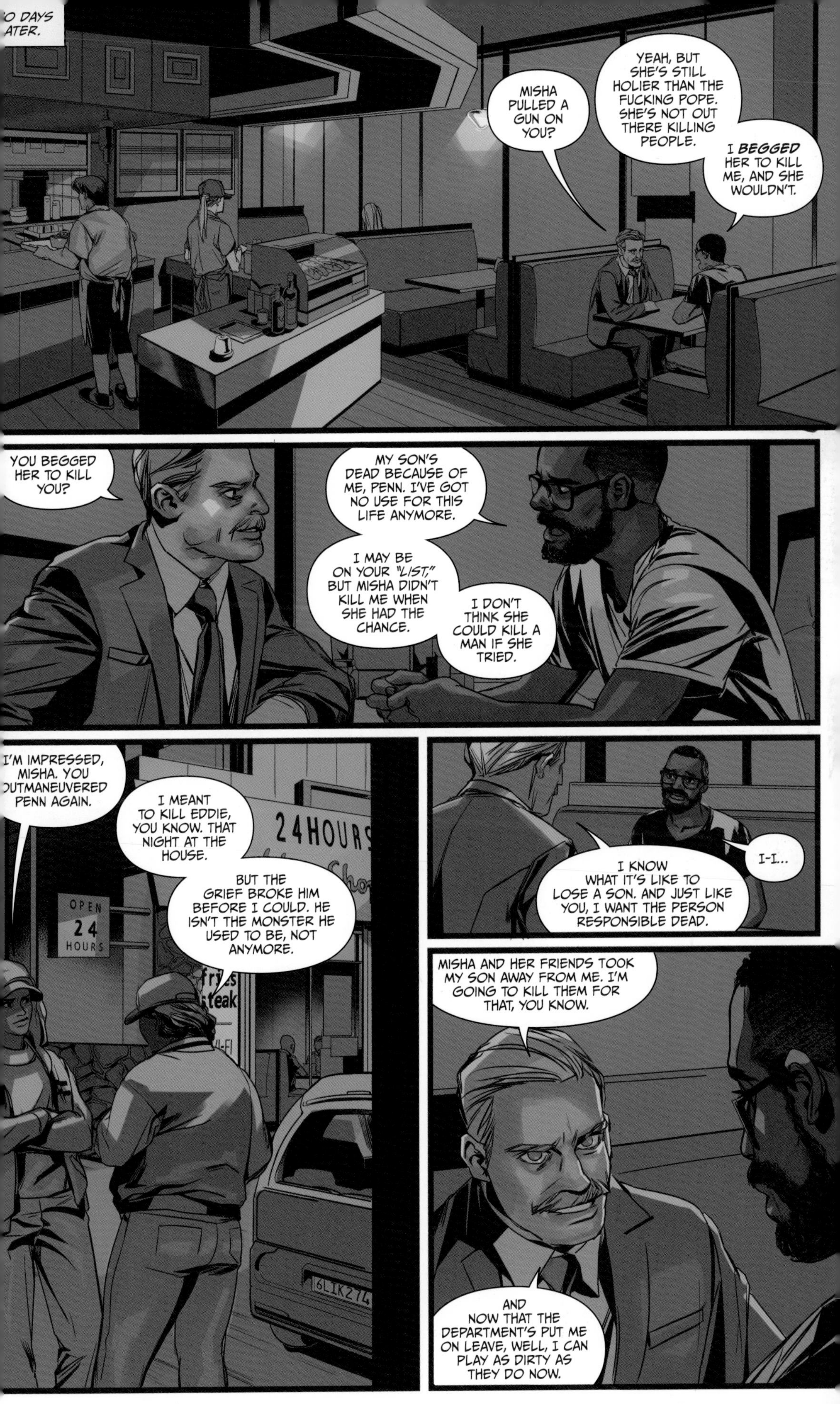

O DAYS
ATER.
MISHA PULLED A GUN ON YOU?
YEAH, BUT SHE'S STILL HOLIER THAN THE FUCKING POPE. SHE'S NOT OUT THERE KILLING PEOPLE.
I *BEGGED* HER TO KILL ME, AND SHE WOULDN'T.
YOU BEGGED HER TO KILL YOU?
MY SON'S DEAD BECAUSE OF ME, PENN. I'VE GOT NO USE FOR THIS LIFE ANYMORE.
I MAY BE ON YOUR "LIST," BUT MISHA DIDN'T KILL ME WHEN SHE HAD THE CHANCE.
I DON'T THINK SHE COULD KILL A MAN IF SHE TRIED.
I KNOW WHAT IT'S LIKE TO LOSE A SON. AND JUST LIKE YOU, I WANT THE PERSON RESPONSIBLE DEAD.
I-I...
MISHA AND HER FRIENDS TOOK MY SON AWAY FROM ME. I'M GOING TO KILL THEM FOR THAT, YOU KNOW.
AND NOW THAT THE DEPARTMENT'S PUT ME ON LEAVE, WELL, I CAN PLAY AS DIRTY AS THEY DO NOW.
I'M IMPRESSED, MISHA. YOU OUTMANEUVERED PENN AGAIN.
I MEANT TO KILL EDDIE, YOU KNOW. THAT NIGHT AT THE HOUSE.
BUT THE GRIEF BROKE HIM BEFORE I COULD. HE ISN'T THE MONSTER HE USED TO BE, NOT ANYMORE.
24HOURS
OPEN 24 HOURS
6LIK274

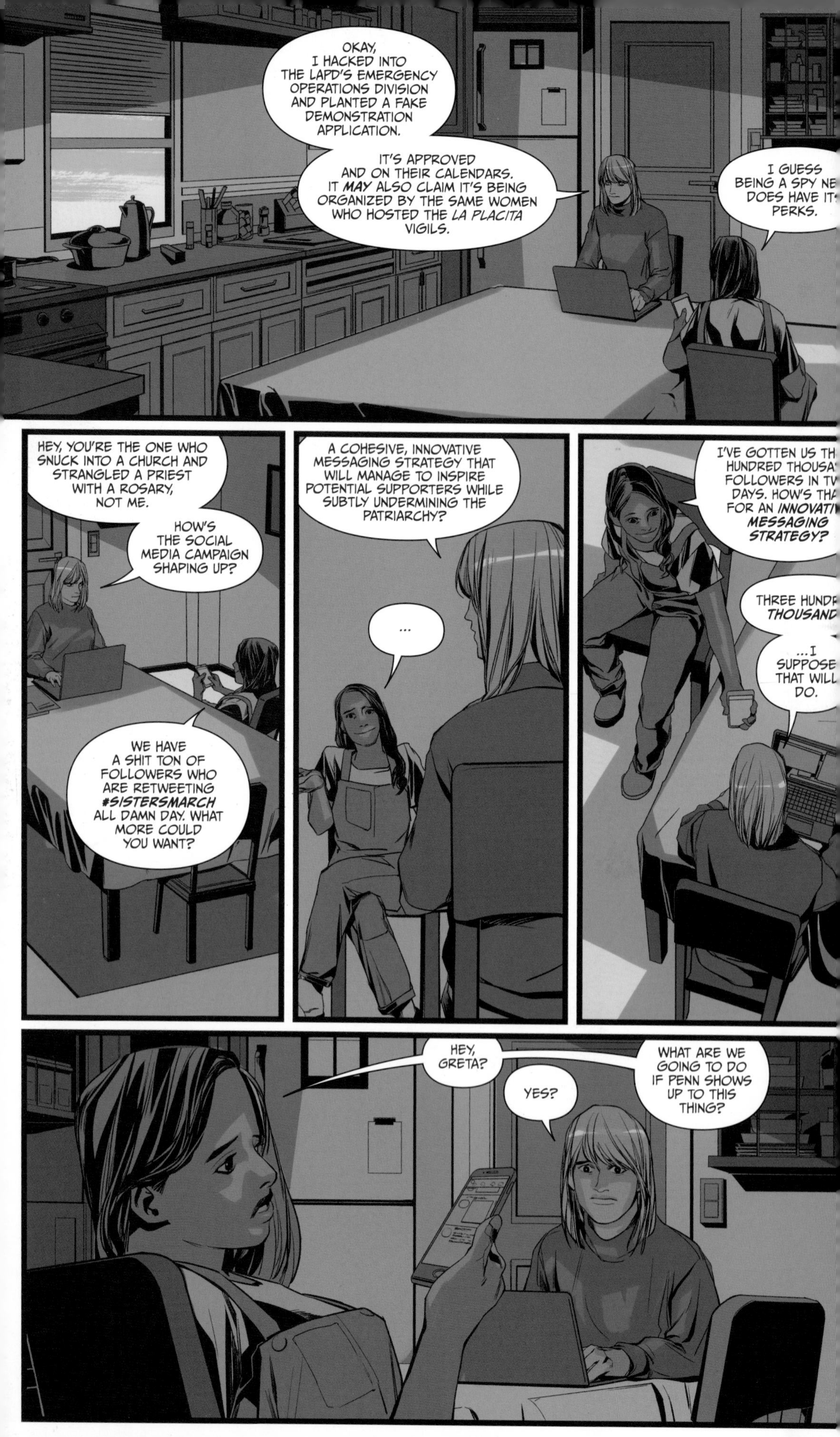
OKAY, I HACKED INTO THE LAPD'S EMERGENCY OPERATIONS DIVISION AND PLANTED A FAKE DEMONSTRATION APPLICATION.
IT'S APPROVED AND ON THEIR CALENDARS. IT MAY ALSO CLAIM IT'S BEING ORGANIZED BY THE SAME WOMEN WHO HOSTED THE LA PLACITA VIGILS.
I GUESS BEING A SPY NE DOES HAVE IT PERKS.
HEY, YOU'RE THE ONE WHO SNUCK INTO A CHURCH AND STRANGLED A PRIEST WITH A ROSARY, NOT ME.
HOW'S THE SOCIAL MEDIA CAMPAIGN SHAPING UP?
WE HAVE A SHIT TON OF FOLLOWERS WHO ARE RETWEETING #SISTERSMARCH ALL DAMN DAY. WHAT MORE COULD YOU WANT?
A COHESIVE, INNOVATIVE MESSAGING STRATEGY THAT WILL MANAGE TO INSPIRE POTENTIAL SUPPORTERS WHILE SUBTLY UNDERMINING THE PATRIARCHY?
...
I'VE GOTTEN US TH HUNDRED THOUSA FOLLOWERS IN TW DAYS. HOW'S THA FOR AN INNOVATI MESSAGING STRATEGY?
THREE HUNDR THOUSAND
...I SUPPOSE THAT WILL DO.
HEY, GRETA?
YES?
WHAT ARE WE GOING TO DO IF PENN SHOWS UP TO THIS THING?

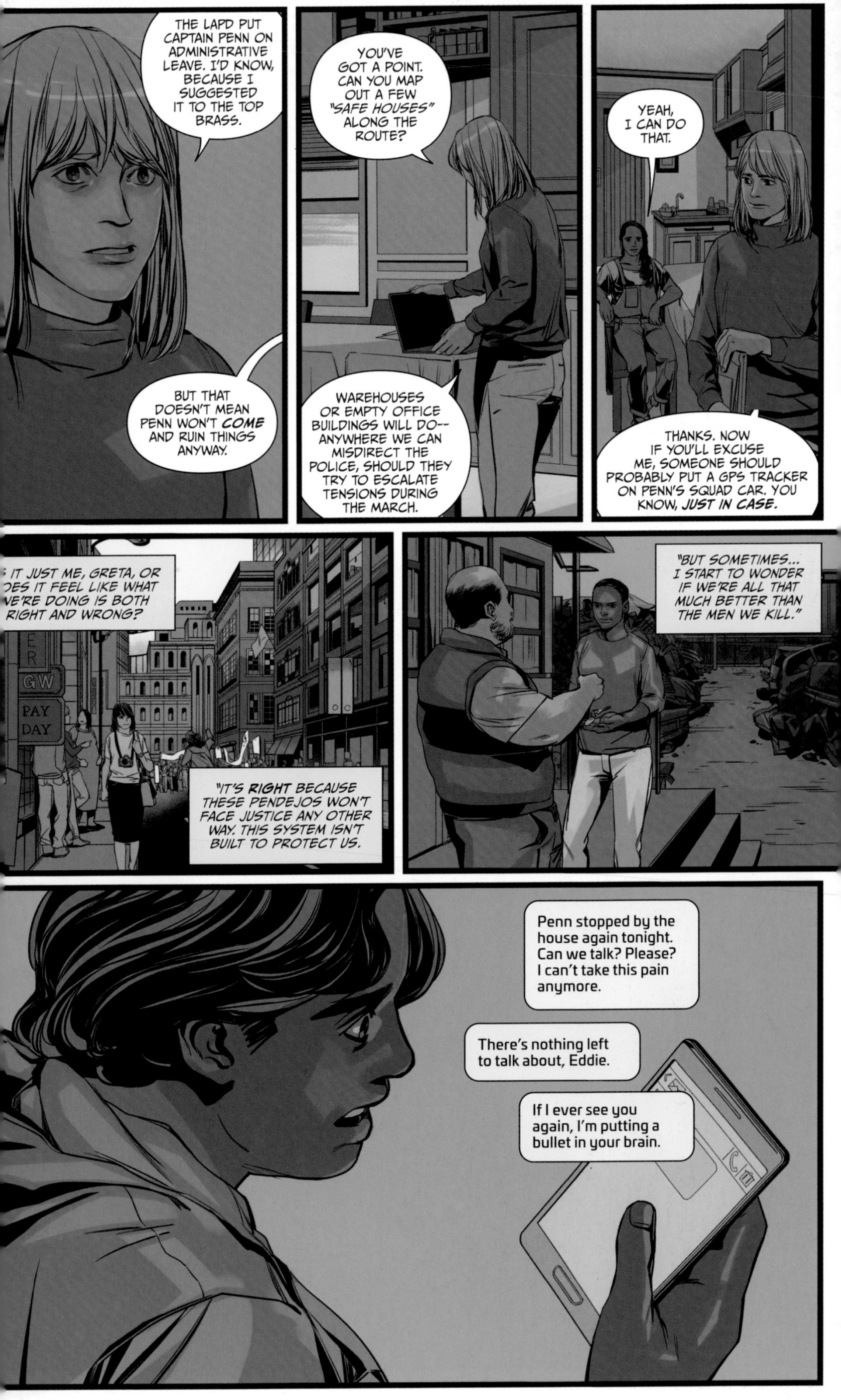
THE LAPD PUT CAPTAIN PENN ON ADMINISTRATIVE LEAVE. I'D KNOW, BECAUSE I SUGGESTED IT TO THE TOP BRASS.
BUT THAT DOESN'T MEAN PENN WON'T COME AND RUIN THINGS ANYWAY.
YOU'VE GOT A POINT. CAN YOU MAP OUT A FEW "SAFE HOUSES" ALONG THE ROUTE?
WAREHOUSES OR EMPTY OFFICE BUILDINGS WILL DO-- ANYWHERE WE CAN MISDIRECT THE POLICE, SHOULD THEY TRY TO ESCALATE TENSIONS DURING THE MARCH.
YEAH, I CAN DO THAT.
THANKS. NOW IF YOU'LL EXCUSE ME, SOMEONE SHOULD PROBABLY PUT A GPS TRACKER ON PENN'S SQUAD CAR. YOU KNOW, JUST IN CASE.
IT JUST ME, GRETA, OR DES IT FEEL LIKE WHAT VE'RE DOING IS BOTH RIGHT AND WRONG?
PAY DAY
"IT'S RIGHT BECAUSE THESE PENDEJOS WON'T FACE JUSTICE ANY OTHER WAY. THIS SYSTEM ISN'T BUILT TO PROTECT US.
"BUT SOMETIMES... I START TO WONDER IF WE'RE ALL THAT MUCH BETTER THAN THE MEN WE KILL."
Penn stopped by the house again tonight. Can we talk? Please? I can't take this pain anymore.
There's nothing left to talk about, Eddie.
If I ever see you again, I'm putting a bullet in your brain.

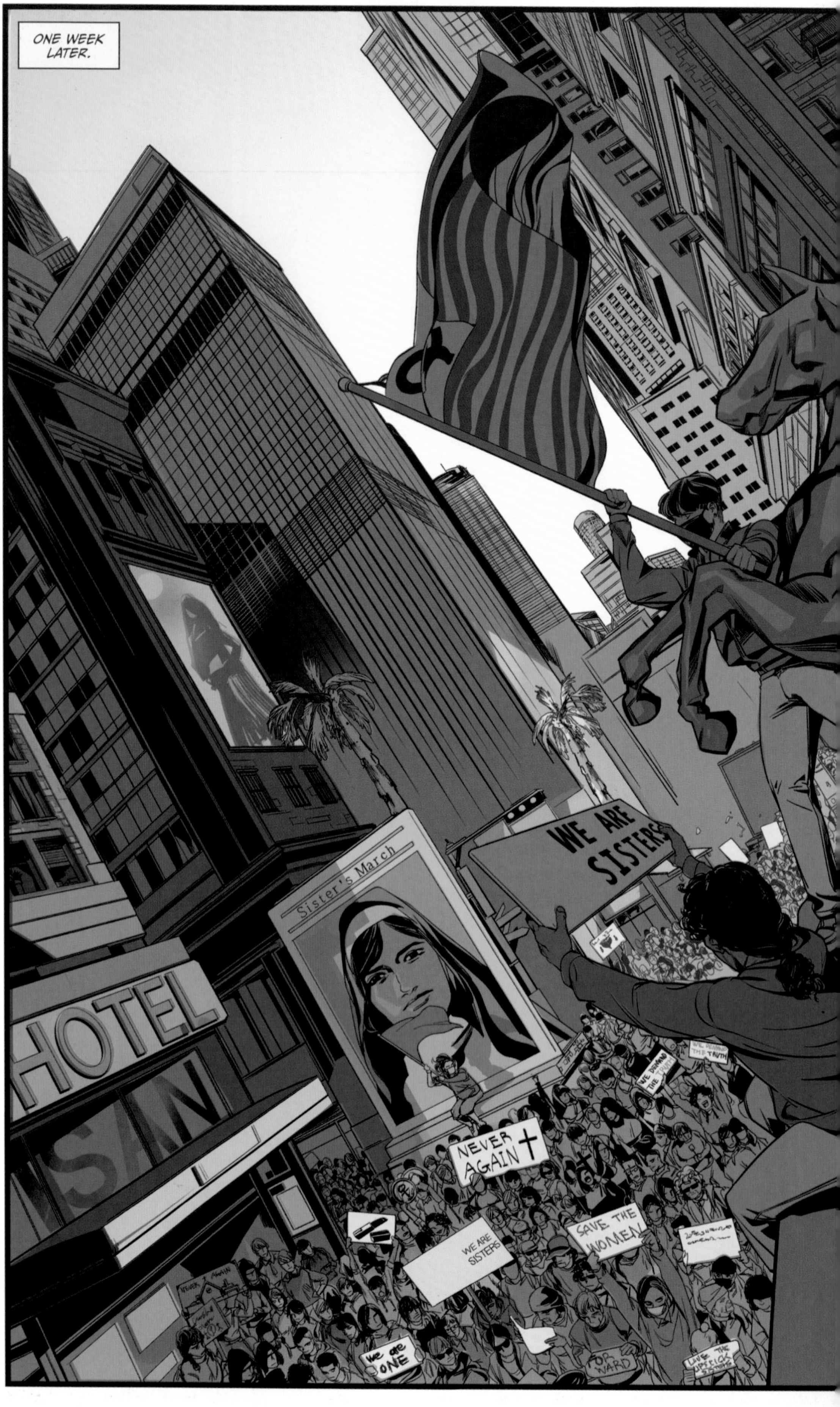
ONE WEEK LATER.
WE ARE SISTERS
Sister's March
HOTEL
WE DEMAND THE TRUTH
WE DEMAND THE TRUTH
NEVER AGAIN
WE ARE SISTERS
SAVE THE WOMEN!
we are ONE
FOR WARD
LIVE THE LIPSTICK SISTERS

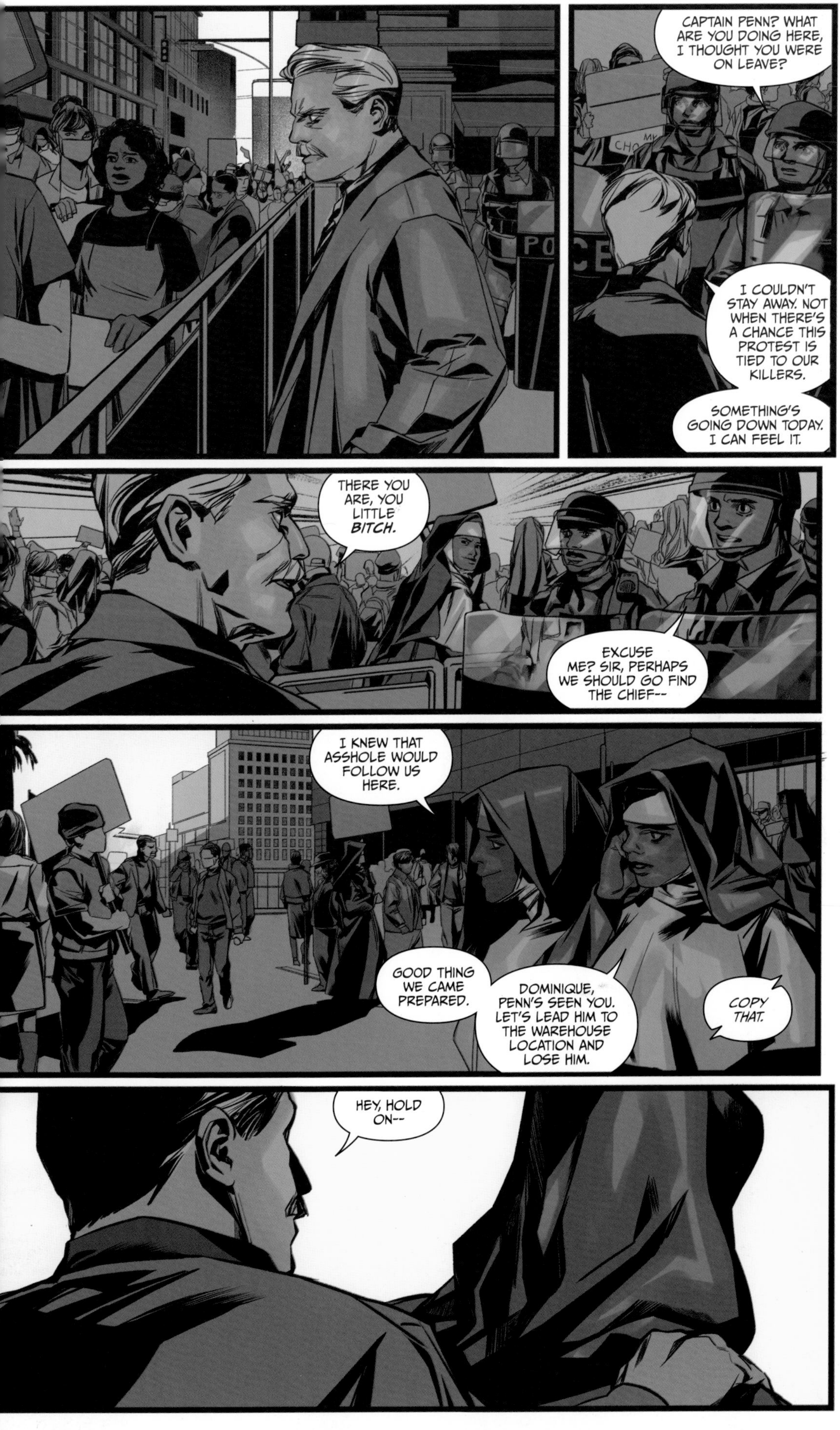
CAPTAIN PENN? WHAT ARE YOU DOING HERE, I THOUGHT YOU WERE ON LEAVE?
I COULDN'T STAY AWAY. NOT WHEN THERE'S A CHANCE THIS PROTEST IS TIED TO OUR KILLERS.
SOMETHING'S GOING DOWN TODAY. I CAN FEEL IT.
THERE YOU ARE, YOU LITTLE *BITCH.*
EXCUSE ME? SIR, PERHAPS WE SHOULD GO FIND THE CHIEF--
I KNEW THAT ASSHOLE WOULD FOLLOW US HERE.
GOOD THING WE CAME PREPARED.
DOMINIQUE, PENN'S SEEN YOU. LET'S LEAD HIM TO THE WAREHOUSE LOCATION AND LOSE HIM.
COPY THAT.
HEY, HOLD ON--

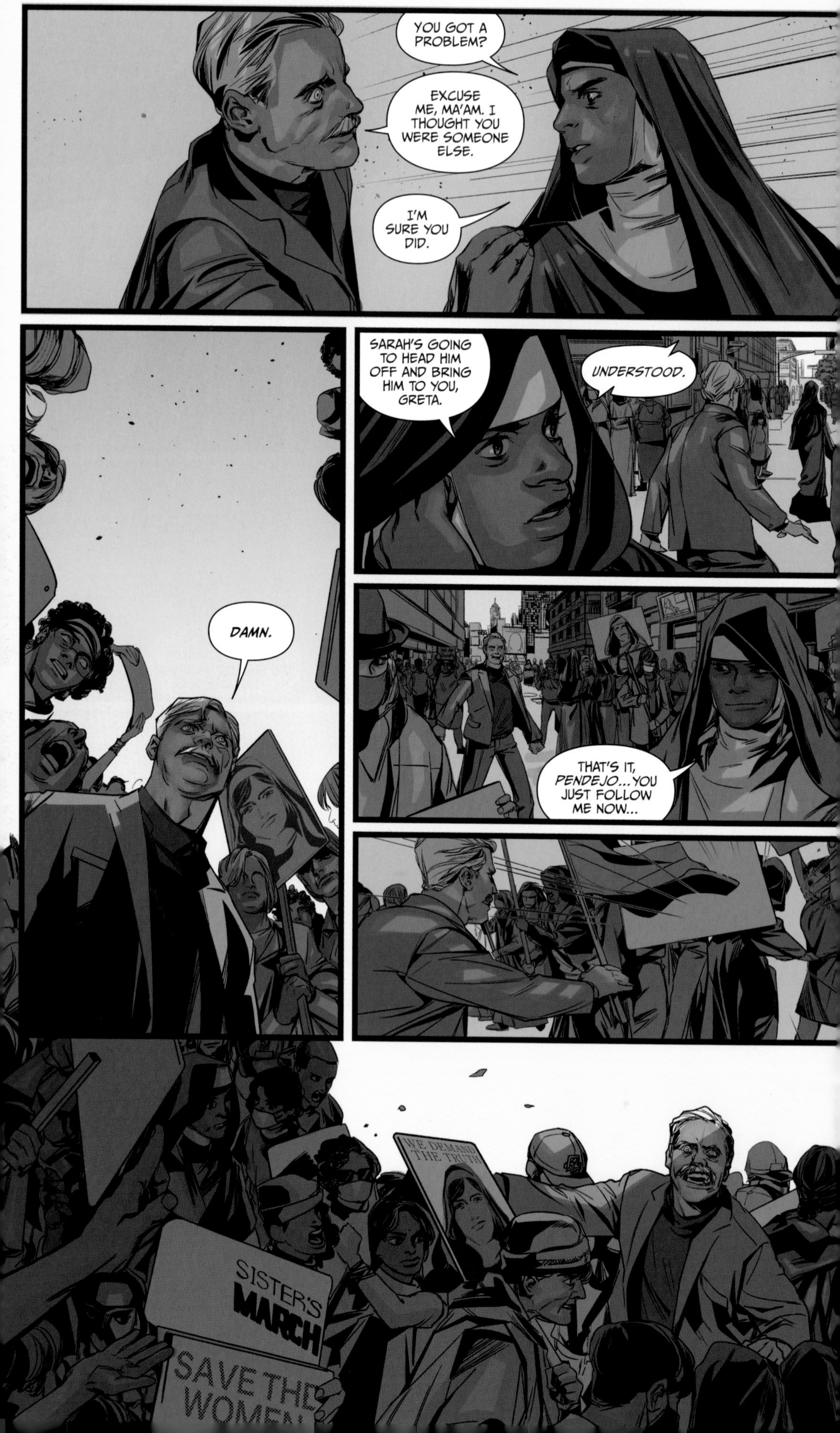

YOU GOT A PROBLEM?
EXCUSE ME, MA'AM. I THOUGHT YOU WERE SOMEONE ELSE.
I'M SURE YOU DID.
DAMN.
SARAH'S GOING TO HEAD HIM OFF AND BRING HIM TO YOU, GRETA.
UNDERSTOOD.
THAT'S IT, *PENDEJO*...YOU JUST FOLLOW ME NOW...
WE DEMAND THE TRUTH
SISTER'S MARCH
SAVE THE WOMEN

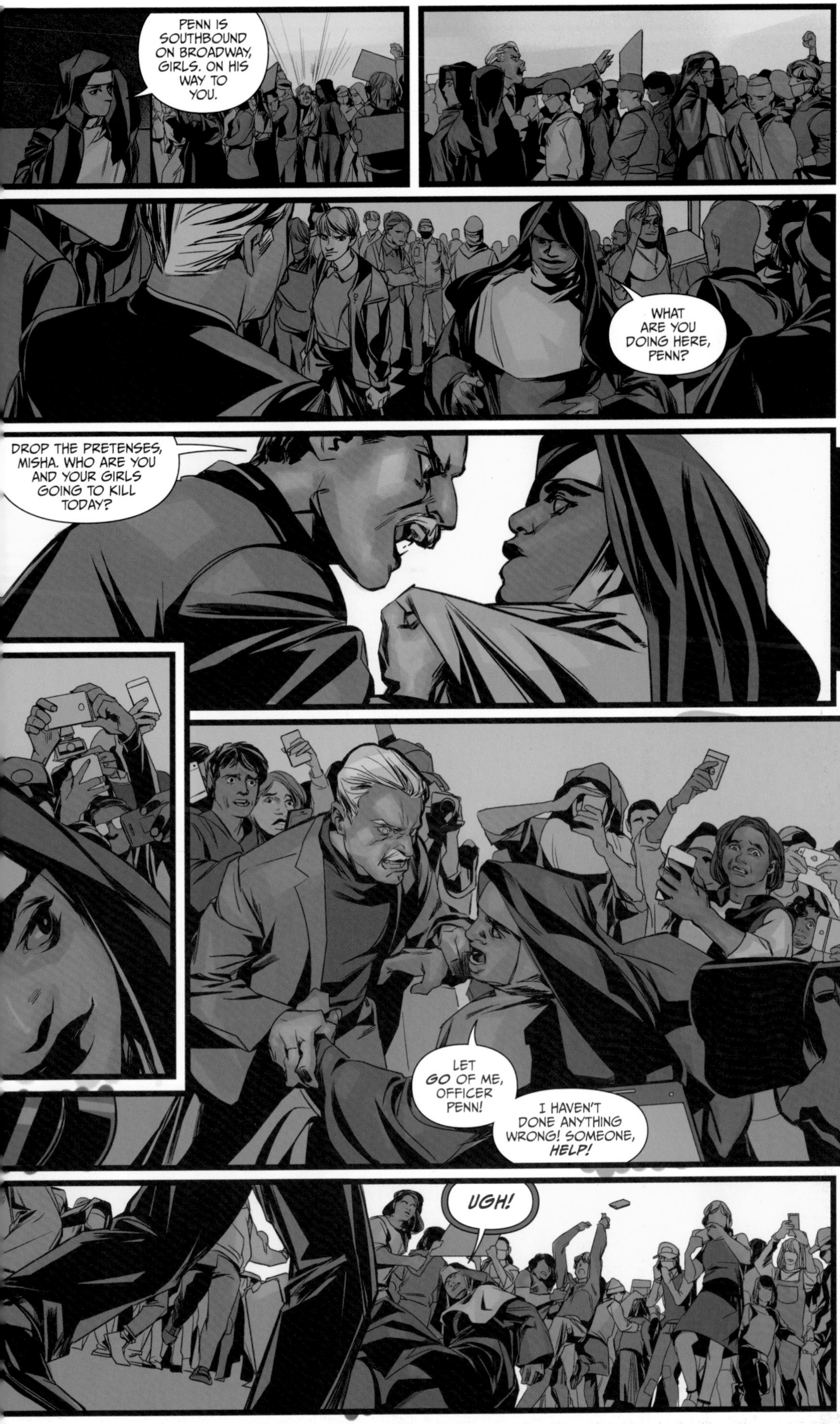
PENN IS SOUTHBOUND ON BROADWAY, GIRLS. ON HIS WAY TO YOU.
WHAT ARE YOU DOING HERE, PENN?
DROP THE PRETENSES, MISHA. WHO ARE YOU AND YOUR GIRLS GOING TO KILL TODAY?
LET GO OF ME, OFFICER PENN!
I HAVEN'T DONE ANYTHING WRONG! SOMEONE, HELP!
UGH!

WHERE ARE YOU GOING NOW?

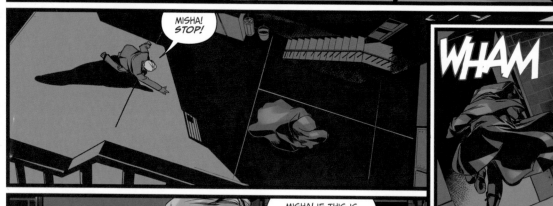

MISHA! STOP!

WHAM

MISHA! IF THIS IS ANOTHER PRANK, I'M NOT JUST GOING TO ARREST YOU.

I'LL KILL YOU. WRITE I'M SORRY ON YOUR FOREHEAD IN LIPSTICK. THAT'S THE WAY YOU AND YOUR GIRLS LIKE TO DO THINGS, RIGHT?

THAT'S WHAT YOU DID TO FATHER VEGA, AND TO MARTIN HOLT, AND TO MY SON.

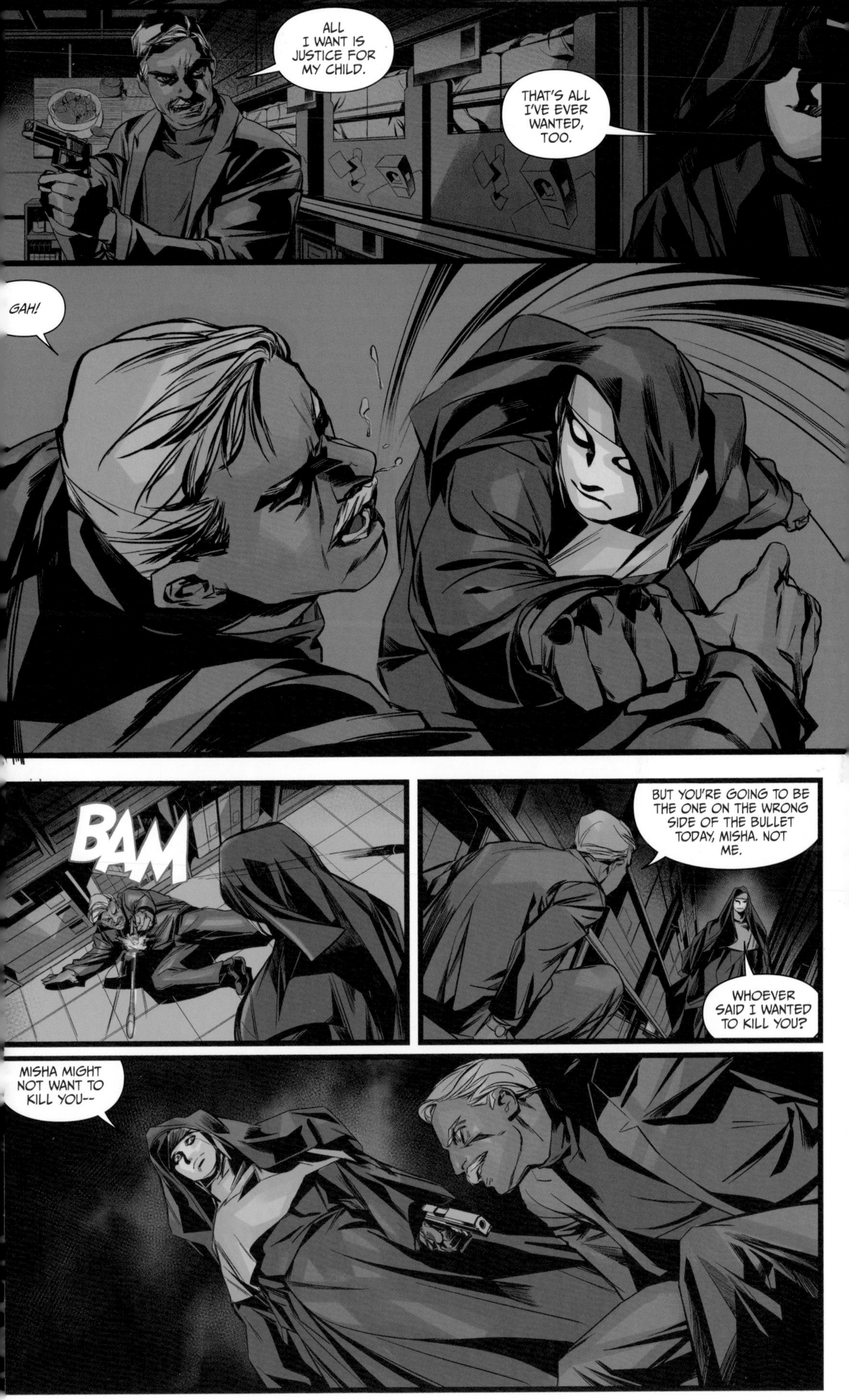
ALL I WANT IS JUSTICE FOR MY CHILD.
THAT'S ALL I'VE EVER WANTED, TOO.
GAH!
BAM
BUT YOU'RE GOING TO BE THE ONE ON THE WRONG SIDE OF THE BULLET TODAY, MISHA. NOT ME.
WHOEVER SAID I WANTED TO KILL YOU?
MISHA MIGHT NOT WANT TO KILL YOU--

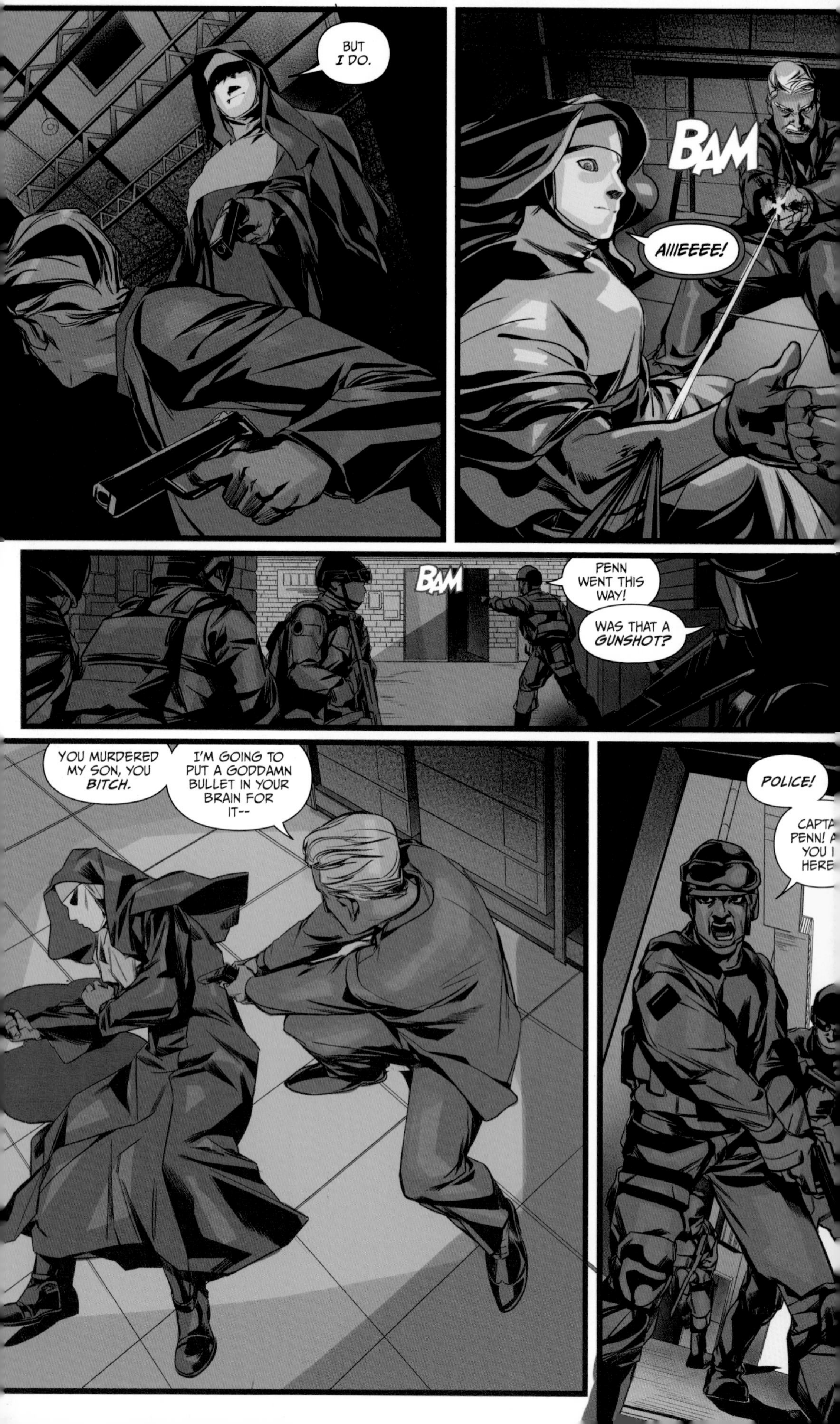
BUT
I DO.
BAM
AIIIEEEE!
BAM
PENN WENT THIS WAY!
WAS THAT A GUNSHOT?
YOU MURDERED MY SON, YOU BITCH.
I'M GOING TO PUT A GODDAMN BULLET IN YOUR BRAIN FOR IT--
POLICE!

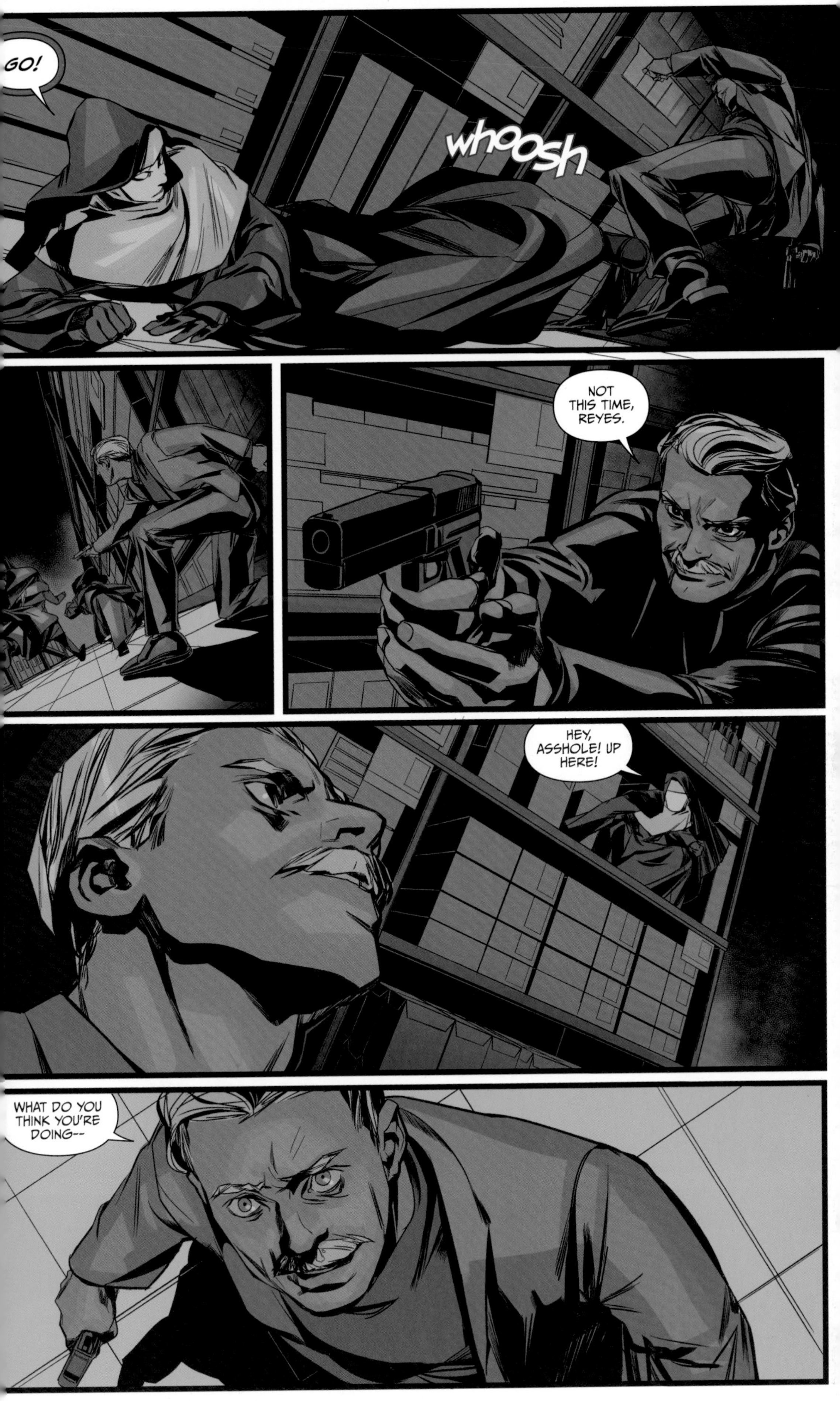
GO!
whoosh
NOT THIS TIME, REYES.
HEY, ASSHOLE! UP HERE!
WHAT DO YOU THINK YOU'RE DOING--

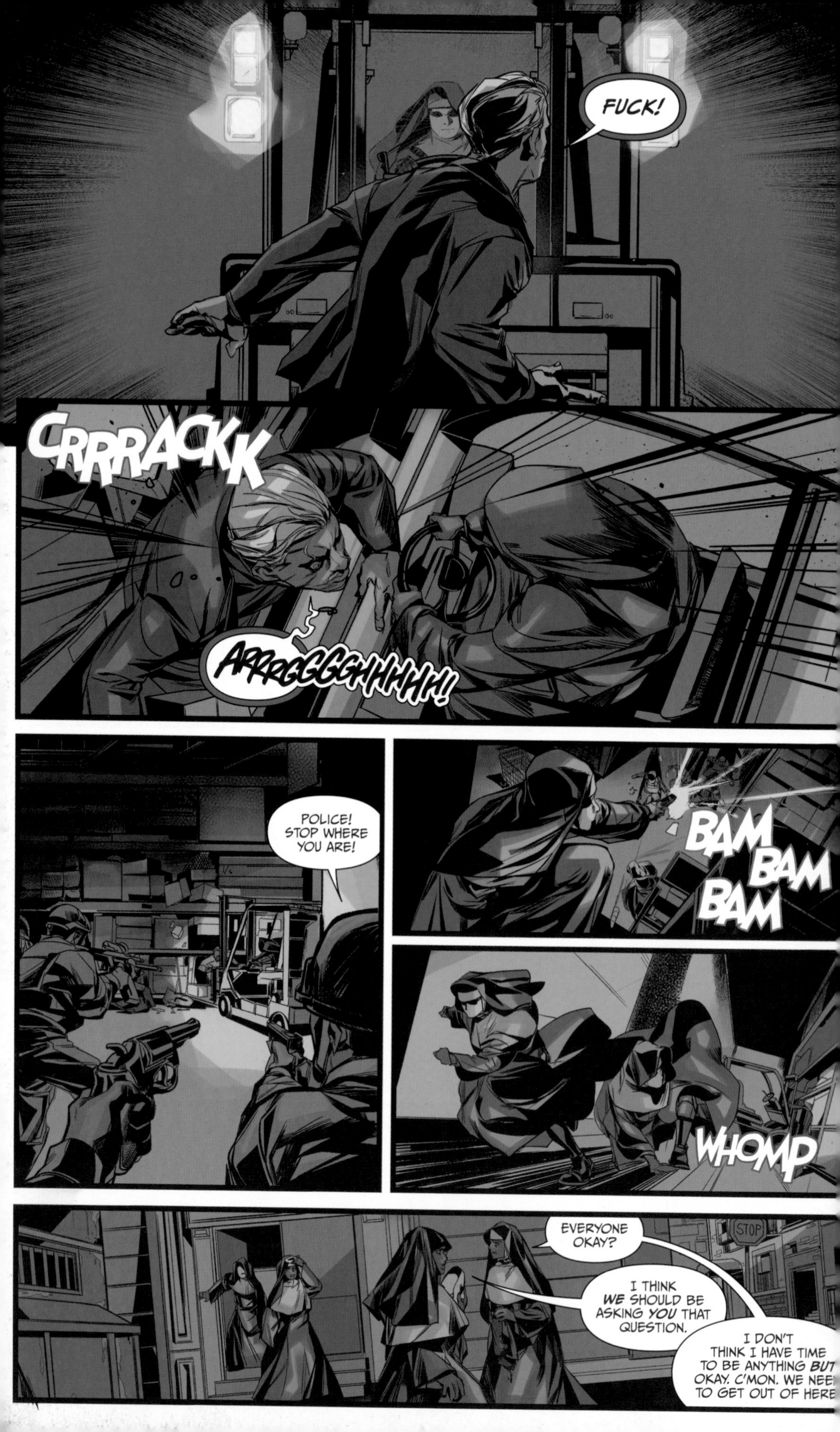
FUCK!
CRRRACKK
ARRRGGGGHHHHH!
POLICE! STOP WHERE YOU ARE!
BAM BAM BAM
WHOMP
EVERYONE OKAY?
I THINK *WE* SHOULD BE ASKING *YOU* THAT QUESTION.
I DON'T THINK I HAVE TIME TO BE ANYTHING *BUT* OKAY. C'MON. WE NEED TO GET OUT OF HERE
STOP

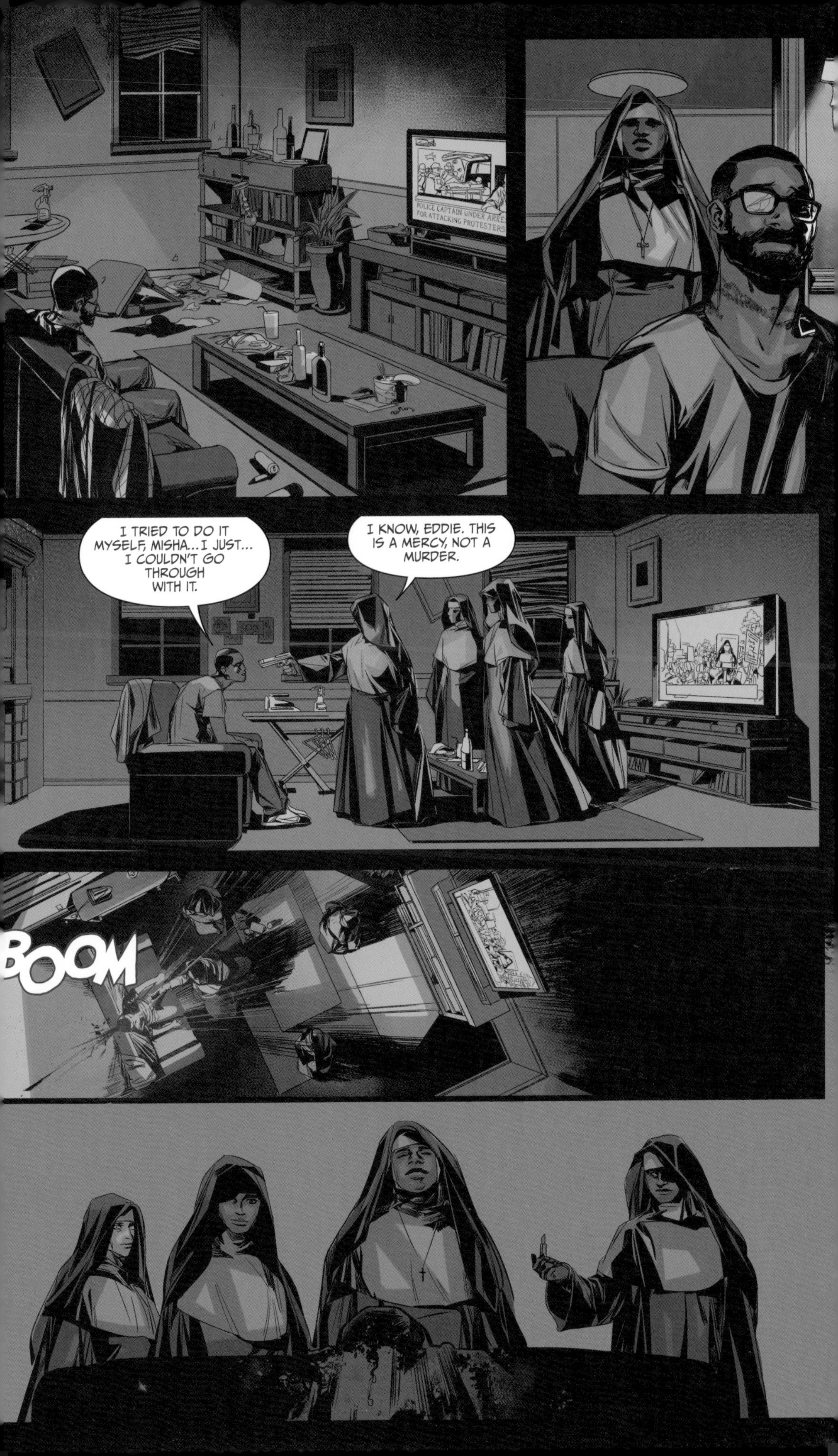
POLICE CAPTAIN UNDER ARRE
FOR ATTACKING PROTESTERS
I TRIED TO DO IT MYSELF, MISHA... I JUST... I COULDN'T GO THROUGH WITH IT.
I KNOW, EDDIE. THIS IS A MERCY, NOT A MURDER.
BOOM

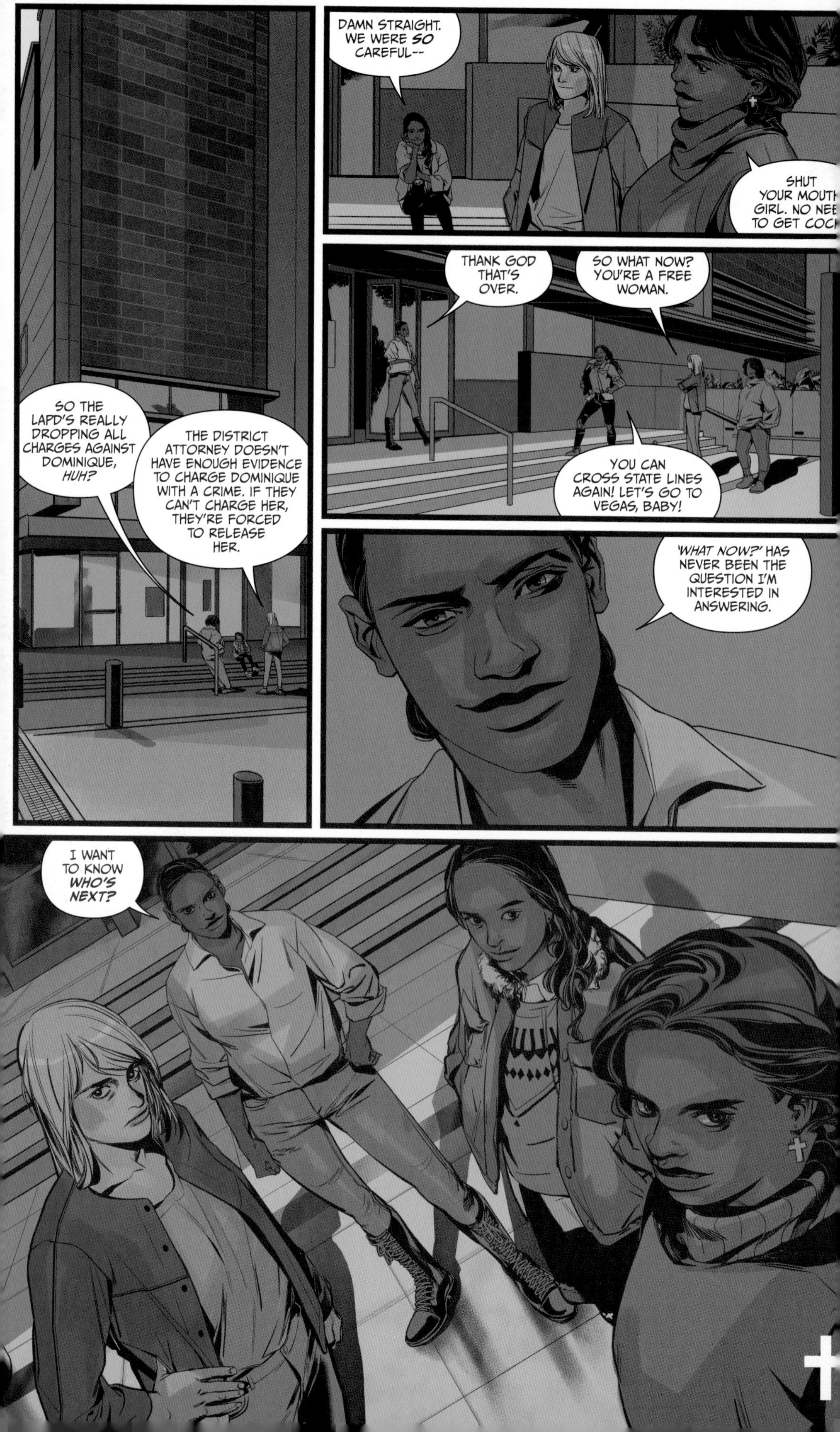
DAMN STRAIGHT. WE WERE *SO* CAREFUL--
SHUT YOUR MOUTH GIRL. NO NEE TO GET COC
SO THE LAPD'S REALLY DROPPING ALL CHARGES AGAINST DOMINIQUE, *HUH?*
THE DISTRICT ATTORNEY DOESN'T HAVE ENOUGH EVIDENCE TO CHARGE DOMINIQUE WITH A CRIME. IF THEY CAN'T CHARGE HER, THEY'RE FORCED TO RELEASE HER.
THANK GOD THAT'S OVER.
SO WHAT NOW? YOU'RE A FREE WOMAN.
YOU CAN CROSS STATE LINES AGAIN! LET'S GO TO VEGAS, BABY!
'WHAT NOW?' HAS NEVER BEEN THE QUESTION I'M INTERESTED IN ANSWERING.
I WANT TO KNOW *WHO'S NEXT?*

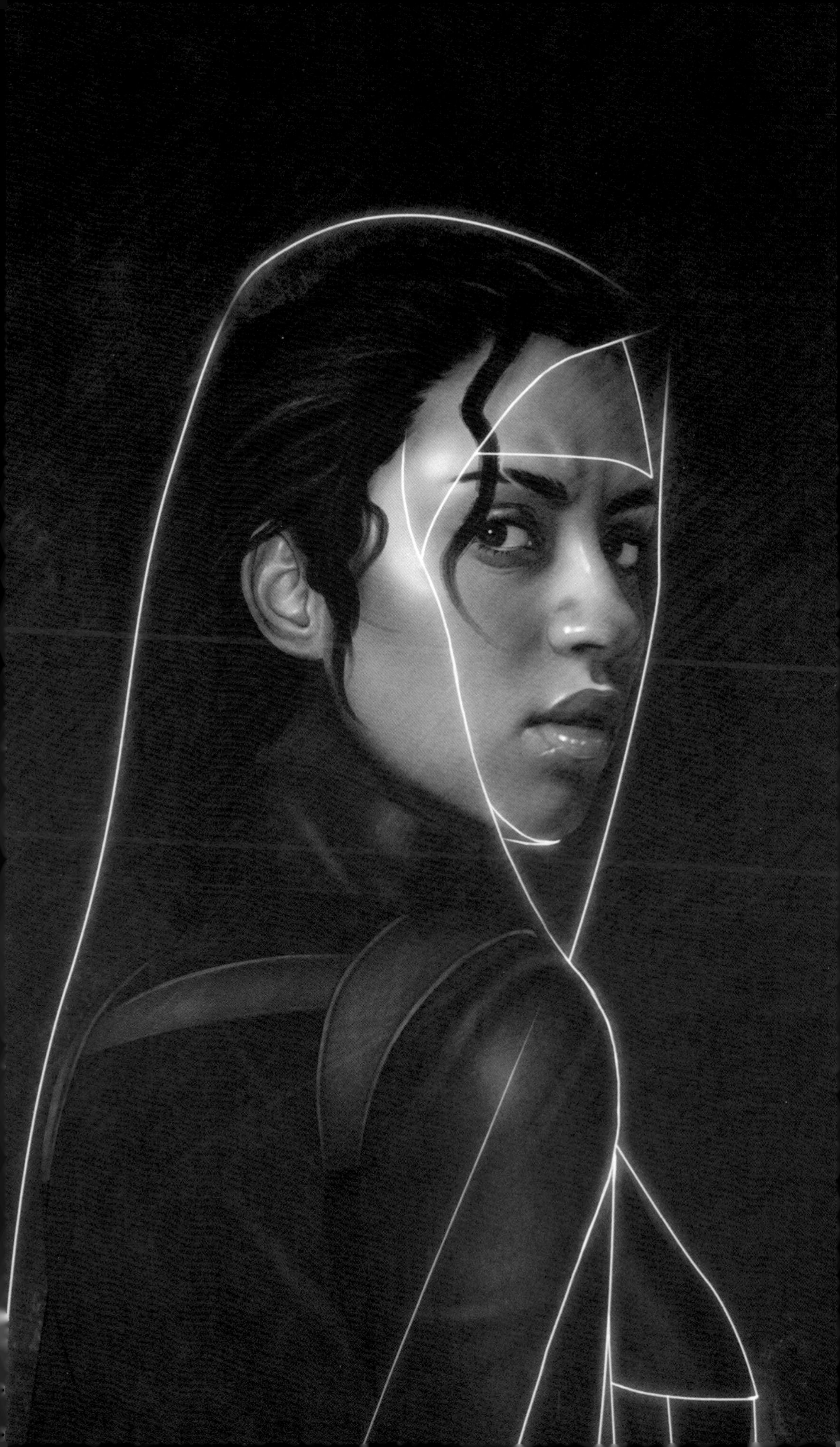

ISSUE ONE COVER BY
JAE LEE & JUNE CHUNG

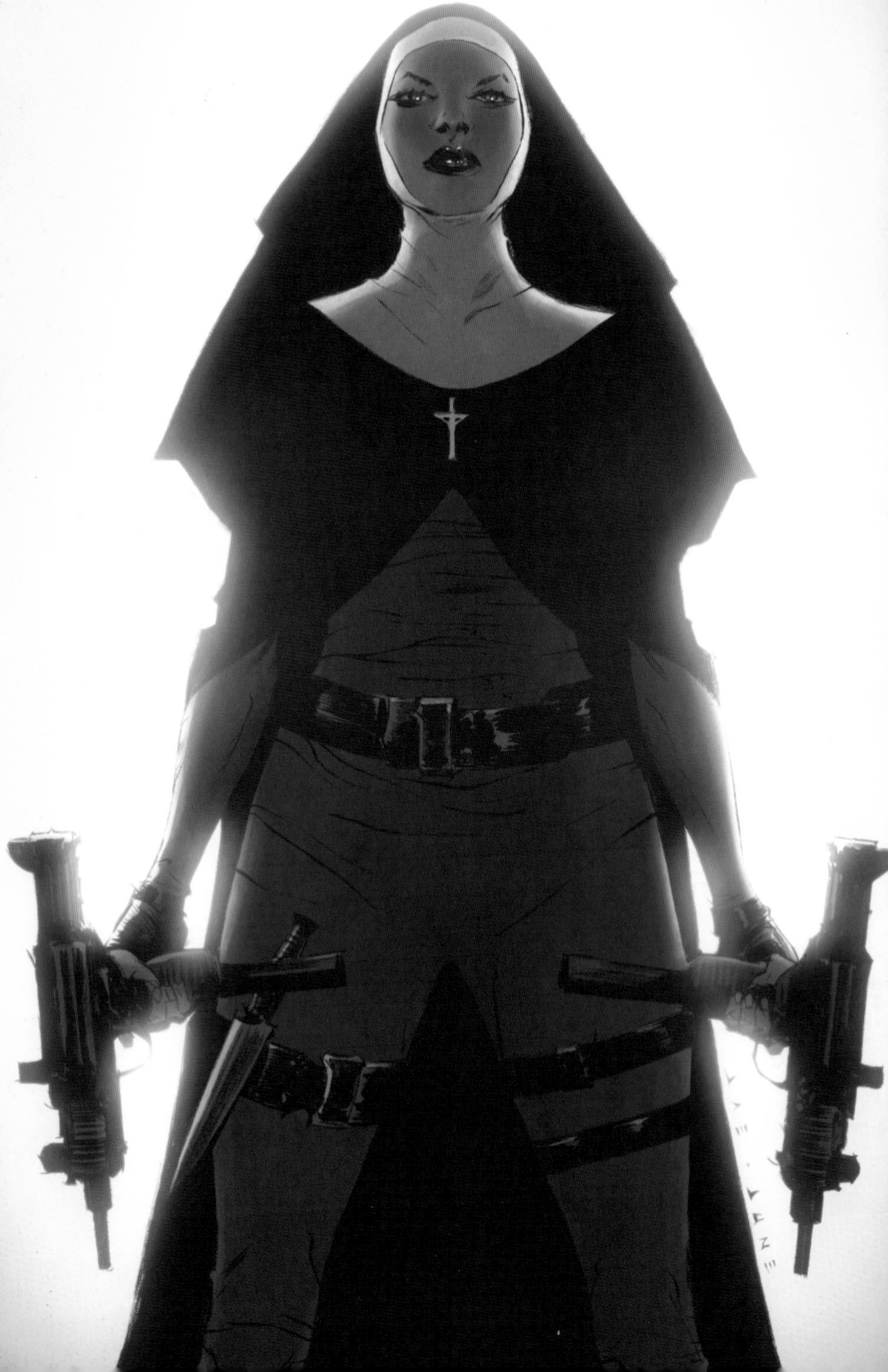

ISSUE ONE COVER BY
ANDRE DE FREITAS

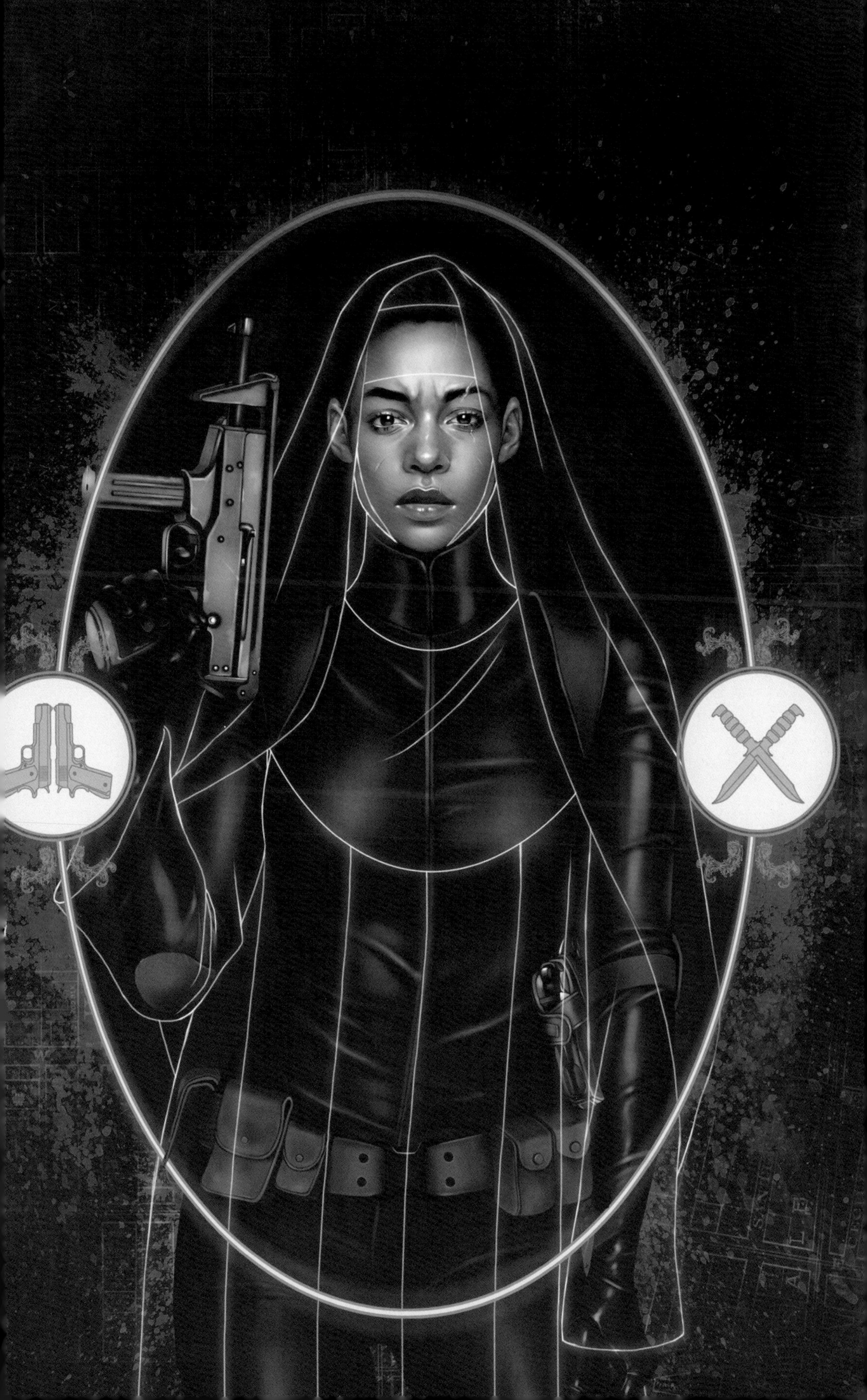

ISSUE ONE UNLOCKED RETAILER VARIANT COVER BY
VALENTINE DE LANDRO

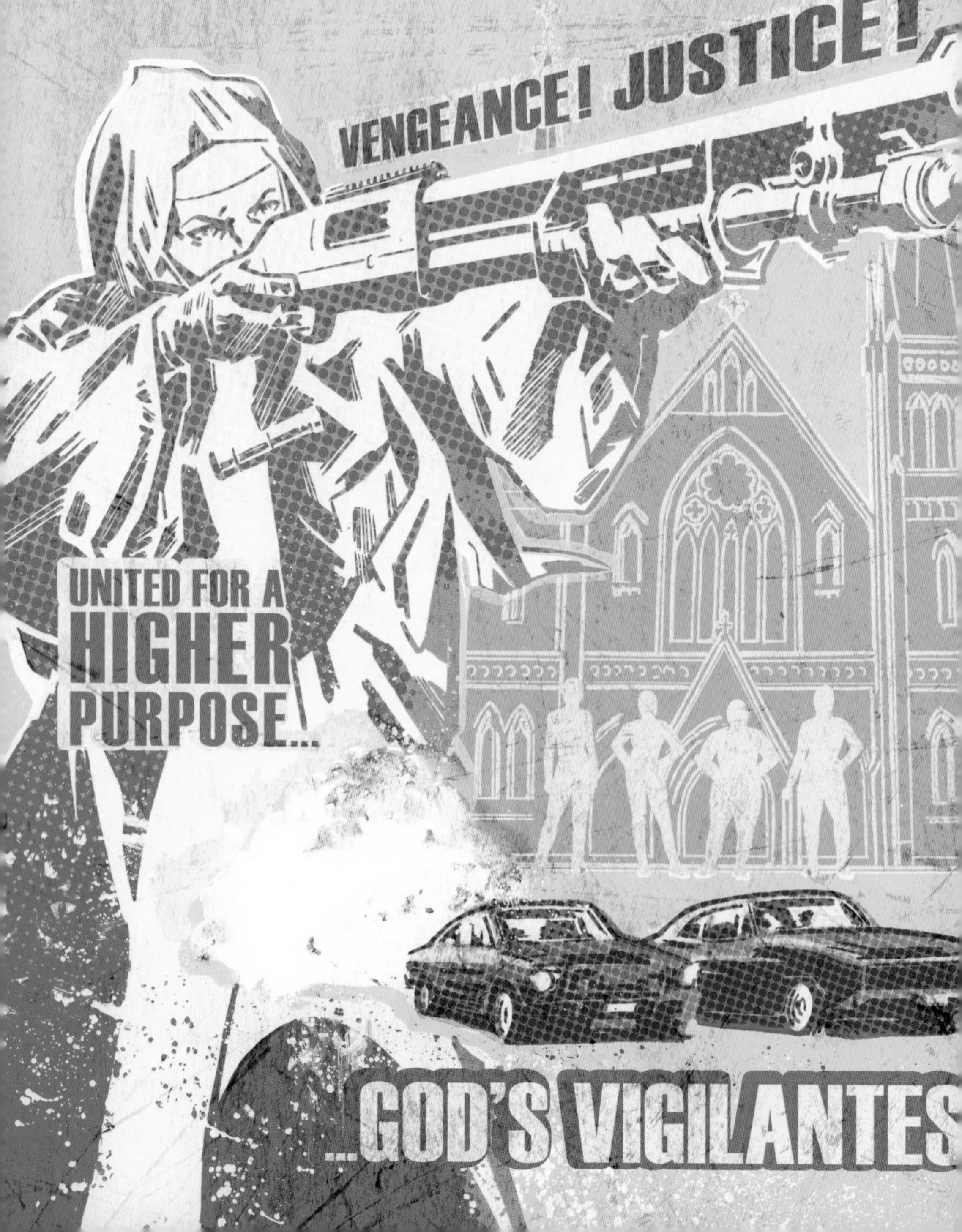
VENGEANCE! JUSTICE!
UNITED FOR A HIGHER PURPOSE...
...GOD'S VIGILANTES

ISSUE ONE CONVENTION EXCLUSIVE COVER BY
VANESA R. DEL REY

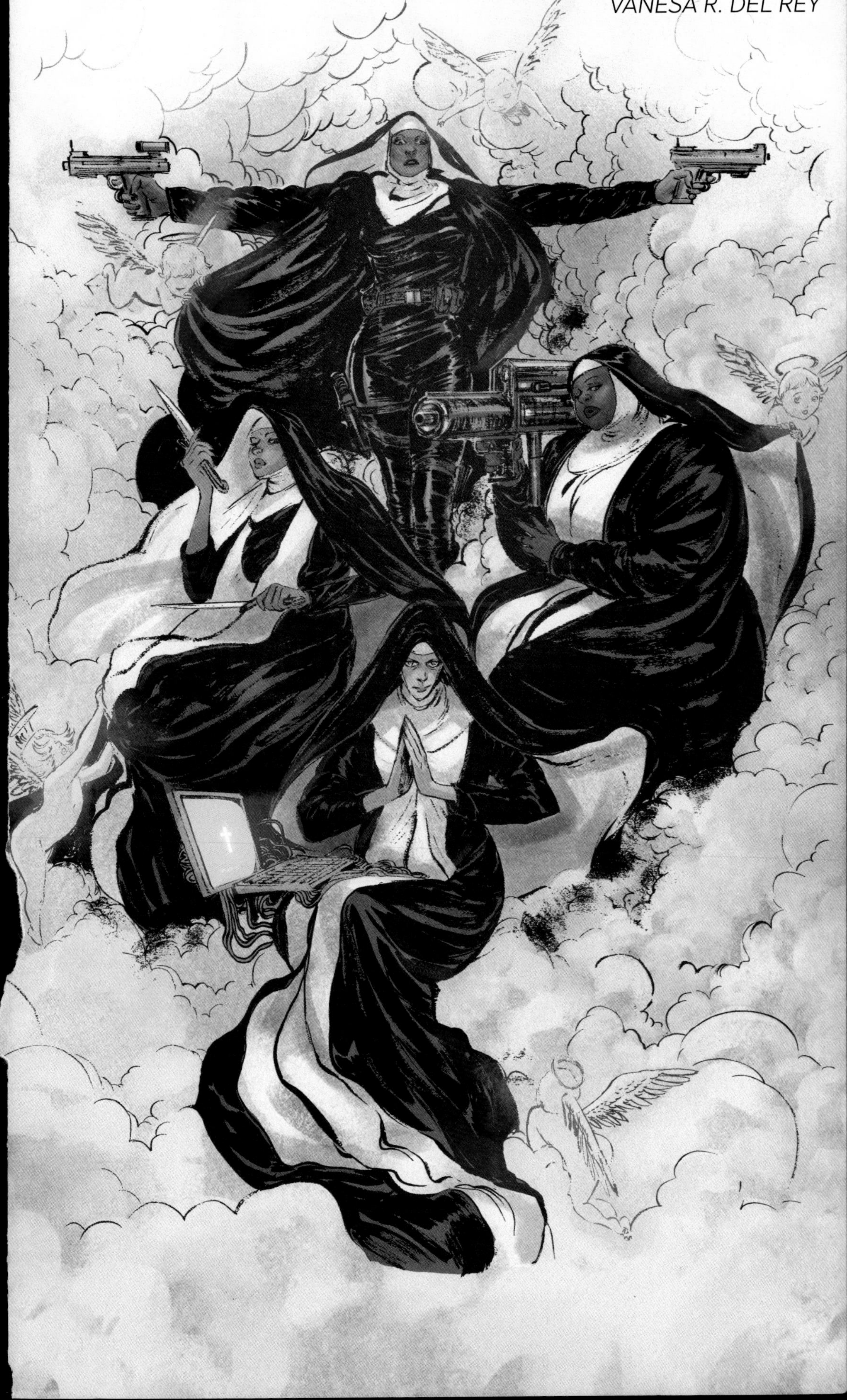

ISSUE TWO COVER BY
TAJ TENFOLD

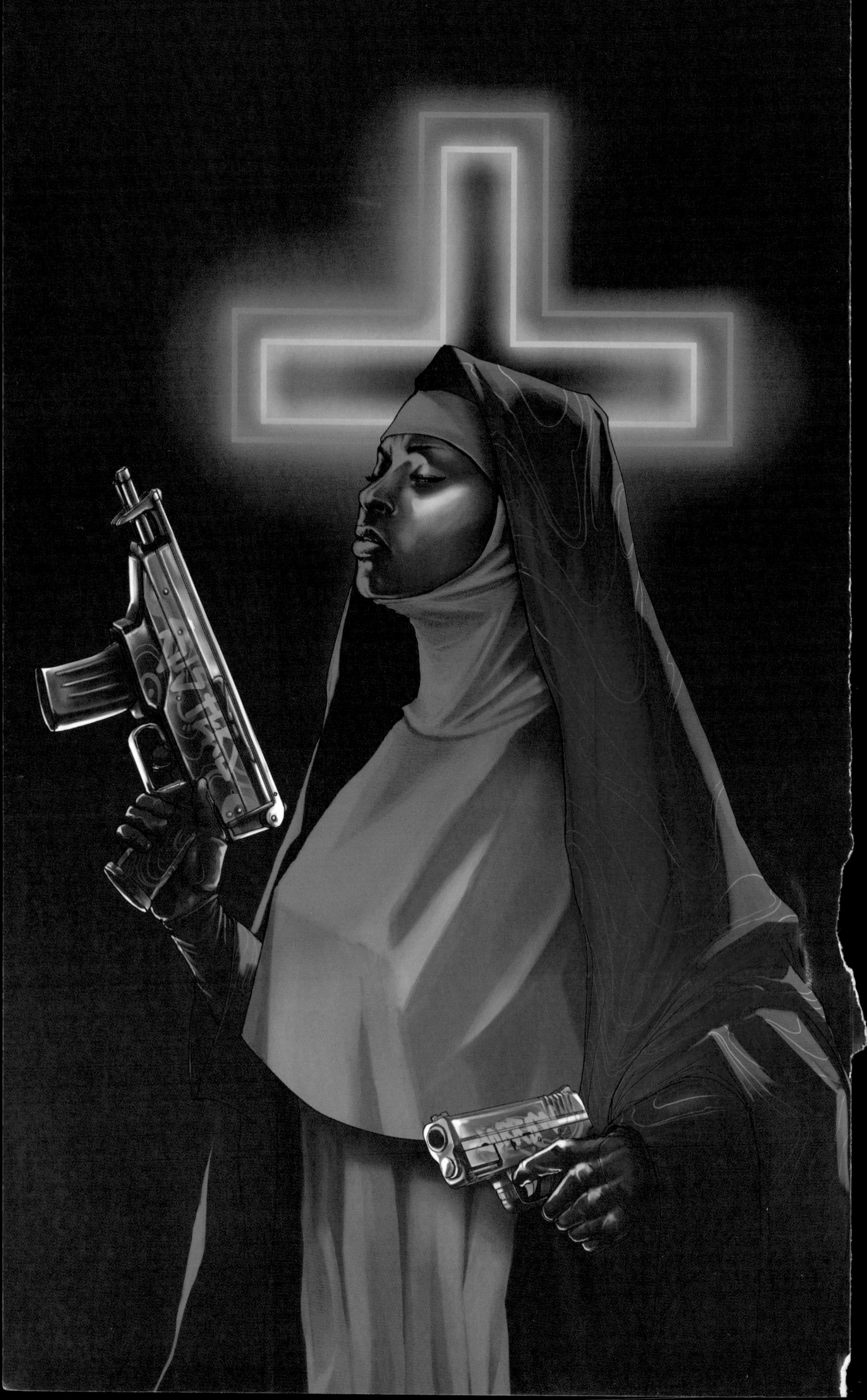

ISSUE TWO COVER BY
ANDRE DE FREITAS

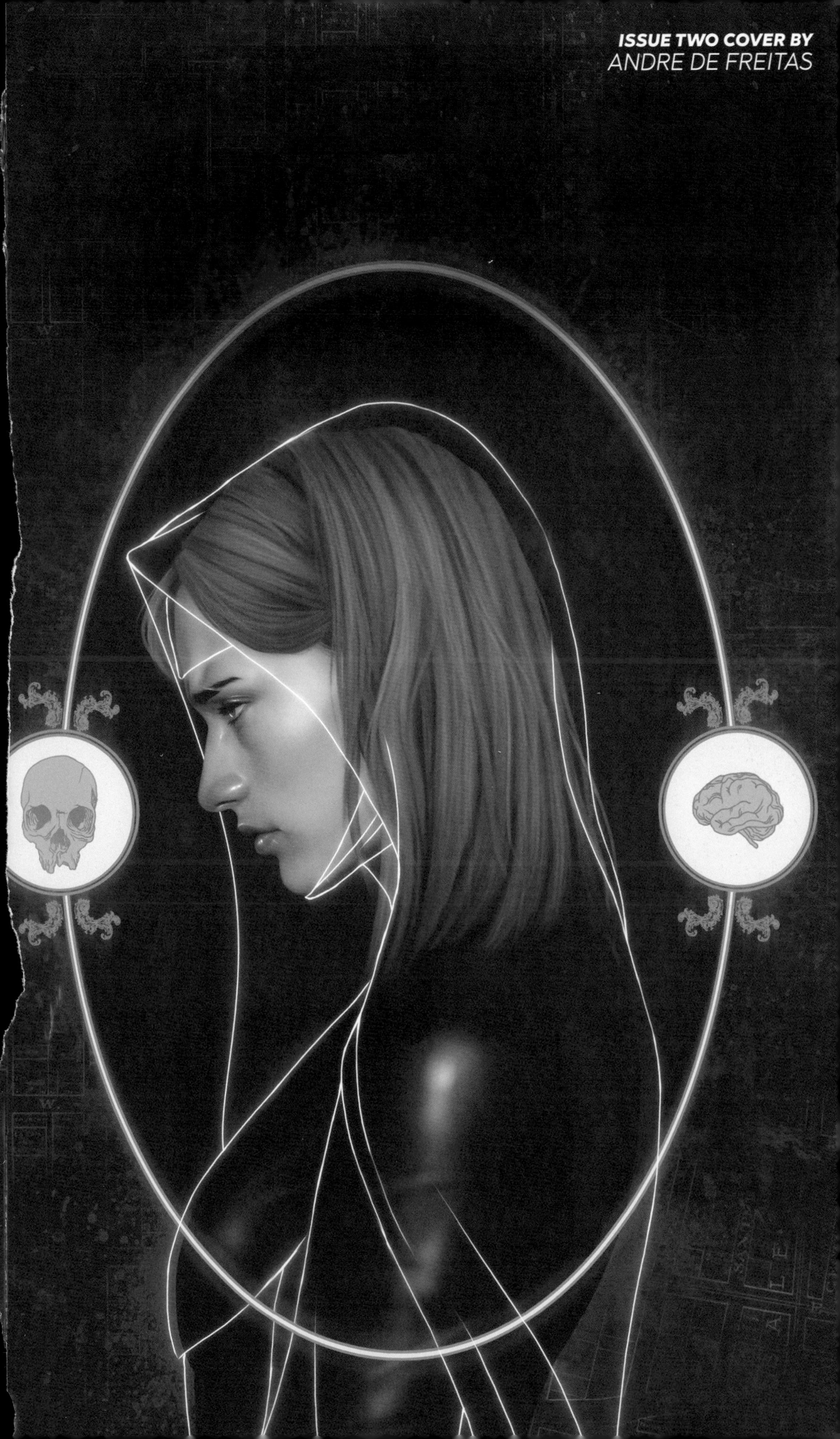

ISSUE THREE COVER BY
TAJ TENFOLD

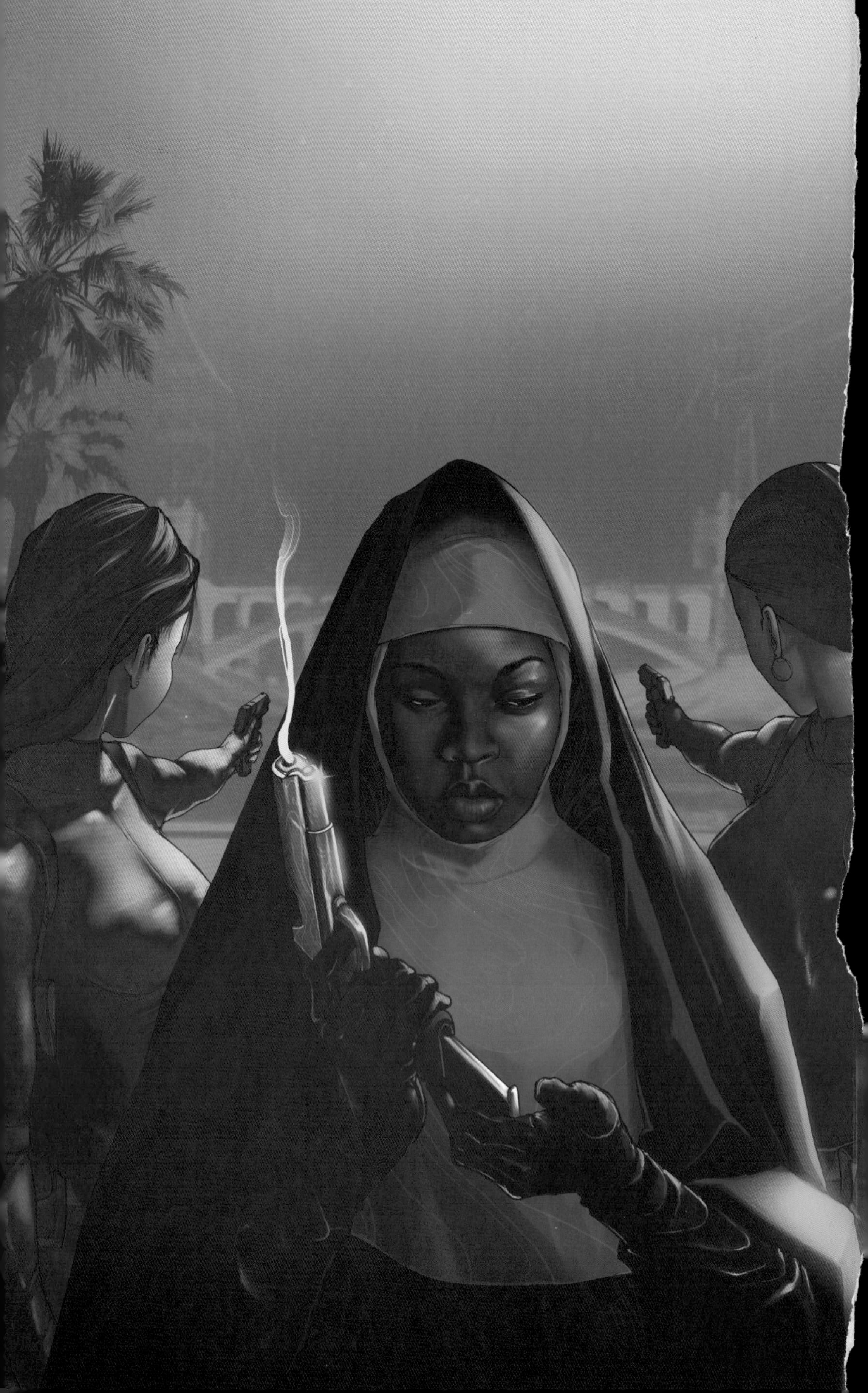

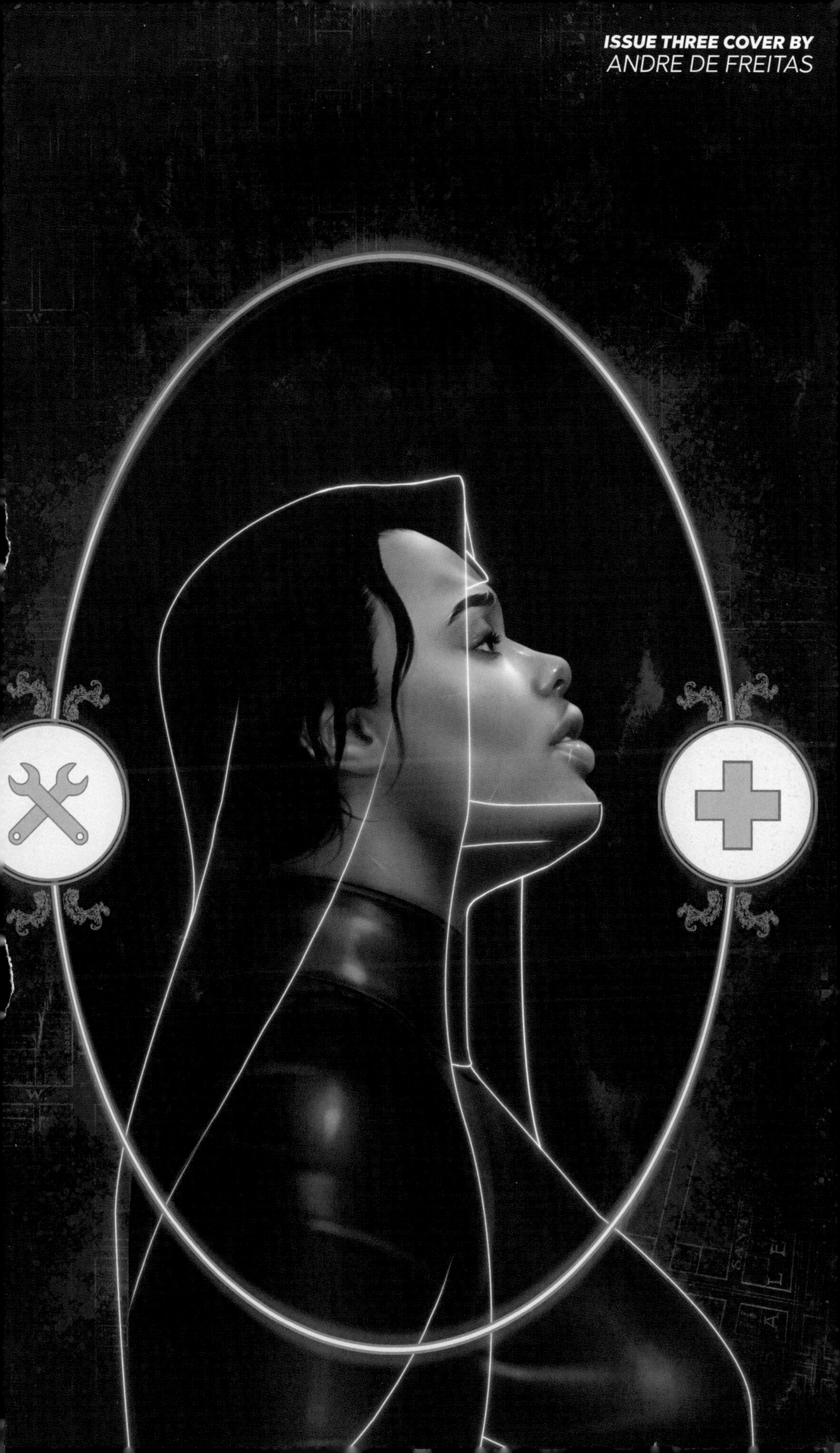

ISSUE THREE COVER BY
ANDRE DE FREITAS

ISSUE FOUR COVER BY
TAJ TENFOLD

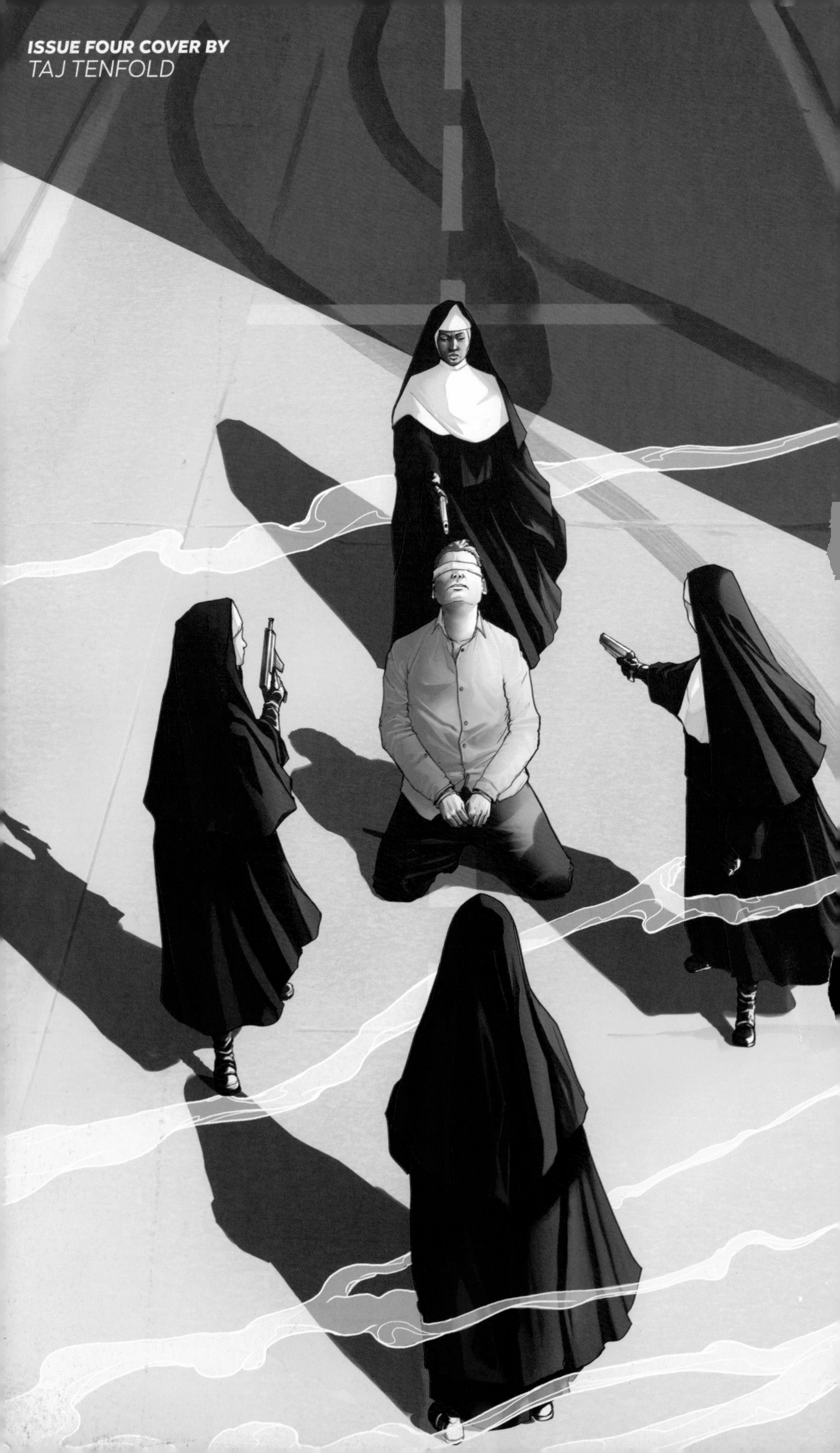

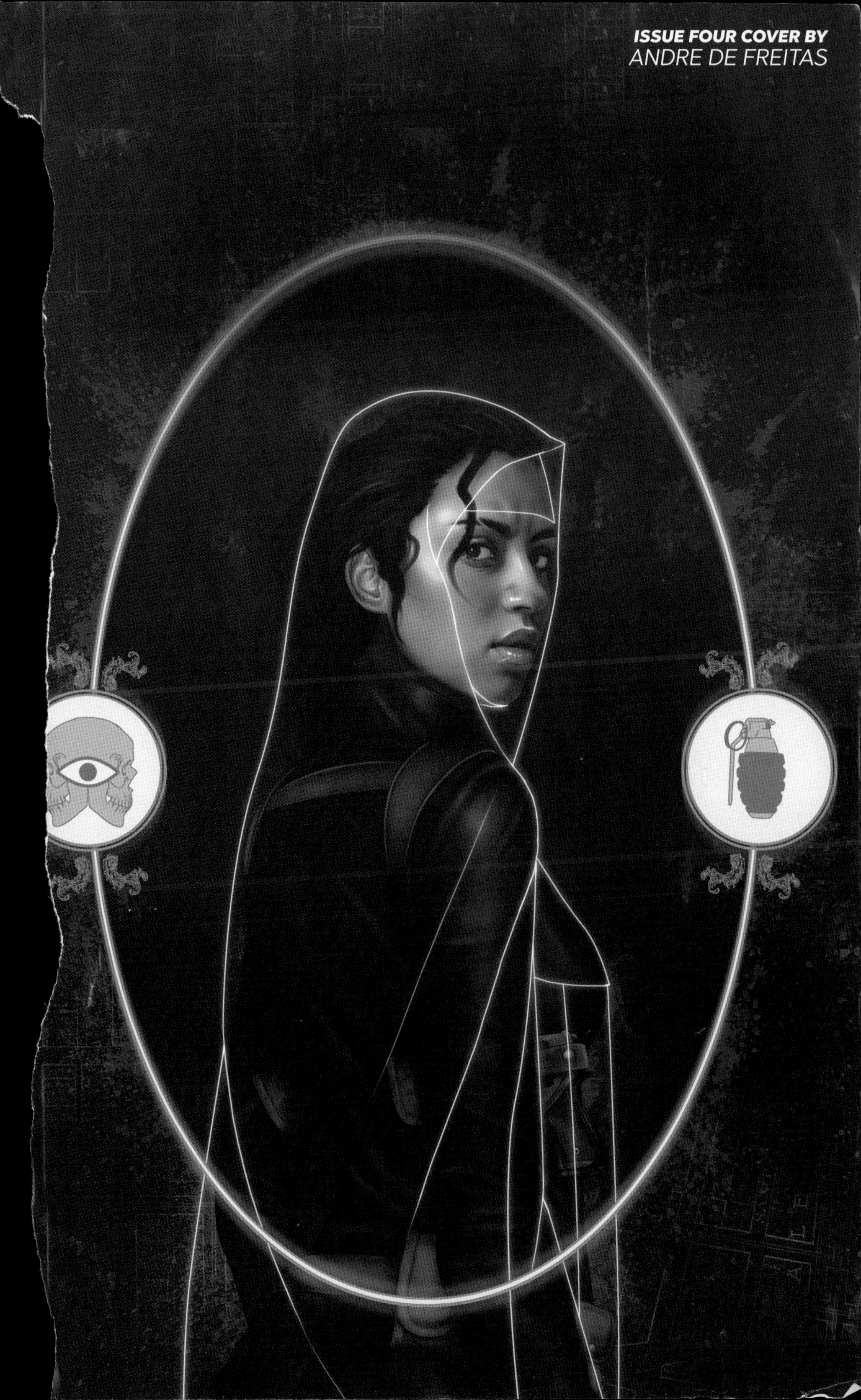

ISSUE FOUR COVER BY
ANDRE DE FREITAS